ANTHROPOLOGY
EXPLORED

Edited by
Ruth Osterweis Selig
and Marilyn R. London

Illustrated by
Robert L. Humphrey

With a Foreword by
David W. McCurdy

SMITHSONIAN INSTITUTION PRESS

Washington and London

ANTHROPOLOGY
EXPLORED

The Best of
Smithsonian
AnthroNotes

Acquiring editor: Daniel Goodwin
Editor: Vicky Macintyre
Production editor: Jack Kirshbaum
Designer: Kathleen Sims

Library of Congress Catalog-in-Publication Data

Anthropology explored : the best of Smithsonian "AnthroNotes" / edited
  by Ruth Osterweis Selig and Marilyn R. London ; illustrated by
  Robert L. Humphrey ; with a foreword by David W. McCurdy.
      p.   cm.
    Includes bibliographical references and index.
    ISBN 1-56098-763-4 (alk. paper). — ISBN 1-56098-790-1 (pbk. :
  alk. paper)
    1. Anthropology—Study and teaching.   I. Osterweis Selig, Ruth.
  II. McCurdy, David W.   III. AnthroNotes.
  GN31.2.A57   1998
  301'.071—dc21   97-47715

British Library Cataloging-in-Publication data available

04   03   02   01   00   99   98   5   4   3   2   1

∞ The paper used in this publication meets the minimum requirements of the American
National Standard for Permanence of Paper for Printed Library Materials Z39.48-1984.

For permission to reproduce any of the illustrations, correspond directly with the artist.
Smithsonian Institution Press does not retain reproduction rights for these illustrations
individually or maintain a file of addresses for image sources.

The chapters in this collection are based on the following issues of *AnthroNotes: The
National Museum of Natural History Bulletin for Teachers* (editors: Alison S. Brooks,
P. Ann Kaupp, JoAnne Lanouette, Ruth O. Selig; guest editor, Marilyn R. London, 1994–
97; illustrator, Robert L. Humphrey).

1: vol. 8, no. 3, 1986	11: vol. 9, no. 3, 1987	21: vol. 7, no. 3, 1985
2: vol. 13, no. 1, 1991	12: vol. 14, no. 2, 1992	22: vol. 14, no. 1, 1992
3: vol. 18, no. 2, 1996	13: vol. 5, no. 1, 1983	23: vol. 11, no. 1, 1989
4: vol. 14, no. 3, 1992	14: vol. 12, no. 3, 1990	24: vol. 12, no. 1, 1990
5: vol. 7, no. 2, 1985	15: vol. 12, no. 1, 1990	25: vol. 10, no. 2, 1988
6: vol. 17, no. 3, 1995	16: vol. 15, no. 2, 1993	26: vol. 13, no. 3, 1991
7: vol. 11, no. 2, 1989	17: vol. 19, no. 1, 1997	27: vol. 16, no. 1, 1994
8: vol. 18, no. 3, 1996	18: vol. 12, no. 2, 1990	28: vol. 18, no. 3, 1996
9: vol. 14, no. 1, 1992	19: vol. 19, no. 2, 1997	29: vol. 15, no. 3, 1993
10: vol. 16, no. 2, 1994	20: vol. 6, no. 1, 1984	

To the memory of
Rollyn Osterweis Krichbaum
and
Bruce Richard Markle

CONTENTS

FOREWORD

nthropology provides a unique and powerful way to look at human experience. Unlike other social scientists, such as psychologists or sociologists, economists or political scientists, anthropologists use the broadest possible framework to study human physical and cultural development and variation. The field is holistic and comprehensive and its subdisciplines interdependent—as is reflected in many of this volume's essays, which defy easy classification into one subfield or another and could easily be placed in any of the book's three major sections.

Culture is the central concept of anthropology; not surprisingly, culture is explored throughout this volume. Culture is the knowledge that humans acquire and share with other people and use to interpret experience and to generate behavior. It is the patterns, rules, and customs of acting, thinking, feeling, and communicating. We only come to understand our common capacity for Culture as we see it expressed with unique identity in a specific culture. As Kathleen Gordon's essay, "'Ape-ing' Language," demonstrates, the roots of human culture go far back into our primate ancestry.

The anthropological perspective infusing the contributions to this volume reveals that our own culture is one of many cultures created by the human species. Anthropology's comparative approach helps us understand other cultures and other peoples within our own community, as well as ourselves. It is in this context that the chapters in this volume speak forcefully, illuminating, first, our primate ancestry and our evolutionary development; second, the emergence of various ancient societies, reconstructed by archaeologists using increasingly sophisticated methodologies, technology, and dating techniques; and, third, the diversity of human languages and cultures around the globe.

ANTHRONOTES

For almost 20 years, the Smithsonian Institution's Department of Anthropology has published *AnthroNotes*, which is dedicated to bringing anthropology—its subject matter, concepts, and theory—to as broad an audience as possible. As past president of the General Anthropology Division of the American Anthropological Association and coeditor of the division's publication, *General Anthropology,* I have recommended *AnthroNotes* on numerous occasions. I am pleased to see this volume of *AnthroNotes* selections produced in a format that will be widely available to students, teachers, anthropologists, and members of the general public.

The book spans the entire field of anthropology and offers an alternative or supplement to the traditional introductory textbook. Its twenty-nine chapters, all based on material previously published in *AnthroNotes*, provide short, concise, and excellent syntheses of topics of broad interest. Many include updates detailing research developments since the selections first appeared. These updates not only inform the reader of current discoveries but also shed light on the process of research and discovery itself. The book has an excellent introduction, which summarizes the selections and highlights the major questions, concepts, and contemporary relevance of the field.

AnthroNotes editors believe that research-based articles convey their information best through nontechnical language, and that even the most sophisticated concepts can be communicated through clear analysis and concise narrative. The authors include Smithsonian anthropologists as well as other distinguished specialists in the field. Robert L. Humphrey, anthropologist and artist from the George Washington University's Department of Anthropology, provides the illustrations, each one inspired by a specific chapter.

Anthropology Explored: The Best of Smithsonian AnthroNotes will take you into the world of anthropology and anthropologists. The chapters should illuminate not only the world around you but much about your own self as a member of the human family. I invite you to enjoy this anthropological journey through time and space.

David W. McCurdy
Macalester College

THE ART OF ANTHROPOLOGY

A Note from the Artist

W hy use cartoons to illustrate serious articles in an anthropological publication? One of the most important attributes that differentiates our species from the rest of the animal kingdom is our ability to laugh, and even more important, to laugh at ourselves. The enormous variety of human behaviors observed and recorded by anthropologists should teach us, if nothing else, the infinite capacity for human folly. The ability to make and understand cartoons represents some of the most complex symbolic thought, expression, and self-reflection of which we humans are capable.

Admittedly, it is sometimes difficult to find the humor in some of the articles in *AnthroNotes*. Not all cartoons are meant to be funny, but they *are* intended to combine visual elements in such a way as to startle—to capture our attention and focus it momentarily on a new idea, or on a familiar idea seen from a new perspective. By synthesizing multiple elements into a single focus, cartoon art causes us to see an event or phenomenon through new eyes, making us laugh, or even to think!

The first cartoons appeared on the walls of Upper Paleolithic caves in France and Spain more than 30,000 years ago, and the artists who created those images worked much as cartoonists do today. A good cartoon simplifies, distills, and refines an event until it instantly communicates a moment in time that the artist has singled out as being different from the preceding moment or the next one. Immediacy is the essence of a successful cartoon.

Simplicity underlies all cartoons, but the process of creating that simplicity is highly complex. First comes the development of a single idea through its visual representation in the mind; only then can drawing begin. I often make 20 or 30 sketches of the same face just to perfect an expression, and the caption is so critical to the timing of the humor that it may take days and multiple revisions to complete. Researching the setting, costumes, and props; eliminating every detail not absolutely necessary to the final impression; developing the expressions and words—these are all hidden from the viewer, who may think the cartoon was completed in a moment's time. If the cartoon is successful, the hard work of the cartoonist should be completely concealed from the viewer.

As an anthropologist, I particularly enjoy drawing for *AnthroNotes* because I am able to work as an artist and anthropologist simultaneously. Every drawing is an ethnography or archaeological site of its own—a specific time and place, a complete environment peopled by thinking, behaving, interactive beings. Further, I suspect there is no better guide to the morality, politics, religions, social issues—in short, the culture—of our times than our cartoons. Each idea in a good cartoon may be every bit as complex as the theoretical research on which a paper for an academic journal is based and may take just as long to emerge. In fact, writing an academic paper bears similarities to cartooning: the activity consists of focusing on a single idea worth exploring in detail and then developing the right language, verbal or visual, to express it.

As an anthropologist, I realize it is important to symbolize without stereotyping, to lampoon a serious topic without becoming tasteless, since the cartoonist's goal is to communicate ideas, not just to amuse the reader. The most amazing part of this experience is what others read into my cartoons; they find humor in things I did not anticipate or, worse, they miss what I meant to be most obvious. Unlike my academic papers, my cartoons often do distort ordinary perceptions by violating some kind of cliché and looking at something familiar in an off-kilter way. To do this while remaining sensitive to an extraordinarily eclectic and critical readership can be quite a challenge.

Nevertheless, cartooning is well worth the challenge. If we can learn to laugh at ourselves, it becomes very easy to see through racism, sexism, fundamentalism, and all the other nasty "isms" that our species is too often prey to. One of the favorite quotations of cartoonists is a comment on the cartoons of Thomas Nast by the corrupt political leader of old Manhattan, Boss Tweed: "Stop them Damn pictures," Tweed said. "I don't care so much what they write about me . . . my constituents can't read—but damn it, they can see pictures!"

Robert L. Humphrey

ACKNOWLEDGMENTS

Because this book is based on 20 years of work developing *AnthroNotes*, there is no way to thank all the anthropologists, teachers, students, Smithsonian colleagues, friends, and family members whose advice and assistance helped bring this volume into being. Certain individuals, however, must be named: Beatrice Kleppner, who first introduced me to the tremendous potential anthropology has for enlivening a classroom; my *AnthroNotes* coeditors, Alison S. Brooks, P. Ann Kaupp, and JoAnne Lanouette, with whom I have worked so long, first when they were a wonderful teacher training team in the late 1970s and 1980s helping to create the National Science Foundation–funded Anthropology for Teachers Program out of which *AnthroNotes* grew, and then, in more recent years, when they were an editorial team pushing me to "finish the book"; and Robert L. Humphrey, mentor, friend, and colleague, who believed in *AnthroNotes* from the beginning and proved the ideal artistic collaborator for all the *AnthroNotes* editors these many years. Department of Anthropology Chairmen William W. Fitzhugh, Douglas H. Ubelaker, Donald J. Ortner, and Dennis J. Stanford; National Museum of Natural History director Richard S. Fiske; and educator Louise Harper Schuchat each supported *AnthroNotes* at a critical juncture in its development. I owe a special debt to Daniel H. Goodwin, director of the Smithsonian Institution Press, who encouraged me seven years ago to create a collection of *AnthroNotes* articles to introduce the field to a wider audience.

Several anthropologists with whom I worked on the Task Force on the Teaching of Anthropology for the American Anthropological Association (AAA) offered continuous ideas and support, particularly Patricia J. Higgins, Jane J. White, Lawrence B. Breitborde, Paul A. Erickson, Patricia C. Rice, and Charles Ellenbaum. Conrad P. Kottak and David W. McCurdy, during each one's presidency of the AAA's General Anthropology Division, provided much appreciated encouragement for the wider dissemination of anthropology in schools. Colleagues in the Public Education Committee of the Society for American Archaeology also offered support through many years.

Given my full-time responsibilities as a Smithsonian administrator, it was not possible to do this book alone. It took the organizational talents of Macalester student intern Andrea List in January 1994, Yale student intern Katherine Westgate the summer of 1994, and particularly Marilyn R. London in 1995–96 to make this book a reality. Marilyn effectively managed the project, creating and organizing numerous paper and computer files, obtaining author updates, verifying citations and bibliographic references, and writing author biographies. For her work on and commitment to this project, I will always be grateful.

An advisory committee (teachers Jessie Diffley, Jack Caussin, Carolyn Gecan, Margot Zahner, and Jeanne Jarvis, along with science writer Laura Kennedy) worked through 1994–95 to help shape the selection of essays for the book as well as select other *AnthroNotes* materials for the Department of Anthropology's revised *Teachers Packet in Anthropology*, which is available as an educational companion to this volume. Anthropologists William C. Sturtevant and Bruce D. Smith provided advice and carefully reviewed the manuscript. Marcia Bakry drew maps, and Vera Chase assisted with some of the details of final manuscript preparation. Ann Kaupp gave assistance, ideas, and support, as she has throughout our 20 years of working together. Marilyn and I are grateful for the talent and expert advice of editors Vicky Macintyre and Jack Kirshbaum, designer Kathleen Sims, and editorial assistant Robert Lockhart at the Smithsonian Institution Press. Finally, I want to thank Dennis O'Connor, provost, and Robert S. Hoffmann, former acting provost and assistant secretary for research (and science) at the Smithsonian Institution, for whom I worked for 10 years, who offered unwavering support for my work on *Anthro-Notes* and the *AnthroNotes* book project.

Ruth Osterweis Selig

INTRODUCTION

Investigating the Origins, Nature, and Cultures of Humankind

Ruth Osterweis Selig

How can we best understand ourselves and others?
How did the human species develop over time and space?
How can we explain and understand the diverse cultures that share
  our globe?

Creation stories, widespread throughout human societies, attest to the universal human passion for understanding ourselves and the world around us. Where did we come from and where are we going, as individuals, as a society, as a species that developed on earth? How did the incredible variety of human beings—physically, culturally, linguistically—develop through time? How have human societies adapted to a wide range of changing environments, cultural contacts, and technological innovations?

The search for the answers to these fundamental questions lies at the heart of the field of study called anthropology. As David McCurdy explains in his Foreword, anthropology looks at peoples and cultures from a broad perspective, seeking to understand the nature and development of human beings—through all human history and in all cultures around the earth. Whether specialized in biological, cultural, or applied anthropology, linguistics, or archaeology, most anthropologists have a deep and abiding interest in understanding their fellow human beings—their past, present and future, their physical development and variation, and their diverse cultures around the globe.

Since 1979, the Smithsonian Institution's Department of Anthropology has been publishing *AnthroNotes*. Dedicated to the wider diffusion of original, recent research in anthropology in order to help readers stay current in the field, *AnthroNotes* began as part of a joint museum and university teacher training program (Selig and Lanouette, 1983; Selig and Higgins, 1986; Selig, 1995). The editorial team of *AnthroNotes*— P. Ann Kaupp, Ruth O. Selig, Alison S. Brooks, and JoAnne Lanouette— is the same team that created the National Science Foundation–funded *George Washington University/Smithsonian Institution Anthropology for Teachers Program*; Marilyn R. London joined us from 1994 to 1997 and served as one of the editors for this volume. Today, more than 8,400 people receive *AnthroNotes*. Although many of them are professional anthropologists and teachers, an increasing number in this country and abroad are general readers interested in anthropology, archaeology, and museums. The *AnthroNotes* mailing list comprises a national network of anthropologists, archaeologists, teachers, and museum and other profes- sionals interested in the wider dissemination of anthropology, particularly in schools (Selig, 1997).

Anthropology Explored: The Best of Smithsonian *AnthroNotes*
The volume consists of three main sections. The first, "Human Origins," focuses on primates, human origins, and human variation. The contribu- tions here address the questions "Who are we?" "Where did we come from?" and "How do we know?" The second section, "Archaeologists Examine the Past," highlights archaeologists' understanding of the past, both in the old and new worlds, by examining such questions as "How do we learn about the past?" and "What do we know about the past?" Sev- eral chapters consider the question of origins: of the earliest Americans, of agriculture in the New World, of the earliest South Americans, of Es- kimo/Inuit societies. The discussions of African American archaeology and ethnoarchaeology bring a contemporary view to the question of how archaeologists help us understand the past through each new generation's perspectives.

The third section, "Our Many Cultures," begins with chapters on the ethnohistory of Northern Mexico and Plains Indians. The section looks at how anthropologists study other cultures in diverse societies around the world. The culture change affecting both those societies and cultural an- thropology as a discipline will become evident to readers. Finally, a bit of Smithsonian history is offered within the context of working with Native Americans; the Institution's long involvement with anthropology is clear from the history of the discipline itself, which emerged largely within a Smithsonian context in the nineteenth century, well before there were any university departments devoted to it.

Although the essays here can be read separately and in any order, they were selected to provide an introduction to the field of anthropology, including physical anthropology, archaeology, cultural anthropology, applied anthropology, and linguistics. The volume concludes with short biographies of the contributors and the *AnthroNotes* editors. Many other *AnthroNotes* materials particularly relevant to teachers (including teaching activities, guides to further resources, and fieldwork opportunities) are available as part of a revised *Teachers Packet in Anthropology,* which can be obtained by writing: *AnthroNotes,* Department of Anthropology, MRC 112, Smithsonian Institution, Washington, D.C. 20560.

In order to bring the contributions up to date, authors were asked to review their original essays and make whatever changes they considered appropriate. In most cases, new bibliographic references were added and minor corrections made. In addition, most authors chose to add an "update" section discussing recent discoveries or concepts. These update sections are designed to demonstrate the process by which new knowledge accumulates through scholarly research. In three chapters (13, 16, and 25) that focus on the contributions of a particular anthropologist, that scholar provides the update.

SECTION 1: HUMAN ORIGINS

Few of us ever stop to think about the most fundamental questions regarding the human species: Who are we? Where did we come from? How have we changed over the millions of years through which our ancestors developed? Why do we come in so many different shapes, sizes, and colors? How do scientists explore the answers to these puzzling questions? These are the topics addressed in section 1.

The anthropologists who seek answers to these questions are called physical or biological anthropologists. Like all biologists, they have trained for many years to carry out research on animal organisms; in this case, the animal species is called *Homo sapiens.* Like other scientific disciplines, physical anthropology has undergone revolutionary changes in recent years. New technologies developed in molecular biology are now used to explore the DNA structure of once living tissue, and other advanced technologies—such as scanning electron microscopes, high-speed computers, and sophisticated X-ray machines—have expanded our knowledge immeasurably.

Although the order in which the contributions appear is based on their chronological context, it is helpful to see how they relate to the questions outlined above. From an introductory point of view, chapter 5, by Kathleen Gordon, provides an excellent review of the work of physical anthropologists, detailing not only the range of their work but also the variety of fascinating stories and information that they have uncovered. Whether discussing diet, disease, or demography, or the story of the Japanese Ainu, or African American history, Gordon demonstrates that "the study of modern, historic, and prehistoric skeletons has made it possible for anthropologists to contribute an enormous and diverse array of information about human behavior and morphology past and present." At the end of her essay, written in 1989, the author predicts that "many more new approaches to reconstructing past lives from bones will be discovered in the future." In her 1997 update, Gordon has the opportunity to fulfill her prophecy, as she details the exciting recent discovery that scientists can extract DNA not only from soft tissue but also from ancient bone.

In chapter 1 Gordon introduces the reader to the field of primatology and the story of humans teaching their primate cousins to communicate through human language. In the process of discovering that speech and language are not synonymous (apes seem utterly incapable of the first but quite capable of the rudimentary forms of the second), researchers learned a great deal not only about themselves and the chimpanzee's capacity for language but much about our possible early preadaptation to a cultural way of life.

Alison Brooks, long-time editor of *AnthroNotes,* writes an article for the publication every two to three years, detailing the most recent information about our earliest ancestors. Her 1997 update, presented in chapters 3 and 4, is a model of synthesis and clarity in a field notorious for its complexity and ever-changing "family tree." Chapter 3 focuses on the earliest period of human evolution, and chapter 4 on the past 200,000 years, which is when fully modern humans emerged.

Clearly, one of the great challenges for scientists is to understand the physical emergence of our earliest ancestors. As chapter 5 explains, it may be even more difficult to uncover information about early human behavior. Much of that behavior is subject to interpretation, not only by scientists but also by artists whose representations shape how we view not only our early ancestors but ourselves today. In chapter 6, Diane Gifford-Gonzalez discusses the various motifs dominating the visual representation of our ancient past—motifs such as "The Drudge-on-the-Hide" and "The Guy-with-a-Rock"—and argues for closer collaboration between scientists and artists, who must together acknowledge the "social power of the visual assertions about our ancestors that populate our museums and popular books." Gifford-Gonzalez has much praise for the few artists who closely collaborate with scientists and attempt to portray the past with the richness of detail it deserves.

Finally, in chapter 8, George Armelagos, physical anthropologist at Emory University, Atlanta, along with two colleagues, discusses a topic of abiding interest to all physical anthropologists: disease. Taking a broad synthetic view, the chapter details three epidemiological revolutions in human history. The first occurred with the emergence of agriculture and urban centers, and the second with the industrial revolution and modern technology; the third, which is under way today, is marked by growing resistance to multiple antibiotics. "The emergence of infectious disease has been one of the most interesting evolutionary stories of the last decade, and has captured the interest of scientists, the general public, and the media, through such films as *Outbreak*."

Interestingly, chapter 8 could have been placed in any of the volume's three sections. This underscores the point made by David McCurdy in his Foreword about the interdependency of all of anthropology's subfields. The chapter covers the entire span of human history and thereby demonstrates one of anthropology's greatest strengths, namely, its ability to look at human physical and cultural development through all time and across all space, in both its biological and cultural dimensions.

As a unit, section 1 traces the emergence of humans through millions of years and details many of the methods and techniques scientists use today to study our origins. The contributions here tell fascinating stories, are consistently well written, and together can help us better understand ourselves and the mysteries of our distant past.

SECTION 2: ARCHAEOLOGISTS EXAMINE THE PAST

Archaeologists help us answer the questions: What can we know about the past? How can we learn about the past? Archaeologists tell us stories about our past, stories they develop through their examination of the material remains of our ancestors. Despite the glamour of archaeology in the popular press as well as in films such as *Raiders of the Lost Ark*, it is because of the scientific methods of this discipline that we know about so much of human history. Only in the last 5,000 years, after all, have we had written records, but our human ancestry began almost 4 million years ago! We are indeed indebted to archaeology.

The chapters in this section reflect this debt and convey much of the richness and excitement of the field. Because of the importance of dating and chronology in archaeology, the essays are arranged in chronological order. The first two, chapter 9 by Mark Cohen and chapter 10 by Melinda Zeder, focus on the earliest evidence of domestication and its consequences for the human species. Chapter 10 also demonstrates the enormous changes that high-speed computers have brought to archaeological analysis and the painstaking work involved in such investigations.

Chapter 11 turns to the Old World and to Africa. Archaeologist John Fisher details his ethnoarchaeological research among the hunter-gatherer Efe peoples of tropical Africa, comparing his findings with similar research among the !Kung (San) peoples of Botswana, people made famous by Elizabeth Marshall Thomas in her classic 1959 study, *The Harmless People.* Fisher worked about 100 kilometers from where Colin Turnbull studied the Pygmy peoples, as detailed in his 1961 book, *The Forest People.* Fisher was part of the Ituri Project, codirected by Irven DeVore, who also ran the Harvard Kalahari study. "The Ituri Project, one of the first comprehensive studies of human ecology, demography, and health and nutrition among hunter-gatherers (and horticulturalists), was designed to build on and further explore some of the results of the Kalahari study." Both studies examined the lifeways of modern hunter-gatherers, partly to better understand how to interpret "the ancient pieces of bone and stone and other clues of archaeological sites to reconstruct what life was like in the past." Ethnoarchaeology combines insights of both ethnography and archaeology. It demonstrates the dependency of archaeological interpretations on the description and analyses of ethnographic (both historical and modern) cultures around the world, both for specific interpretations of evidence and for models of reasonable culture systems, since both are needed to fill in the inevitable gaps in the archaeological record.

Many of the essays in this section deal with the Americas, since that is where American archaeology had its beginnings and was nourished over the last 150 years. Stephen Williams, emeritus professor, Harvard University, takes on one of the more contentious issues in chapter 12. Williams details the evidence and lack of evidence for contact before the Vikings; I leave it to our readers to find out his conclusions. Evidence of the earliest inhabitants of North and South America continues to be of abiding interest for New World archaeologists, and two of the country's leading specialists in this field, Dennis Stanford for North America and Tom Dillehay for South America, report on their investigations in chapters 13 and 14. Stanford also provides an update that discusses not only his current thinking but the way knowledge changes over time as new discoveries are made and new concepts emerge. Tom Dillehay's update explains his work at Monte Verde, which was in the news during 1997, while chapter 15, by John Verano, relates further interesting work in South America, this time on the Moche, an ancient Peruvian people who predated the more famous Inca.

My discussion in chapter 16 moves north again, to describe Bruce D. Smith's groundbreaking documentation of Eastern United States as a fourth center of the discovery of agriculture. His update details the recent refinements in this research area since the essay first appeared. Moving still farther North, chapter 17 by Smithsonian archaeologist William W. Fitzhugh focuses on the origins of the Eskimo peoples, and more generally on new perspectives of Arctic studies.

Chapter 18, the last one in this section, looks at a subject of increasing interest to historians and anthropologists: the daily lives of enslaved African Americans, as reflected in their material remains. A relatively new field of study when Theresa Singleton first wrote this essay for *AnthroNotes,* her 1997 update details significant developments in both research directions and theoretical frameworks that have occurred since 1990.

Although the general public often associates "archaeology" with romantic images of fieldwork, the search for hidden treasures, and the recovery of lost civilizations, this section demonstrates the realities of archaeology as a subfield of anthropology, with its rigorous field study, painstaking laboratory analysis, and careful scholarship. The result of all this effort is the unfolding of an ever more complex story of human cultural development through time—as amply demonstrated by the chapters in this section.

SECTION 3: OUR MANY CULTURES

Many of the presentations in the first two sections reflect broad synthetic approaches to specific topics in physical anthropology and archaeology. Those in the third section are quite different. Cultural anthropologists, although interested in broad questions of cultural adaptation and cross-cultural comparisons, generally write about specific cultures, at specific times and places. In addition, because of the nature of these different cultures, they tend to focus on one or two aspects of the society under discussion.

Nonetheless, the enormous variety of human societies and cultures stands out clearly in these chapters. They transport the reader to Sonqo, a Quechua-speaking community in the highlands of southern Peru (chapter 20); to Wyoming and Montana, to the Arapahoes on the Wind River Reservation, and the Gros Ventres at Fort Belknap (chapter 21); to Bissel, in the Kajiado district in Kenya, where native anthropologist and former Smithsonian fellow Naomi Kipury experienced her rites of passage, first into adulthood and then into anthropology (chapter 23); to Chiapas, Mexico, and the Passamaquoddy Indian reservation at Pleasant Point, near Perry, Maine (chapter 24), where projects in linguistic survival bring anthropologists and native speakers together to work in new ways.

Section three also explains how cultural anthropologists go about doing their work. Several essays elucidate the methods of cultural anthropologists, including ethnohistorical analysis of documents (chapter 19); ethnographic interviewing (chapter 22); new work in applied linguistics (chapter 25); and working with native peoples (chapter 28). The section also takes a look at the changes in anthropology over the past few decades, particularly in relation to the shift from an emphasis on objectivity and facts to subjectivity and points of view, as described in relationship to ethnographic filmmaking (chapter 27). This shift also can be seen in ethnographic writing, since most anthropologists today believe that understanding another culture can be at best only partial, since it always is filtered through one's own cultural perspectives and experiences. Finally, chapters 26 and 29 remind us of the inseparability of our biological and cultural heritage. The former looks at the process of aging in several different societies and the latter discusses the emergence of different races and the difficulties of dividing human populations that differ genetically.

This section underscores the value of traditional anthropological methods—participant learning, interviewing informants, fieldwork, and cross-cultural comparison—which provide anthropologists with a special perspective and a set of highly useful skills. These skills offer a unique way to gather and analyze information, and they can be developed, practiced, and applied not only by anthropologists but by all those who have the opportunity to live among other cultures, as well as students who are able to do ethnographic projects in their own communities.

As our world becomes increasingly diverse and as more and more people from varied cultural backgrounds live and work side by side, these anthropological perspectives and methods will find useful applications in many settings. Tremendous challenges await those who endeavor to understand other cultures, but tremendous enrichment awaits them as well. The anthropological perspective offers one important avenue toward this increased understanding and awareness.

CONCLUSION

Anthropology means "the study of people." Anthropologists study the physical and cultural development of people, and their diversity. The *AnthroNotes* contributions to this volume present specific case studies that take you with anthropologists as they investigate the origins, nature, and cultures of humankind. Although each chapter focuses on a specific topic, issue, or subject, the volume as a whole provides a view of the entire field of anthropology, a field that is becoming increasingly relevant to the modern world.

Human diversity, whether physical, cultural, or political, is among the most pressing issues in our shrinking world; of all the scholarly disciplines, anthropology is perhaps best equipped to shed light on that diversity, its origins, manifestations, and implications. Anthropology thus provides an

important lens for examining the dynamic complexity, diverse cultures, and global changes in our world today.

REFERENCES

Selig, Ruth O. 1995. "Teacher Training in One Wyoming Community: An Argument for Anthropologists' Involvement in American Schools." In *Wyoming Contributions to Anthropology*, 4, University of Wyoming.

Selig, Ruth O. 1997. "The Challenge of Exclusion: Anthropology, Teachers and Schools." In Conrad P. Kottak, Jane J. White, Richard H. Furlow, and Patricia C. Rice, eds., *The Teaching of Anthropology: Problems, Issues, and Decisions*. Mayfield.

Selig, Ruth Osterweis, and Patricia J. Higgins, eds. 1986. "Practicing Anthropology in PreCollege Education." *Practicing Anthropology* 8(3–4) (special double issue).

Selig, Ruth Osterweis, and JoAnne Lanouette. 1983. "A New Approach to Teacher Training." *Museum News* 61(6):44–48.

Thomas, Elizabeth Marshall. 1959. *The Harmless People*. Alfred A. Knopf.

Turnbull, Colin. 1961. *The Forest People*. Simon and Schuster.

HUMAN ORIGINS

Who Are We?
Where Did We Come From?
How Do We Learn about Early Humans?

1 "APE-ING" LANGUAGE

Experiments and Communication with Our Closest Relatives

Kathleen D. Gordon

What would other animals tell us about themselves if only they could speak? What could a close relative such as the chimpanzee tell us about ourselves and our history? Like Dr. Doolittle, researchers have long dreamed of communicating with other species. Over the past years, numerous experiments have shown that a capacity for symbolic language is not necessarily the sole preserve of *Homo sapiens,* and that it may indeed be possible to have meaningful communication across species boundaries.

It has become increasingly clear to anthropologists in the past decade that although there are dramatic differences between the overall behavior and lifeways of humans and the great apes, many of the characteristics once thought to be unique to humankind are being discovered, albeit in a very limited form, in the behavioral repertoires of the chimpanzee, gorilla, and orangutan.

For instance, it used to be thought that only humans used tools. Then Jane Goodall at the Gombe Stream Reserve in Tanzania electrified the world with the news that chimpanzees used rudimentary tools in the wild, to fish for termites and to sponge up water. Others have observed chimpanzees elsewhere using rocks as hammers and anvils to crack open palm nuts. Some anthropologists countered that only humans actually made tools, but, once again, chimpanzees were found to prepare their termite sticks with considerable care and foresight. One captive orangutan was even taught to chip stone tools. Clearly, no other animal species depends

on tools for survival to the extent that the human species does (and has done probably for millions of years), but it is nonetheless true that at least our closest relatives are capable of tool-using and tool-making behavior that foreshadows that of human beings.

In the same way, it now appears that the ability to think about and refer to things in the abstract, or by means of symbols, may be due in part to a common substrate of intelligence that we share with the chimpanzee, gorilla, and orangutan. Although it is not yet clear whether any of the great apes make use of this capacity in the wild, recent experiments in laboratories and primate colonies have shown that all apes are able to learn symbolic systems of communication modeled after human language. Further, apes can communicate with humans and other apes about objects, persons, places, and activities using these "artificial" languages. For those who believed that language and the ability to communicate about something other than one's immediate emotions were the sole province of human beings, these experiments have provided a fascinating glimpse into the minds of apes and perhaps have given us clues to the communicative potentials of our last common ancestor.

TEACHING CHIMPANZEES LANGUAGE

The first attempts to teach chimpanzees how to speak took place in the 1940s. The method used mimicked the way human infants learn language.

Baby chimpanzees were raised in human homes, by human caretakers, and were treated as if they were human. One such chimpanzee, Viki, was eventually able to use pictures to ask for objects or activities. On tests of conceptual discrimination, she was as accurate as similarly aged human children. But Viki was never able to pronounce more than three words, even after years of training and constant exposure to human speech. Her surrogate mother summed up the experiment in the 1951 book *The Ape in Our House*: "We said that if an ape had proper upbringing, it might learn to speak spontaneously. But we were wrong. You can dress an ape in the finest of finery, buy it a tricycle, and kiss it to death—but it will not learn to talk."

Viki's inability to master spoken language was not a training problem, we now know. It has since been demonstrated that in addition to some differences in their vocal tracts, apes simply lack the special brain connections that make human speech possible. In the 1960s, psychologists began to realize that language had to be distinguished from speech when thinking about primate communication abilities. Because human language is expressed through speech, we tend to equate one with the other, but any formal communication system is a language.

If chimps cannot speak, perhaps they can use a different form of language. As a result of further fieldwork among chimpanzees in their natural habitat, some observers noticed that chimpanzees use hand signals in their natural communications with one another. Suggesting that chimpanzees might be more successful at learning methods of communication that used the chimpanzee's native gestural abilities, Allen and Beatrice Gardner, working at the University of Nevada in the 1960s, taught their chimp infant, Washoe, to make hand signals in American Sign Language (ASL). The success the Gardners were able to achieve excited anthropologists, psychologists, and linguists everywhere. During her four years of training, Washoe learned 150 signs, signed them in combinations (though never in such a constant order as to resemble a real sense of syntax), and, apparently by imitation and observation learned some signs that were never taught to her (such as "smoke"). She also invented some signs on her own and adapted others.

Washoe's success with sign language was not unique. Over the past 15 years, similar experiments have been conducted with other common chimpanzees and with the bonobo (or pygmy chimpanzee), the gorilla, and the orangutan. Most of the experiments have focused on sign language, but such studies are difficult to control scientifically, and utterances must be filmed to be preserved. Hoping to avoid these methodological problems, some experimenters devised artificial languages, based on plastic tokens or keyboard symbols, in order to better control and record the animals' actual utterances. Sarah, a common chimpanzee, was taught by David and Ann Premack to manipulate plastic discs of various shapes and colors to name and ask for objects and to make simple sentences. Another chimpanzee, Lana, at the Yerkes Primate Center in Atlanta, Georgia, was taught "Yerkish," an artificial language using "lexigrams" (or graphic symbols) on a keyboard connected to a computer. This system had the advantage of eliminating the human trainer, and with it, the possibility that humans were unconsciously cuing the animals to make appropriate responses, a criticism that continues to cloud some of the results of the sign language studies.

The artificial language systems have had their share of critics too. With such narrow training, some say, the animals have little opportunity to use language in the important ways in which humans use it, namely, to construct a world, to obtain desirables, and to regulate the behavior of others. "Language" it may be, but it is divorced from the open social context that makes language a meaningful phenomenon instead of a trivial game.

Although the sign language experiments are difficult to conduct, to maintain, and to verify by objective means, they still provide us with the most compelling evidence of the apes' capacity for symbolic language. Because these studies are relatively open, they also document the ability of trained animals to use symbolic communication in innovative and productive ways, such as to convey spontaneous or novel thoughts and desires. Koko, a lowland gorilla who was raised from infancy and taught ASL by Dr. Francine Patterson, now has a sign vocabulary of some 500 words and recognizes 500 more. This is the largest vocabulary of any of the signing apes. Most important, Koko uses her abilities to joke with, lie to, and insult her human and animal companions, as well as to perform the more mundane vocabulary exercises and comprehension tests, which are administered to obtain objective information about her language skills. Koko has used sign language to protest to trainers about boring vocabulary drills, to ask for a kitten as a pet (which she got), and to insult her young male gorilla companion Michael ("Michael stupid toilet devil").

To be sure, not all authorities have been willing to accept that the behavior being taught and used is truly "language." Before these studies were first undertaken, it was assumed by many prominent linguists that human language was so distinct and qualitatively different from all other forms of communication that it could not be explained as an evolutionary development from any more primitive communication system. But the language studies showed that ape language did share some of the important components of human communication. Apes could use a symbolic

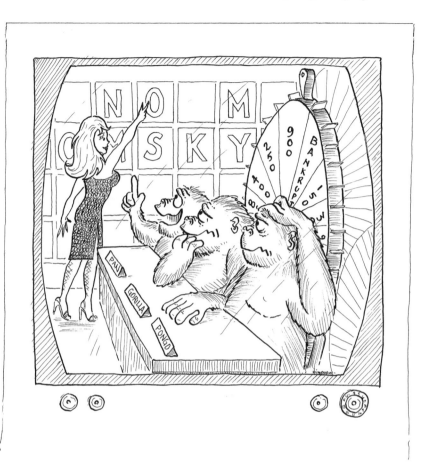

system of arbitrary referents, could generalize (that is, transfer meaning from one context to another appropriate one, as in the use of the word "coke" to mean all sweet dark drinks), and could use signs or symbols to create new words or combinations of words spontaneously in response to unfamiliar objects. As a result, some linguists began to draw ever stricter definitions of what constitutes "real" language and claimed the apes were merely "aping" their trainers and not producing intentional, patterned, or grammatical language at all. One experimenter, Herbert Terrace, who had worked with the chimpanzee Nim, concluded that his experiments showed only that Nim was mimicking his trainers and at best could use signs as simple demands.

Workers who had experience with raising infant apes countered that Nim, in particular, had an unstable environment with so many changes in personnel that his language training may have been compromised. Problems with objectively verifying tests of any ape's language comprehension and usage also occur when the animals are bored, or when the tester is a stranger to the animal. Motivation and emotional state contribute to ape testing performance just as they do to that of human children.

OVERCOMING METHODOLOGICAL OBSTACLES

Fortunately, the researchers at the Yerkes Center have found ways around these various methodological impasses. The latest results of the work of Sue Savage-Rumbaugh and her colleagues are the most impressive yet. Dr. Savage-Rumbaugh worked for many years training two common chimpanzees, Sherman and Austin, to use Yerkish. Their training was considered successful, but nonetheless the two chimpanzees required intensive conditioning to first acquire symbols and then to progress from a simple stage of symbol association to the more abstract representational use of symbols. In sum, although common chimpanzees clearly can deal with symbolic usage on a conceptual level, they still do not learn language in the same way, at the same pace, or with anywhere near the same facility as do human children, even with the kind of intensive conditioning that children never undergo.

More recently, the Yerkes group has worked with the bonobo, or pygmy chimpanzee, a little-known ape that until recently was considered to be merely a smaller version of the common chimp. Startling behavioral differences between the two closely related species have been found, both in field studies and in laboratory colonies, and the bonobo's language abilities are remarkably advanced in comparison with those of the common chimpanzee. Kanzi, a young male being raised by his mother, showed spontaneous use of the Yerkish keyboard and recognition of symbols without any training or conditioning behavior. His sole experience with language came by observing his mother, who was actively trained during his infancy. When it became clear that Kanzi was able to learn the Yerkish lexigrams independently, the research project was altered so that Kanzi would never be trained in the same manner as previous study subjects. Instead, he was given full access to the keyboard, both inside the laboratory and outside as he roamed the 55-acre enclosure. Kanzi requests all food, activities, and personal contact with his human and ape companions by means of the keyboard. Because of this research design, the criticism of past studies, that the apparent linguistic behavior is only a conditioned response, has been avoided.

Kanzi's language use differs from that of Austin and Sherman. Unlike them, Kanzi will name objects he does not want immediately, so his responses are not reward-dependent. He frequently uses gestures and vocalizations in conjunction with lexigrams, and his gestures are more controlled and precise. Most fascinating is the fact that Kanzi understands spoken English. Although it seemed that Austin and Sherman did also, it was not until their English comprehension was tested (in the absence of the usual contextual and gestural cues) that their performance on identification tests dropped to slightly better than chance. Using lexigrams improved their scores once more to almost 100 percent. Kanzi's performance shows no drop with the switch to English, and in fact he seems to use the spoken English as an additional cue to the meaning of lexigrams. More recent studies of Kanzi's younger sister, Mulika, indicate that Kanzi's abilities are not unique, leading Savage-Rumbaugh to conclude that the bonobo has some innate language abilities not shared with the common chimp, abilities that seem more like those of humans.

What do these results tell us about how animals communicate naturally among themselves? Very little is known about how wild chimpanzees communicate with each other, or about the complexity of their messages. These studies would seem to indicate that chimpanzees very likely use several types of cues simultaneously, such as vocalizations, gestures, and eye contact. No study in the wild has yet documented the range of chimpanzees' natural communications, but that may simply be a question of the human observers not knowing what to look for.

Some surprising results have been obtained from studies of monkey calls. Recording both vocalizations and behavior of wild vervet monkeys, Robert Seyfarth and Dorothy Cheney have shown that these monkeys have different alarm calls for each of their four major predators and different vocalizations for different types of social interactions. The calls seem to be a simple kind of representational signaling. Interestingly, while some of these calls are acoustically distinguishable to the human ear, others are not. If wild monkeys are capable of such unsuspected behavior, it seems likely that apes may also be able to communicate some types of information to each other, some of which we may not be able to hear.

Do these experiments provide any clues about how language might have begun in the human past? From these studies, and from observations of human infants, it seems clear that the ability to conceptualize and to hear complex vocalized messages can exist before the ability to produce actual speech is present. The ape experiments also show that once started, language use and learning can continue, even without further human training. For instance, Washoe, now living in a colony with other signing apes, has learned a few signals from her companions. They have also invented or modified signs on their own. Washoe has even taught signs to her adopted son, Louis, who continues to pick up additional vocabulary by imitating the other apes. Roger Fouts, the researcher in charge of the colony, reports that Jane Goodall has remarked on the low levels of aggression among the signing chimps, compared with chimps in other situations. This is an especially telling observation, since one of the theories about why language evolved in humans suggests that language became necessary to regulate social behavior. Whatever its origin, language, even among apes, may be an important diffuser of the tensions of group living. These experiments make it seem likely that the ability to symbolize might well have been present in the last ancestor we share with all the living great apes (that is, about 11 to 12 million years ago). It is now possible to see human language not as a trait without a past, unique to human beings, but rather as one extreme development of primitive communicative abilities and potential shared with our nearest relatives, the great apes.

UPDATE

Do apes have language? The answer to this question, of course, is that they don't. But what would we say of a one-year-old human infant? Does she have language? A two-year-old? A five-year-old? Language emerges as the infant matures, and so it seemed reasonable for us to take a developmental approach in our study. . . . We need to look for parallels between ape language and human language in the earliest stage of development and, having established these, see how far the apes can travel down the path toward human language.

Savage-Rumbaugh and Lewin (1994b:157)

Sue Savage-Rumbaugh's ongoing language studies with the bonobo Kanzi continue to challenge previous results and assumptions. Kanzi's precocious success with the Yerkish lexigram language shows that at least some apes can learn language systems spontaneously, without training, conditioning, or rewarding. The critical factors—as with human children— seem to be early exposure to language and an environment that is both highly social and language-rich.

Much of the scholarly world continues to reject the notion that animals are capable of any kind of "language," and attempts to publish the work with Kanzi have frequently been rejected by major scientific journals. Undaunted, Savage-Rumbaugh and her collaborators have continued to uncover fascinating aspects of Kanzi's language abilities. With linguist Patricia Greenfield, she learned that Kanzi's multiword utterances began to follow some formal syntactic, or grammatical, rules. He not only follows an English grammatical rule of word order (first action, then object, e.g., "hide peanut," not "peanut hide"), presumably picked up from his human companions, but he has also invented some unique grammatical rules himself. For instance, when he wants to engage someone in an action, he specifies the action first ("tickle") by choosing a lexigram on the keyboard, and then specifies the agent who is to do the tickling with a gesture. Not only does he follow this pattern of action-via-lexigram then agent-via-gesture even when he has to travel across the room to get to the keyboard, and the agent is sitting next to him, but it is also a rule that runs counter to the word order of the English spoken around him. These observations, that Kanzi's language use follows some arbitrary grammatical rules and that he is capable of making up some of these rules, satisfy some of the most important requirements for deeming language behavior truly grammatical.

Even more astounding is the discovery that Kanzi also shows substantial comprehension of spoken English, about 150 words by the age of six. Yerkes researchers began to get a hint of this when, in the midst of researchers-only conversations in English about room lights, Kanzi would run up to the light switch and turn the lights on and off. In fact, Kanzi learned the association between the spoken word "light" and the light switch *first,* and only later began to associate the light switch (or flashlight or other lights) with the lexigram for light. In other words, like human infants, Kanzi seems to have learned to decode spoken language first, and only later moved on to "reading" the code through lexigrams. Kanzi's comprehension of spoken English has been tested exhaustively with sophisticated methods designed to avoid the problems of bias noted in other ape-language experiments. During testing, only Kanzi hears the test word or sentence through headphones, so that the tester noting his responses does not know what question he was asked. In this situation, the tester does not know what the correct response is, and cannot inadvertently cue Kanzi to selecting the right answer.

Kanzi's latest exploits have been in the realm of toolmaking and archaeology. Some theories of human evolution have held that the development of language and the development of stone toolmaking may have gone hand in hand, both of them results of a unique human capacity for conceptual thought. Archaeologist Nick Toth had long wondered whether the earliest human toolmakers were doing something cognitively beyond the conceptual abilities of apes, or if they were merely applying an apelike intelligence to nonapelike problems and activities. The continuities between apes and humans that Savage-Rumbaugh has uncovered in language ability inevitably lead to questions about other supposedly unique human behaviors requiring conceptual ability. Could Kanzi learn to make stone tools, as the earliest hominids did?

Toth and Savage-Rumbaugh devised an experiment with three components: motivation to make stone tools (in the form of a food treat in a transparent plastic box tied up with string); the materials to make sharp stone flakes capable of cutting the string (a mound of rocks and cobbles in his compound); and instruction in producing stone flakes (stone-knapping demonstrations by Toth). However, Kanzi was never trained or coached in this new activity; he was merely provided with the opportunity to participate if he wished.

Kanzi learned to appreciate the usefulness of flakes quickly, and also to discriminate between sharp and dull ones. However, producing flakes himself took much longer—after two months, he was regularly producing small flakes of up to 1 inch long. To maintain his motivation to make better flakes, the string securing the treat box was made thicker and thicker, requiring larger flakes to cut through it. But Kanzi confounded the researchers when, instead of improving his stone-knapping technique to get better and larger flakes, he innovated and started throwing the cobble down on the hard tile floor, where it would shatter into a number of usable flakes.

Toth the archaeologist was frustrated by this innovation. While from a psychologist's point of view, Kanzi got high marks for problem-solving, this new production method was never going to result in an Oldowan-type tool. Carpeting was installed on the floor. Once again, Kanzi found a way around the research design—he simply pulled back the carpeting at a seam and hurled the cobbles on the exposed floor. Finally, however, when the weather improved and tool experiments were moved outside, Kanzi was forced to abandon the throwing technique, and produced ever-better flakes. But he eventually reverted to his original solution, when he figured out how to throw one rock at another one he placed on the ground. Again, he produced flakes, but in his own way and on his own terms.

Despite his proficiency at solving the problem at hand, Kanzi has not yet produced flakes that are the technical equals of real Oldowan stone tools. If nothing else, this experiment has inspired anthropologists with a new respect for the complexity of this earliest human stone tool culture. And it has inspired Toth to wonder what kind of tools preceded the Oldowan—and whether we would even be able to identify them. Kanzi's primitive cores and flakes, which look more like naturally fractured rock than like human artifacts, have opened a window on this earlier horizon.

FURTHER READING

Cheney, Dorothy L., and Robert M. Seyfarth. 1990. *How Monkeys See the World*. University of Chicago Press.

Gardner, R. A., and B. T. Gardner. 1969. "Teaching Sign Language to a Chimpanzee." *Science* 165:664–72.

Gibson, Kathleen R., and Tim Ingold, eds. 1993. *Tools, Language and Cognition in Human Evolution*. Cambridge University Press.

Hayes, Cathy. 1951. *The Ape in Our House*. Harper.

Linden, Eugene. 1974. *Apes, Men and Language*. Saturday Review Press/E. P. Dutton. (A survey of the sign language studies with apes.)

Parker, Sue T., and Kathleen R. Gibson, eds. 1990. *"Language" and Intelligence in Monkeys and Apes: Comparative Developmental Perspectives*. Cambridge University Press.

Patterson, F. G., and Eugene Linden. 1981. *The Education of Koko*. Holt, Rinehart, and Winston. (Describes the training of Koko the gorilla and the controversies about language experiments.)

Savage-Rumbaugh, E. Sue. 1986. *Ape Language: From Conditioned Response to Symbol*. Columbia University Press. (A somewhat technical but thorough account of the work of the Yerkes Primate Center.)

Savage-Rumbaugh, E. Sue, and Roger Lewin. 1994a. "Ape at the Brink." *Discover* 15 (September): 90–98.

Savage-Rumbaugh, E. Sue, and Roger Lewin. 1994b. *Kanzi: The Ape at the Brink of the Human Mind*. John Wiley and Sons.

2 POLITICS AND PROBLEMS OF GORILLA AND CHIMP CONSERVATION

Alison S. Brooks and J. N. Leith Smith

Of all the world's endangered species, gorillas and chimpanzees possibly receive the most sympathy, and the widest public support for their conservation. In large part, public empathy with these animals stems from the long-term efforts of Jane Goodall, Dian Fossey, and other primatologists who have demonstrated the close kinship between these animals and ourselves and made us aware of the dangers these primates face in a developing Africa. While elephant conservation in Zimbabwe has resulted in large population increases in some areas, the number of apes has not increased despite greater local and worldwide conservation efforts throughout the 1980s. Why are there only 310 mountain gorillas left in the wild?

WHY IS APE CONSERVATION SO DIFFICULT?

Anthropologists are deeply involved in primate conservation efforts. As Vernon Reynolds notes in a recent issue of *Anthropology Today,* we are responsible for the survival of chimpanzees (and other apes) in the wild if only because "they have helped us. Simply by existing, chimpanzees speak to us of our evolution, of our past, a past our ancestors shared with theirs. Thousands of Ph.D. students owe their thinking to chimpanzees. Careers have been, and continue to be, built on chimpanzees. . . . It is time we started to acknowledge the debt, to do something for them in return" (1990:3).

APE CONSERVATION AND MEDICAL RESEARCH

Ironically, one of the greatest obstacles to conservation efforts for great apes derives from the very same feature that has brought them within the anthropologist's orbit, namely, their close biological relationship to ourselves (they share 99 percent of our genes). This genetic makeup means that they are susceptible to many of the same disease organisms as humans. Not only does this susceptibility make apes harder to protect in the wild, but it makes them commercially valuable in the developed world as subjects for all kinds of experimentation. Geza Teleki, an anthropologist and chairman of the Committee for Conservation and Care of Chimpanzees, told us that

> even though it is illegal to capture and sell wild chimpanzees, the market demand for medical experimentation is so great that a dealer in a developed country can command an asking price of between $10,000 and $25,000 for a single chimpanzee. The African who caught the chimpanzee illegally might receive a payment of $30 to $50, equal to one to two month's wages, so that, even with shipping expenses, the profit margins are in the same league as those of the international trade in illegal drugs. How can African governments defend their endangered wildlife against this overwhelming economic incentive from the developed world?

The conservation effort for the great apes is two-pronged: protect the remaining populations of wild apes from local encroachment, and at the same time attack the international trade in animals caught in the wild. Teleki, who has worked closely for many years with Jane Goodall, is particularly involved in the attack on the international trade. One week he might be testifying in Europe against an illegal dealer caught with a shipment of wild chimpanzees. The next week he might be in Washington testifying before a congressional committee on the relatively small numbers of chimpanzees that remain in the wild and on the need for an international trade ban (Teleki, 1989b: 312–53).

In his work, Teleki also talks with the medical establishment to help

ensure that researchers use great apes from already established captive breeding colonies and not from wild populations. DNA "fingerprinting" of chimpanzees can demonstrate that particular animals come from a breeding colony and are not "illegal." The high price for chimpanzees also supports humane housing for captive animals, since no one wants to lose a $10,000 item of research "equipment."

In a National Geographic film about Jane Goodall, produced by Judith Dwan Hallet, we see how painful it is for those who have lived with chimpanzees in the wild to visit them in captivity. Yet both Teleki and Goodall believe, for the ultimate conservation of these animals, it is important to work *with* the medical establishment as much as possible, since medical research drives much of the deliberate poaching of wild chimpanzees.

FOREST CONSERVATION IN AFRICA

The human population in most African countries is expanding at the rate of 3 to 4 percent per year, which amounts to a doubling of the population every generation. The demands of an expanding population for food and fuel are resulting in widespread destruction of wild habitats, particularly those forested habitats that harbor the remaining ape populations. Furthermore, the need to generate hard currency reserves through the export of timber or cash crops has seriously depleted forest areas, thus reducing the land available for local subsistence.

Many African countries inherited from colonialism large tracts of undeveloped land set aside as game reserves. In several cases, notably in the Virunga National Park in the Democratic Republic of the Congo (formerly Zaire), these tracts were not uninhabited when the reserve was created but were home to indigenous peoples who were resettled outside their boundaries. When cash-poor African governments succeeded colonial ones, they found themselves in the difficult position of defending these reserves against the legitimate land requirements of their own people. In many cases, the people who run the central government of an African country and those who live in a distant rural area in close proximity to wild gorillas or chimpanzees do not share the same language or culture. Decisions made in the capital may not take local needs and interests into account and may be difficult to enforce from a distance, across cultural and linguistic boundaries. In order for a conservation effort to succeed, both the national government *and* the local population must support it.

For many Africans the special land rights demanded for endangered species by Western conservationists have sometimes been seen as a new form of imperialism, under which Africa will continue to supply the raw material for Western needs, albeit spiritual in nature rather than material. The Western search for self-renewal in a pristine wilderness, the quest for a deeper knowledge of the self in a confrontation with the primitive or animal "other" is not universally shared (see Haraway, 1989). How, then, can conserving apes benefit Africans and African countries directly?

Over the last decade most primatologists have come to accept that conservation efforts will succeed only if such efforts provide direct and visible economic benefits to both the local people and the national government. How can wild apes replace local food and fuel or hard currency earned from timber operations? The answer has been tourism. For some African countries (Zimbabwe, Botswana, Kenya, Tanzania) with large, easily accessible and relatively well-maintained savanna game reserves, tourism is the second or even the first source of foreign currency. In some cases, such as at Amboseli Park in Kenya, the cooperation of local people, in this case the Maasai, has been ensured, or at least made likely, through their direct participation in providing housing, food, and guides for foreign tourists. Can this model be applied to forest reserves and their elusive animals?

GORILLAS: TOURISM AND CONSERVATION

The most financially successful and well-known tourist experience in an African forest is the mountain gorilla project in the Parc National des Volcans, Rwanda. In 1990 about 6,500 tourists climbed the steep slopes of the Virunga volcanoes in search of a one-hour encounter with our largest relative. Each of the four habituated gorilla groups is visited by up to five tourists daily. Gorilla tourism is not for the tourist traveling on a shoestring but is designed to extract the maximum foreign currency from each visitor. Local people may have cornered some jobs as guards and guides, but the tourist dollars appear to be flowing primarily to the capital. First, the tourist pays $160 in entrance and gorilla visit fees directly to the park office. The base of the nearest gorilla visit site is at least two to three hours' drive from Kigali, the capital, in an expensive private taxi or rental car; inexpensive local buses drop you about 10 miles from the mountain in the nearest town of Ruhengeri.

Since tours leave early in the morning, to catch the gorillas during their most active period most tourists also end up paying, in the requisite foreign currency, for at least two nights' lodging in Rwanda. The total tab is usually about $400 to $500 each; even the most determined French-speaking tourist in good physical shape is unlikely to get away for less than $300. If 6,500 tourists spend at least $500 each in Rwanda, the total foreign currency revenue generated by gorilla tourism per year is more than $3.2 million dollars. This represents a minimum of $10,000 per "wild" gorilla. Gorilla tourist dollars, moreover, are a perennial resource rather than a one-time windfall. Not surprisingly, the government of Rwanda has strongly supported the development of gorilla tourism, accompanied by antipoaching and education measures.

The popularity of gorilla tourism is extraordinary, given its physical demands. Visitors to the clouded forest of the Virungas cannot experience the landscape or its animals from the comfort of a zebra-striped safari van. Instead the trip is exhausting and often uncomfortable, and the contact with the forest and its inhabitants far more direct than the usual savanna bus ride, but perhaps, for that very reason, more rewarding for the nature pilgrim.

In 1985 Alison Brooks (author of this chapter) and Catherine Smith (wife of its coauthor) visited the gorillas of Mt. Visoke. Although we had spent the previous two months excavating various levels of 100-foot cliffs at an altitude of 3,000 feet, we were quite unprepared for four or more hours of extreme physical exertion at 9,000 feet. During the climb to the nests where our gorilla group had spent the previous night, we began to understand why gorillas have such strong arms. For the most part, we progressed by pulling ourselves upward and forward over a tangled wet and slippery mass of tree roots, vines, and stinging nettles. In about three hours of constant motion, our feet almost never touched the ground. Once we located the nests, distinguished by the piles of feces gorillas always deposit in their nests before moving on, Catherine Smith immediately slipped on the wet leaves and fell in. From the nests, the trail was much clearer, although still covered in stinging nettles and definitely not designed for hairless bipeds. About an hour later, we finally made contact with the gorilla group.

Mountain gorillas are ideal subjects for forest tourism, since they are very large, live in groups, spend most of their time on the ground, move slowly, and rarely travel more than a few miles per day. Their energy budget dictates that they spend most of the day lying around digesting their relatively low-quality diet of leaves and shoots. Many tourists have made arduous climbs of five or more hours only to watch gorillas sleep. We were lucky; ours were just finishing off a morning meal of stinging nettle tops.

GORILLA CONSERVATION IN THE DEMOCRATIC
REPUBLIC OF THE CONGO (FORMERLY ZAIRE)

In the Democratic Republic of the Congo, a country 90 times the size of Rwanda, conservation efforts are strongly supported at the national level, but the local people charged with carrying out the government's edicts are much further removed culturally, linguistically, and physically from the government seat in Kinshasa 1,500 kilometers west of the Virungas. Four habituated gorilla groups at two sites in the Parc National des Virungas (Djombe and Rumangabo), which abuts Rwanda's Parc des Volcans, are visited by up to six tourists daily for one hour. At $150 apiece in park fees, plus substantial costs for transportation by a tour operator, gorilla tourists in the Congo provide a significant source of foreign income to the national government.

When we (authors Brooks and Smith) subsequently visited habituated groups in the Congo in 1986, 1988, and 1990, the park guards were increasingly proud of their conservation efforts as well as of their roles as brokers between gorillas and Western tourists. Over the years, the gorillas became increasingly "habituated," rarely charging or fleeing from the daily scrutiny of strangers, while the tourists were taught how to behave like submissive gorillas, moving only slowly and quietly, hunched down and grunting. The European Economic Community and Frankfurt Zoological Society provided incentives directly to local personnel, both in bonuses and in durable equipment (vehicles, two-way radios, on-site office buildings, etc.). In addition, the largest tour operator at Djombe was a local Congolese.

As in Rwanda, however, the rich volcanic soils immediately surrounding the small gorilla refuges in Congo are farmed intensively for both commercial (tea and coffee) and subsistence (manioc, bananas, potatoes) crops. The population density here approaches 300 people per square mile. Protein- and cash-poor farmers and BaTwa pygmies in close reciprocal relationships with farmers continue to set wire snares for small game inside the forest reserve, snares that occasionally maim or kill gorillas. For the landless pygmies, whose traditional life is tied to the forest, life outside the declining forest areas holds few possibilities. In Rwanda, the number of snares discovered by antipoaching patrols did decline from 2,500 in 1988 to 1,500–1,600 in 1989.

Since gorillas (unlike tourists) can travel freely across the Congo-Rwanda border, antipoaching efforts need to be coordinated internationally, but they are hampered by political instability and armed insurrection in both countries. In the summer of 1990, an armed Tutsi force invaded Rwanda from Uganda across the eastern part of the Virunga range. As of February 1991, all conservation and tourist activities in the Parc des Volcans had been abandoned and the research facilities at Karisoke (established by the late Dian Fossey) burned to the ground. The effect on the small gorilla population confined in the Virungas could be devastating.

TOURISM AND GORILLA HEALTH: A VET'S DILEMMA

Is tourism succeeding as a conservation strategy? Are mountain gorilla numbers at least stable, if not increasing, and does the commitment of the governments and wildlife organizations involved appear solid? During a flight from Nairobi to Frankfurt in early September 1990, Liz MacFie, a veterinarian with the Virunga Veterinary Center in Ruhengeri, and Jeff Seed, of the Karisoke Research Center, talked about these questions. MacFie's organization, funded by the Morris Animal Foundation, is responsible for the surveillance and care of mountain gorilla health, while Seed oversees the antipoaching patrols.

They pointed out that the gorilla census of November 1989 indicated a total population of at least 310 animals in about 30 groups, which was up about 20 percent from 1981. But with such a small total population, extinction is possible at any moment. Gorillas, like chimps, are close enough to humans to catch their diseases. The small size of the reserves, the large numbers of humans on their peripheries, and the close daily contact of gorillas with tourists, guards, and others makes it almost impossible to isolate the gorilla population from human disease organisms. Even though regulations stipulate that humans must keep at least 1 meter distance between themselves and the gorillas in the Congo, and more in Rwanda, gorillas can and do initiate direct physical contact across these distances. A severe epidemic or an infection centered in one of the larger groups could easily disrupt the population and tip the balance toward rapid extinction.

What can or should a vet do about a sick or injured gorilla living in the "wild" in its natural habitat? After all, should natural selection not be allowed to weed out less fit or weaker individuals? If humans intervene, will they not be condemning future generations descended from weak or sickly individuals to constant veterinary intervention? Should MacFie attempt to save the life of a subordinate male injured by another male? Last year a respiratory epidemic struck one group of 34 animals, representing 11 percent of the *entire* population of mountain gorillas. The dominant silverback male died in April. At this point, a decision was made to treat the seriously ill animals with long-acting and broad-spectrum antibiotics. The gorilla veterinarian faces a constant dilemma: too much intervention will create a weakened, medically dependent population, while no intervention will almost surely lead to rapid extinction.

CHIMPANZEES: TOURISM AND CONSERVATION

Could the gorilla model of forest tourism be used to set aside and patrol forest reserves for the common chimpanzee, and to mobilize local governments to support conservation measures more effectively? This possibility is currently being explored by several countries, including Tanzania, Burundi, and the Democratic Republic of the Congo. Gombe National Park in Tanzania, the locus of most of Jane Goodall's studies, has been inundated by the most intrepid tourists who find their own way there (on foot or by water taxi), camp on the beach, and attempt to make their own arrangements with the underpaid park staff. This situation compromises the research program at Gombe and also endangers the chimpanzees, who are even more susceptible than gorillas to human diseases. In 1966 a polio epidemic that began among the human population in Kigoma district killed about 10 to 15 percent of the Gombe chimpanzee population in one year, and in 1988, an additional 14 animals died from an introduced respiratory infection. Bacteria, parasites, and other infectious organisms can be transmitted both by tourists and by resident staff.

In Burundi, Jane Goodall has been working to help set up a tourism program in a small vestige of forest that has been turned into a sanctuary for chimpanzees confiscated from poachers and dealers. Given the demand for chimpanzees as medical research subjects, the threat of illegal recapture is constant. One group of 30 vagabond animals is followed around full-time by 10 armed guards. Goodall and others involved in this conservation effort hope that the greater visibility of the chimpanzees and daily contact with tourists when the program is well established will help deter poachers.

One of the greatest problems with marketing chimpanzee tourism is delivering the chimpanzee experience on a predictable daily schedule. Chimpanzees are much more mobile than gorillas, and, unlike gorillas, live in fluid social groupings whose membership is changing constantly. Not only do individuals move up to 25 kilometers per day, but they often travel above ground level, leaving little or no trail for an earthbound tourist to follow. The chimpanzee tourism project set up by Conrad Aveling and Annette Lanjouw in the Congo illustrates how chimpanzee tourism differs from gorilla tourism.

Chimpanzee poaching was relatively common in eastern Congo when our archaeological research there began. In 1987 Conrad Aveling, who had just set up the gorilla tourism site at Djombe, heard about a group of chimpanzees in Tongo, a small salient area of the Parc National des Virungas, whose habitat was threatened with total destruction because of charcoal cutting. In a country where almost everyone cooks their food with wood or charcoal, and where the basic staples (manioc and plantains) are inedible unless they are cooked for a considerable time, the pressure on the remaining forest areas is enormous, even if people are not allowed to farm there. Aveling and Lanjouw had to provide alternate firewood or charcoal sources before the Tongo chimpanzees could be protected and developed as tourism subjects. The funding agencies involved, the World Wildlife Fund and the Frankfurt Zoological Society, were persuaded to support two reforestation projects outside the park area at Tongo. In addition to providing a continuing source of firewood, these projects yielded both fruit for immediate human consumption and exotic wood species for commercial sale.

As a result, the local people appear very supportive of the chimpanzee project at Tongo, which began to accept tourist groups at the end of 1989. Twenty-six villagers are directly employed as guides and project staff, others as construction workers and staff for a new hotel recently developed there by a local contractor. When tourists arrive, they are asked if they have come to see "our chimps." Few other wildlife conservation projects in Africa are "owned" by the local community to this degree.

Initially, one trail was cut into the forest to aid in tracking the chimps; this was soon followed by a cross-cutting network of trails at 200-meter intervals, which provide human trackers rapid access to all parts of the chimpanzees' range. Trackers fan out in the early morning before the tourists arrive, following the chimpanzees by their calls. When a group is located, the trackers radio the tourist guide, who brings the tourists directly to the chimps' location. Occasionally tourists fail to see chimpanzees, but during the first eight months of tourism (January through August 1990), 98 percent of all visiting tourists had experienced at least a sighting of chimpanzees. This phenomenal success rate is due not only to the hard work of the trackers and guides but also to the unusual ecological situation of the Tongo site. The chimps occupy an ecological "island" of mature forest surrounded by the open desolation of recent lava flows. The forest island is dense with mature fruit-bearing trees, especially the chimps' favorite: figs. The resulting population density of chimps, about 4 per square kilometer, is among the highest known.

Because the chimps can retreat into the tree tops, visitors must often be content with glimpses of black shapes in the green canopy. This is particularly true on rainy days, when the chimps spend most of their time aloft. Since encounters cannot be guaranteed, the fee has been set much lower than for gorillas, at $40 per visit, and the number in the daily group is limited to four. It is unclear whether chimps can generate enough foreign currency to win the kind of government support provided to gorilla conservation.

Clearly, unlike mountain gorilla tourism, chimpanzee tourism can never provide an umbrella of protection over the total chimpanzee population. It is a quandary that awaits another solution.

UPDATE

Catherine Cockshutt Smith and J. N. Leith Smith

In the 1991 version of this chapter, Robert Humphrey's lead cartoon showed two gorillas lounging carefree and satiated in the fork of a tree while two human guerrillas fight viciously below. At the close of 1996, this cartoon remains, sadly, all too appropriate. Standing silently at center stage in a tragic human drama of genocide and political instability is the last remaining stronghold of the mountain gorilla, and so the issue urgently becomes whether the gorillas, as depicted by Humphrey, can remain carefree and well fed.

The last five years have witnessed ethnic genocide in Rwanda and the mass exodus of over a million refugees from this torn nation into the neighboring Democratic Republic of the Congo. Political instability and dire humanitarian problems are also increasing in this refugee-saturated borderland. Ecotourism in Rwanda has all but ground to a halt since the ethnic violence and instability began. In 1995 only about 100 tourists braved political turmoil to glimpse the apes on this side of the border. Since ecotourism is Rwanda's third largest source of international revenue (following coffee and tea sales), its decline has been unfortunate for both humans and gorillas. The impact of lost revenue on the human population

HIGHER PRIMATES

is obvious. Yet, without adequate financial backing, the gorillas also suffer since the park rangers and support staff who monitor and protect them cannot do their jobs. Concern about personal safety during the armed conflicts has also forced the Rwandan park staff to abandon their posts on several occasions. Every time this happens, the fate of the gorillas hangs in the balance.

On the Congo side of the gorillas' home range, the influx of more than a million refugees threatens these great apes. A number of camps are located dangerously close to the gorillas' habitat, and though the refugees are not poaching these animals, they have been entering the park to collect firewood. In addition to destroying the habitat, such close and uncontrolled contact between humans and gorillas can pose potentially devastating health risks for the apes. The refugees are numerous (at the time of writing, repatriation is reducing their numbers radically on the Congo side, but this may simply be carrying the problem back to Rwanda), many are in poor health, and the diseases they carry can be transmitted to gorillas with alarming ease, especially when sanitation is poor. As if to add insult to injury, the fighting between government troops and rebels in eastern Congo has forced the park guards there to abandon their posts. Tragically, several guards were killed in a recent confrontation and the park buildings and property were completely destroyed—once again leaving the gorillas unprotected.

It should also be acknowledged that close contact with great apes can be dangerous for humans. In 1995 a group of chimpanzees under long-term study in the Ivory Coast began dying at an alarming rate. Through autopsies it was learned that the apes had contracted the deadly Ebola virus—but not before one human researcher contracted the disease and nearly died (Morell, 1995). Ebola has drastically reduced the numbers in this unique group of chimpanzees, which possess the most extensive and complex technological repertoire of any nonhuman population. The high number of deaths suffered by these apes argues against the hypothesis that they constitute the disease's hidden reservoir. Nevertheless, fast on the heels of this deadly outbreak came news from Gabon in March 1996 that 13 people in one village had died from Ebola after eating a chimpanzee.

Our similitude with the great apes, whether immunological, genetic, physiological, or even intellectual, simply cannot be ignored, and this has motivated one organization named the Great Ape Project (Cavalieri and Singer, 1994) to go so far as to officially declare that we must "include non-human great apes within the community of equals by granting them the basic moral and legal protection that only human beings currently enjoy." Using the Anti-Slavery Society as its political model, this organization may be rather extreme in its approach, yet there is no denying that the more we know about the great apes, the more the distinction between "self" and "other" becomes blurred.

In such troubled times, is there hope? We believe so. In spite of all the upheavals in Rwanda and the Democratic Republic of the Congo, the gorilla population appears surprisingly stable—or even on the increase! This is very good news. However, the continuing political crisis in this region warns against complacency; the fate of these animals could change quickly and drastically at any moment. Rwanda is working very hard to reestablish ecotourism and has set up programs to involve and benefit the human community through the production and sale of local crafts. Throughout Africa, there is a heightened awareness of the plight of the great apes, and rehabilitation and reintroduction programs are expanding. Finally, new technology such as the World Wide Web and publications such as the IUCN/SSC's Newsletter, *African Primates,* are helping to disseminate critical information around the globe to all who can and are willing to help.

FURTHER READING

Butynski, Thomas M., ed. 1995–. *African Primates. Newsletter of the African Section of the IUCN/SSC Primate Specialist Group.*

Cavalieri, Paola, and Peter Singer, eds. 1994. *The Great Ape Project: Equality beyond Humanity.* St. Martin's Press.

Haraway, Donna Jeanne. 1989. "The Biopolitics of a Multicultural Field." In *Primate Visions: Gender, Race and Nature in the World of Modern Science.* Routledge, pp. 244–75.

Heltne, Paul G., and Linda A. Marquardt, eds. 1989. *Understanding Chimpanzees.* Harvard University Press.

Morell, Virginia. 1995. "Chimpanzee Outbreak Heats up Search for Ebola Origin." *Science* 268:974–5.

National Geographic Society. 1990. *Jane Goodall: My Life with the Wild Chimpanzees.* Film produced by Judith Dwan Hallet.

Nichols, Michael, and George B. Schaller. 1989. *Gorilla: Struggle for Survival in the Virungas.* Aperture Foundation. Distributed by Farrar, Straus, and Giroux.

Reynolds, Vernon. 1990. "Images of Chimpanzees." *Anthropology Today* 6(6): 1–3.

Teleki, Geza. 1989a. "An Etiquette for Ape Watching to Keep Them Healthy." *GEO* 1(2): 135.

Teleki, Geza. 1989b. "Population Status of Wild Chimpanzees (*Pan troglodytes*) and Threats to Survival." In Paul G. Heltne and Linda A. Marquardt, eds., *Understanding Chimpanzees.* Harvard University Press.

3 WHAT'S NEW IN EARLY HUMAN EVOLUTION 5 TO 1 MILLION YEARS AGO?

Alison S. Brooks

Where do we come from? What did our earliest ancestors look like and how did they behave? In the past 10 years, a flood of evidence, accumulating at an increasing rate, suggests new answers to these old questions. Until recently, the hallmarks of "humanness" were thought to have emerged early in human evolution: full bipedalism by 4 million years ago, and tools, nuclear families, division of labor by sex, hunting, long periods of childhood and adolescent dependency, and maybe even primitive language by 2 million years ago. In addition, as recently as five years ago, the family tree itself seemed rather simple and straightforward; the most common model was a tree with only seven or perhaps eight species in all, and only one "side branch."

Most of the time, the hominid "niche" was filled by only one species, except between about 2.6 and 1.3 million years ago, when related species occupied the "side branch." First there was "Lucy" (*Australopithecus afarensis*), from about 3.6 to 2.9 million years ago. Then, there were more "evolved" australopithecines who came in two varieties: the "gracile" type (*Australopithecus africanus*) and the "robust" type with huge teeth and a bony crest on top of the skull (*Australopithecus robustus*, *A. boisei*, and *A. aethiopicus*). The former group was thought to have evolved into an early form of our own species, *Homo*, while the latter "side branch" became more and more specialized, lived alongside early

38

Homo for a while (for perhaps as much as a million years) and then died out. Early *Homo,* in turn, went through a direct progression from *H. habilis* to *H. erectus,* to *H. sapiens,* marked by increasing brain size and decreasing tooth size. Until about 1 million years ago, Africa, specifically eastern and southern Africa, was the only home of our ancestors, or so it was thought.

In the past five years, new finds, new dates, and new analyses have turned this simple tree into a complex bush, full of unseen connections, dead ends, and mysteries. In addition, the bipedalism, bigger brains, omnivorous diets, toolmaking, long period of childhood and learning, indeed, the very "human-ness" of early humans, have been challenged. The result has been a dramatic upheaval in our conceptions of our past. While the African roots of the family tree have remained firmly fixed, the timing and number of migrations out of that continent have been matters of considerable debate. In addition to the "where," "what," and "when" of human evolution, the "why" has also been challenged. Was it really so dry in Africa 4 million years ago that our ancestors *had* to leave the trees for the savanna? Did larger brains evolve so we could make tools?

This review of recent finds covers five topics: the "oldest old" hominids; later stages of australopithecine evolution (news from South Africa); diversity in the early stages of *Homo*; when and why big brains, tools, and long childhoods evolved; and when hominids expanded out of Africa (and where they went).

THE OLDEST HOMINIDS

New finds from two regions have greatly expanded our knowledge of human evolution "B.L." (before Lucy). The first finds, announced in the fall of 1994, come from the Middle Awash region of Ethiopia, just south of Hadar, where Lucy herself was found. Here, Tim White, Berhane Asfaw, and an international team of experts found the scattered and highly fragmentary remains of 16 small creatures with large molar teeth, slightly reduced canines, and a positioning of the skull on the vertebral column (backbone) suggesting upright posture. These features suggested human ancestry and an initial placement in the genus *Australopithecus.* Enough differences exist, however, for these fossils to be placed in a new species, *A. ramidus* (or "root" in Afar, the local language). For example, the enamel on the canines and molars is relatively thin, the canines are

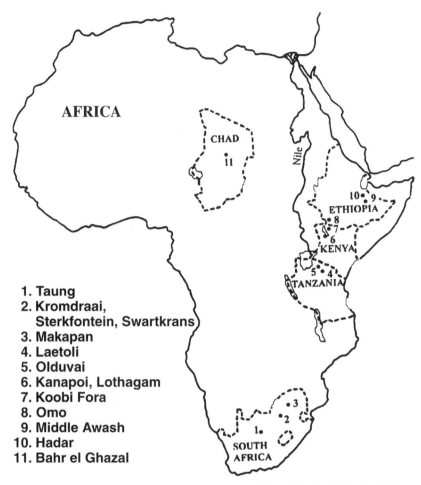

1. Taung
2. Kromdraai,
   Sterkfontein, Swartkrans
3. Makapan
4. Laetoli
5. Olduvai
6. Kanapoi, Lothagam
7. Koobi Fora
8. Omo
9. Middle Awash
10. Hadar
11. Bahr el Ghazal

Early Hominid Sites in Africa

relatively large for hominids, and the molars—especially the lower first deciduous or "baby" molar—are smaller than those of other *Australopithecus* and more elongated than square in shape. The skull opening for the ear is small, as in apes, rather than large, as in *Homo* and *Australopithecus*.

The leader of the geological team, Giday WoldeGabriel, argues that the fossils are close to 4.4 million years old, which is as far back in time from the actual Lucy find (3.18 million years old) as Lucy herself was from the original *Homo habilis* at Olduvai Gorge (1.9 million years old). While the teeth relate *ramidus* clearly to humans, the limb bones remain to be described. In recognition of the dental differences, White and his colleagues (1994) recently suggested that the fossils also be placed in a new genus: *Ardipithecus ramidus* rather than *Australopithecus.* White continued to work in the Middle Awash in 1994, 1995, and 1996, and has announced the recovery of at least one and perhaps several partial skeletons of different individuals.

One of the most interesting features of the *ramidus* find is the apparent *absence* of a savanna environment, at least in the immediate vicinity. The animal bones and plant remains reflect a forest with colobus monkeys, kudus, bats, a primitive bear, and a number of small mammals, but relatively few large savanna mammals such as giraffes, hippos, elephants, rhinos, or primitive horses.

In 1995 paleontologist Meave Leakey and colleagues also announced a new species from about 4.1 million years ago, this one from several localities around Lake Turkana. Called *Australopithecus anamensis* (after "anam," or "lake," in the Turkana language), it was differentiated from *afarensis* because the lower canines were larger, the lower front premolars more asymmetrical, the molars more sloping toward their crowns, the chin region a different shape, and the earhole small, as in *ramidus.* On the other hand, it was distinguished from *ramidus* by the thicker tooth enamel, larger molars, and squarer molar shape.

From the asymmetry and angle of the upper part of the shin bone in the region of the knee, however, this form was clearly bipedal. Bipedal knees are quite distinctive because they are shaped so as to allow the individual to lock ("hyperextend") the knees "straight" while standing and to balance easily over one leg while stepping out with the other. (It was just such a knee joint that led to the finding of Lucy in 1974.) The environment of *A. anamensis* was less densely forested than that of *ramidus,* closer to the open savanna envisioned in the earlier scenarios.

Which of these two led to *Australopithecus afarensis* and thence to *Homo habilis*? This may be a moot question, inasmuch as *Australopithecus afarensis* and *Homo habilis* themselves are challenged as single species stages on the road to modern humans. Is there more than one variant of Lucy, as is the case for the multiple species of monkeys and of chimpanzees that coexist in Africa today? A recent find of a much larger hominid (approximately 24 to 25 percent larger than Lucy) at Hadar was interpreted by Kimbel, Johanson, and Rak (1994) as a male *afarensis,* but could Lucy's son or brother really have been so different? Or are there two dif-

NEW STUDIES OF LUCY'S
ANATOMY SUGGEST SHE
WAS ACTUALLY A "HE"

ferent species of *Australopithecus* at this time as well? A recent argument by Richmond and Jungers (1995) for multiple hominid species in the time range of Lucy suggests that new studies of Lucy's pelvic anatomy indicate that she was actually a "he." Two males of such different sizes would certainly argue for at least two species.

Kimbel and his colleagues, however, contend that Lucy's pelvic shape is due to her posture while walking and not to an incorrect determination of her sex. Differences in limb anatomy could mean not different species but simply that the heavier males spent more time on the ground while females spent more time in the trees. Furthermore, they argue, not only do all the fossils attributed to *afarensis* belong in a single species, but the species lasted unchanged for almost a million years. This conclusion is based on comparisons between a new, almost complete skull from Hadar dated

to 3.0 million years ago and a new frontal (forehead and brow regions) from Belohdelie in the Middle Awash region just south of Hadar, dated to 3.9 million years ago.

If early australopithecines were not restricted to savanna environments, were they confined to east Africa? A new fossil suggests otherwise. It comes from Bahr el Ghazal in the *west* African country of Chad, more than 1,500 miles west of the east African rift valley sites. The fossil mandible is comparable to *afarensis* but with thinner tooth enamel and other distinctive traits so it could represent another new species. It is dated to around 3.0 to 3.4 million years ago on the basis of the primitive elephants, horses, pigs, hippos, and rhinos found with it. These are interpreted as indicating a mixed forest and woodland with some grassy areas, rather than an open savanna. Further exploration will probably expand both the range of the ancestral hominids and their variety.

NEWS FROM SOUTH AFRICA

The first *Australopithecus* find in 1924 consisted of a child's face, brain cast, and mandible from the South African site of Taung (*Australopithecus africanus*). The first recognition of different robust (r) and gracile (g) australopithecine species was also based on South African sites: Sterkfontein (g) and Kromdraai (r) in the 1930s, Makapan (g) and Swartkrans (r) in the 1940s. Although work has continued at these four sites, the main action in recent years appears to have shifted to east Africa, where periodic volcanic eruptions and rift valley sedimentation have enabled paleoanthropologists to find and date actual surfaces where australopithecines lived. Dates and ancient landscapes were much harder to reconstruct in the cave sites of South Africa. Also, in the 1980s and early 1990s South Africa was isolated from the rest of the scientific community for political reasons.

South Africa is suddenly in the early human news again with new finds that shift the picture of human evolution. There are two new fossil sites: Gladysvale and another site as yet unpublished, each with a new series of human remains. Sterkfontein, the first site to yield an adult australopithecine of the gracile variety ("Mrs. Ples"), now contains evidence that more robust forms were there as well *at the same time*. And at least some of these human ancestors may have been able to hold onto things (like tree branches) with their feet. Newly published foot bones from one of the oldest levels (member 2) at Sterkfontein, comparable in age to Lucy, show a big toe that stuck out at a slight angle to the other toes. Were there any trees to hold onto? New paleobotanical studies at Sterkfontein from the main australopithecine level (member 4) recovered fossilized vines or lianas (the kind that Tarzan swings on in the old movies) that today occur only well inside the tropical forest far to the north. No open savannas here either!

In addition, the younger horizon at Sterkfontein (member 5) has now yielded Oldowan tools dated to about 2.0 million years, slightly older than Olduvai and more "primitive" in their manufacture. Sterkfontein's archaeologist, Kathy Kuman (1994), has suggested most of them were made by smashing quartz cobbles on a hard surface and picking out the good flakes. Who made these tools? Sterkfontein yielded another hominid, younger than the tools and provisionally classified as *Homo,* but Ferguson (1989) has suggested that it may be too robust for *Homo* and might possibly be reclassified with *Australopithecus.*

Was the toolmaker Mrs. Ples, who comes from the underlying horizon dating to 2.5 to 3.0 million years ago (or someone like her but slightly later)? Since gracile australopithecines were supposed to have been ancestral to *Homo,* while the robust forms were on a side branch, many scenarios had the late gracile forms experimenting with tools, despite the absence of any evidence for tools in gracile sites. (Tools do occur with later *robust* forms!) Like Lucy, Mrs. Ples may soon undergo a sex change operation and, at the very least, assume a new identity. A recent careful examination of the top of her skull suggested that something was missing. Fortunately, the piece of rock that once encased her skull had been saved. Stuck into this rock were the remnants of a small sagittal crest. Gracile females did not have this feature. Either "Mrs. Ples" was really "Mr. Ples" or else she is one of the earlier members of the South African robust line.

At this point, the taxonomy becomes really confusing. If the *Homo* from Sterkfontein is really *Australopithecus,* and if the type fossil of an adult *Australopithecus africanus* is really a robust form like *Australopithecus* (or *Paranthropus*) *robustus,* then who is *Australopithecus africanus* anyway? Since the original *A. africanus* was a child's skull and braincase, we really have no way of knowing exactly what it would have looked like when it grew up. There will certainly be many years of arguments before these and other queries surrounding the fossils we now have are resolved, let alone the questions raised by new finds.

One postscript to the Taung story involves a fascinating bit of detective work. Most South African sites consist of the remains of lairs of predators that ate australopithecines for dinner, as suggested by the many carnivore tooth marks on hominid skulls and bones. Taung was always different from the others. Despite the mining of what was probably the entire cave, only the three pieces of the Taung "baby" were recovered. No larger or more complete fossils of anything ever turned up. The damage on the Taung skull was also different: sharp triangular nicks on the edges of the bone, and a distinctive dent in the top of the skull where the thin cranial bone was pushed into the brain. What could have caused this damage?

Lee Berger and Ron Clarke (1995) studied damage from many different types of carnivores and concluded that the only possible agent of destruction was a large eagle, whose talons poked a hole in the skull, and whose curved beak took distinctive bites out of the bone. This would explain why no australopithecine (or other large mammal) adults ever turned up there—they were too big for an eagle to carry.

EARLY HOMO: HOW MANY SPECIES?

The early evolution of our own species was also once thought to be a simple affair. Toolmaking, an enlarged brain, and smaller teeth marked the emergence of *Homo habilis* 1.9 million years ago. These features were functionally linked together by reasoning that teeth could not be smaller on a larger creature unless some "food processing" was done outside the mouth, that is, with tools. By 1.5 million years ago, even larger brains and modern body size marked the appearance of *Homo erectus,* who subsequently spread out of Africa. Finally, by about 500,000 years ago, early forms referred to as "archaic" *Homo sapiens* appeared in both Europe and Africa.

The number of species suggested for our own genus has also increased recently, and the relations between them have grown more complicated. What used to be called *Homo habilis* is divided into at least two, and possibly three, species, while the early *Homo erectus* fossils from Africa are sometimes put in their own species, *Homo ergaster.* In the later stages of *Homo,* once all grouped in the species *sapiens,* some authors place the early "archaics" in a separate species, "*Homo heidelbergensis*" and may further delineate the later Neandertals as "*Homo neanderthalensis.*" These authors reserve the species designation "*sapiens*" for modern humans only. Were all of these groups separate species that could not interbreed and had different adaptations? Did our previous "single species" view of the evolution of *Homo* obscure what was really happening?

Within a few years of finding the original *Homo habilis* at Olduvai, a very different early form had turned up to the north at east Turkana. This form, dated to the same time, had a larger brain but retained rather large teeth. The Olduvai fossils had small teeth, but brain sizes only slightly bigger than those of australopithecines. Bernard Wood (1992) has argued for the name *Homo rudolfensis* (after the old name for Lake Turkana) for the larger-brained Turkana form and retains the name *habilis* for the smaller form, whose skeleton, recovered in 1985, suggests Lucy-like proportions of arms and legs. How did these two differ in their behavior? The record is not yet complete enough to tell. Both used simple stone tools and occur in the same kinds of environments, usually more open and grassy than those prevailing before 2.5 million years ago. The difference is not due to geographical separation; a very early example of *rudolfensis* dating to more than 2.0 million years ago was reported in 1993 from the Malawi sector of the east African rift, well to the south of Olduvai. Which one led to modern humans? This, too, is unclear, and may never be determinable if new early species continue to be found. Perhaps more detailed environmental and behavioral studies now under way will provide some answers.

WHY BIGGER BRAINS?

Theories about the origin of the large human brain have focused on many aspects of behavior that were supposed to have driven this change. An early view pointed to hunting. When it was shown that early humans were more likely to have been scavengers, the focus changed to toolmaking. Recent dates of 2.5 million years ago for the earliest tools, at the Gona sites near Hadar in Ethiopia, predate the earliest evidence for an enlarged brain, and suggest that toolmaking came first, brains may only have followed hundred of thousands of years later. (New early fossils of *Homo* from Malawi, as well as from Ethiopia, may change this perspective as well.) Another theory is that brains became larger to take advantage of a longer period of learning and childhood development. New ways of studying growth rates in early humans, however, have shown that australopithecines were more like apes than like modern humans in their growth patterns, and that even *Homo erectus* was not yet fully human in this respect.

Scholars have tended to assume that the reason that brains did not become larger earlier is that they were not needed. A new theory, the "expensive tissue hypothesis," has argued instead that brains *could not* have become larger earlier, because they used up too much of the body's energy—ounce for ounce, the mammalian brain uses *nine times* as much energy as the rest of the body, on average. Leslie Aiello and Peter Wheeler (1995) point out that five major organs or organ systems use 60 to 70 percent of the body's energy at rest, although they account for only 7 percent of the body's total mass. These "expensive" organs are the gut, the heart, the liver, the kidney, and the brain. (Lungs are also quite "expensive.") Unless the animal eats a lot more high-calorie foods (very unlikely in the case of humans, to judge from the teeth) *or* one of these organs grows smaller, there is no energy budget left to feed a larger brain.

What did become smaller about 2 million years ago that allowed the brain to finally increase in size? The heart, liver, and kidney are scaled to body size (mass); they cannot grow smaller unless the individual does. The only remaining possibility is the gut, which could become smaller *if* foods were either higher in quality or partly "digested" outside the body by tools. Lucy's rib cage suggests that her gut was enormous and that her body proportions were more similar to those of a gorilla than of a modern human. No wasp-waists or hourglass figures among the australopithecines—indeed, no waists at all! On the other hand, the oldest relatively complete skeleton of early *Homo*, the "boy" from Lake Turkana (see my article in *AnthroNotes*, vol. 9, no. 3 [Fall 1987], pp. 11–15), though much larger than Lucy, has both a larger brain and a delicate waist and flattened rib cage, like ours.

But if changing food patterns made big brains possible, what made them desirable? Richard Potts (1996) of the Smithsonian's Human Origins Program argues that the major adaptation of early *Homo* was the ability to deal with rapidly changing climates and diverse environments, what he calls "variability selection." As climate swings became more severe, brain size and body size increased, and learning rather than instinctive behavior was at a premium. The major shift toward greatly expanded brains relative to body size took place not in the early stages of human evolution but about 500,000 years ago, with the onset of the dramatic climate changes associated with major ice ages and subsequent changes in the tropics.

OUT OF AFRICA: WHEN AND TO WHERE?

When did humans first expand out of Africa, and where did they go? Only a few years ago, the general patterning seemed to indicate that the exodus was just before 1 million years ago, that the human type involved was *Homo erectus*, and that the destination was Asia, not Europe. The earliest well-dated sites with definitive traces of human activity in Europe all appeared to cluster in the Middle Pleistocene after about 730,000 or even 500,000 years ago. New dates for both Asia and Europe as well as new finds suggest that this scenario, like the others mentioned in this article, may be far too simplistic.

The most widely accepted early dates in Asia are for 'Ubeidiya, a well-known site in Israel where Oldowan artifacts appear to go back about 1.4 million years based on faunal comparisons with Africa. New chronometric dates for the eastern part of the continent have been even more surprising. Carl Swisher and Garniss Curtis (1994) of the Berkeley Geochronology Center have published several dates older than 1.0 million years for the Modjokerto child, an early *Homo erectus* find from Java. These cluster around 1.8 million years. Some who disagree with these dates have argued that while there is indeed volcanic ash near the site of the find that is of this age, it is far from clear how that relates to the age of the find, which was made by a local farmer in the 1930s. Swisher and Curtis have responded that the ash that lines the skull is a close match chemically to the dated ash; others have either disputed their conclusions or pointed out that *both* the ash *and* the skull could have washed into the site together. In the latter case, the skull could be much younger than the ash. However, the continuing accumulation of new dates for other sites in Java, such as Sangiran, appear to confirm the presence of *Homo erectus* in Java between 1.4 and 1.8 million years ago.

An even more controversial site, Longgupo in South China, was recently described by Huang and others and by Ciochon in *Nature* and *Natural History*. This site contains a small jaw fragment of what the authors argue is early *Homo,* either *habilis* or *ergaster,* the first such fossil outside Africa. The find was associated with early Asian mammals (Late Pliocene to early Pleistocene in age) including a giant ape (*Gigantopithecus*). Also found were two very minimally fashioned objects of stone that the authors argue are tools. The possible attribution to *habilis* is based on the size and forward position of the cusps of the second premolar together with its double root. Others point out that these characteristics are not unknown from *Homo ergaster* or early *erectus,* or even some early Asian apes.

In addition, the dating of Longgupo is based on paleomagnetism, which measures the direction and strength of the earth's magnetic field in samples of earth taken from around the bones. The earth's magnetic field periodically dissolves, reorganizes and changes direction; 800,000 years ago, for example, a compass needle would have pointed south rather than north. These reversals are encoded in newly forming sediments, as the atoms align themselves with the prevailing magnetic field at the time. The ancient magnetic signal is locked into the sediment and can be measured in the lab. Precise dating of reversals in *volcanic* sediments using the potassium-argon technique has led to a sequence of ages for "normal" (north-oriented) and "reversed" (south-oriented) periods. In *nonvolcanic* sediments, such as those at Longgupo, researchers must try to guess which "normal" or "reversed" interval they are looking at, on the basis of the entire sequence. The important levels at Longgupo are "normal," below a layer that is "reversed," and several meters below that is a date of 1.02 million years ago, which is based on the decay of uranium isotopes in a sample of fossil tooth enamel and dentine. The researchers argue that the closest "normal" period before 1.02 million years ago is the one at 1.78 to 1.96 million years ago. If the uranium series age is closer to 0.78 to 0.84 million years ago, which the authors admit is possible, then the earth around the "human" bones could date to 0.9 to 1.0 million years ago, also a normal period, and much closer to the age of other old Chinese hominids.

What about Europe? The oldest European, and the only clear *Homo erectus* fossil from this continent recently turned up in the Republic of Georgia, in the Caucasus Mountains that separate Europe from the Near East. The fossil jaw, which looked very much like one from Kenya, was located in a normally polarized horizon above a basalt flow dating to 1.8 million years ago. One additional problem was that the find was not in some undisturbed cave but in the wall of a medieval storage cellar in the town of Dmanisi. A recent expedition suggested that the fossil came from a series of burrows or dens, excavated by prehistoric mammals. Although the earth where the dens were excavated is of normal polarity, the earth that fills the dens is reversed. This means that the fossil is *younger* than 1.8 million years (when polarity was normal) but must be older than 0.78 million years (polarity has been normal from that time to the present). The most likely estimate at the moment is about 1.4 million years ago, which is about the same age as 'Ubeidiya.

A final European site in the news is much further into Europe than Dmanisi: the site is Atapuerca in northern Spain, where literally hundreds of human bones have been recovered from narrow fissures in the rock. Most relate to Middle Pleistocene times, but in the oldest site, the dating may suggest an age of 800,000 to 900,000 years ago. What is especially interesting is that these are *not* classic examples of *Homo erectus,* but already suggest some specializations in the direction of Neandertals, such as tooth row with a space behind the last tooth, deep pulp cavities in the teeth, semicircular brow ridges, and some enlargement of the middle face. How did all those human bones end up in this area? Excavation and analysis of this site are ongoing, and perhaps further publication will soon enlighten us.

EX AFRICA SEMPER ALIQUID NOVI

Ancient Greek proverb: "Always something new Out of Africa."

Cited by Pliny the Elder and Charles Darwin

Just as we thought that the general picture of human evolution was becoming clear, new finds have suggested that it was too simplistic. The tree is more bushy, the causes more complex, and the migrations multiple and in several directions. These are very exciting times in paleoanthropology, and we look forward with great anticipation to the next few years of research and analysis.

FURTHER READING

Aiello, Leslie C., and Peter Wheeler. 1995. "The Expensive Tissue Hypothesis: The Brain and the Digestive System in Human and Primate Development." *Current Anthropology* 36(2): 199–221. (With comments by nine other scholars.)

Bahn, Paul G. 1996. "Treasure of the Sierra Atapuerca." *Archaeology* 49(1): 45–48.

Berger, Lee R., A. W. Keyser, and P. V. Tobias. 1993. "Brief Communication: Gladysvale: First Early Hominid Site Discovered in South Africa since 1948." *American Journal of Physical Anthropology* 92:107–11.

Berger, Lee R., and Ron J. Clarke. 1995. "Eagle Involvement in Accumulation of the Taung Child Fauna." *Journal of Human Evolution* 29(3): 275–99.

Brunet, M., A. Beauvilain, Y. Coppens, E. Heintz, A. H. Moutaye, and D. Pilbeam. 1995. "The First Australopithecine 2,500 Kilometres West of the Rift Valley (Chad)." *Nature* 378:273–75. (Comment by Bernard Wood on p. 239.)

Carbonell, E., J. M. Bermudez de Castro, J. L. Arsuaga, J. C. Diez, A. Rosas, G. Cuenca-Bescos, R. Sala, M. Mosquera, and X. P. Rodriguez. 1995. "Lower Pleistocene Hominids and Artifacts from Atapuerca-TD6 (Spain). *Science* 269:826–30. (Comment by J. Gutin on pp. 754–55.)

Ciochon, Russell L. 1995. "The Earliest Asians Yet." *Natural History* 104: 50–54.

Clarke, Ronald J. 1988. "A New *Australopithecus* Cranium from Sterkfontein and Its Bearing on the Ancestry of *Paranthropus*." In Frederick E. Grine ed., *Evolutionary History of the "Robust" Australopithecines,* pp. 285–92. Aldine de Gruyter.

Clarke, Ronald J., and Philip V. Tobias. 1995. "Sterkfontein Member 2 Foot Bones of the Oldest South African Hominid." *Science* 269:521–24. (Comment on pp. 476–77.)

Ferguson, Walter W. 1989. "Reappraisal of the Taxonomic Status of the Cranium Stw 53 from the Plio/Pleistocene of Sterkfontein, in South Africa." *Primates* 30(1): 103–9.

Gabunia, L., and A. Vekua. 1995. "A Plio-Pleistocene Hominid from Dmanisi, East Georgia, Caucasus." *Nature* 373:509–12.

Huang, W., R. Ciochon, Y. Gu, R. Larick, F. Qiren, H. Schwarcz, C. Yonge, J. de Vos, and W. Rink. 1995. "Early Homo and Associated Artefacts from Asia." *Nature* 378:275–78. (Comment by Wood and Turner on pp. 239–40.)

Hublin, Jean-Jacques. 1996. "The First Europeans." *Archaeology* 49(1): 36–44.

Kimbel, William H., Donald C. Johanson, and Yoel Rak. 1994. "The First Skull and Other New Discoveries of *Australopithecus afarensis* at Hadar, Ethiopia." *Nature* 368:449–51. (Comment by L. Aiello on pp. 399–400).

Kuman, Kathleen. 1994. "The Archaeology of Sterkfontein—Past and Present." *Journal of Human Evolution* 27(6): 471–95.

Larick, Roy, and Russell L. Ciochon. 1996. "The First Asians." *Archaeology* 49(1): 51–53.

Leakey, Meave G., C. S. Feibel, I. McDougall, and A. Walker. 1995. "New Four-Million-Year-Old Hominid Species from Kanapoi and Allia Bay, Kenya." *Nature* 376:565–71. (Comments by P. Andrews on pp. 555–56.)

Lewin, Roger. 1995. "Bones of Contention." *New Scientist* 148:14–15.

Potts, Richard. 1996. *Humanity's Descent: The Consequences of Ecological Instability.* William Morrow.

Richmond, Brian G., and William L. Jungers. 1995. "Size Variation and Sexual Dimorphism in *Australopithecus afarensis* and Living Hominoids." *Journal of Human Evolution* 29(3): 229–45.

Schrenk, F., T. G. Bromage, C. G. Betzler, U. Ring, and Y. M. Juwayeyi. 1993. "Older *Homo* and Pliocene Biogeography of the Malawi Rift." *Nature* 365: 833–36. (See also comment by Bernard Wood on pp. 780–90.)

Swisher, Carl, C. III, G. H. Curtis, T. Jacob, A. G. Getty, A. Suprijo, and Widi-asmoro. 1994. "Age of the Earliest Known Hominids in Java, Indonesia." *Science* 263:1118–21.

White, Tim D., G. Suwa, and B. Asfaw. 1994. "*Australopithecus ramidus,* a New Species of Early Hominid from Aramis, Ethiopia." *Nature* 371:306–12. (Comments by Bernard Wood on pp. 280–81.)

WoldeGabriel, Giday, T. D. White, G. Suwa, P. Renne, J. de Heinzelin, W. K. Hart, and G. Heiken. 1994. "Ecological and Temporal Placement of Early Pliocene Hominids at Aramis, Ethiopia." *Nature* 371:330–33.

Wood, Bernard. 1992. "Early Hominid Species and Speciation." *Journal of Human Evolution* 22:351–65.

4 MODERN HUMAN ORIGINS

What's New with What's Old

Alison S. Brooks

In a lecture at George Washington University, Washington, D.C., in September 1992, Richard Leakey argued that one of the most controversial and least understood events in human evolution occurs toward the end of the story. Where, when, and why did modern humans like ourselves first appear, and how did they come to occupy most of the earth?

Study of this stage of evolution is not new; in fact, it began more than 160 years ago with the discovery of Neandertal fossils in Belgium in 1830. In 1868, the coexistence of extinct animals such as mammoths with anatomically modern but very robust humans was documented at the site of Cro-Magnon, in southern France.

After all this time, why do we still not know more about an event so close to our own era? And why are the arguments over this event so bitter?

WHAT'S SO MODERN ABOUT MODERN HUMANS?

Anatomically, modern humans are distinguished from their predecessors by their relatively "gracile" (less robust or less muscular) skeletons and smaller teeth. Males, in particular, became smaller and overlapped the female size range to a greater extent than previously. Although the size of the brain itself did not increase in moderns from the preceding "archaic" stage, the braincase became taller, less elongated from front to back, and more sharply flexed at its base, where it joins the face. In essence, the face became almost completely situated under the braincase, rather than sticking out in front of it, as in earlier human ancestors and other primates. Smaller teeth also left the chin sticking out in front, and brow ridges became reduced. Archaic *Homo sapiens,* with modern-size brains but big brow ridges, large faces, and large teeth, occupied Europe, Asia, and Africa before the appearance of modern *Homo sapiens.* The term "Neandertals" refers in some theories to one relatively isolated, cold-adapted population of these "archaics." In other theories, Neandertals refers to *all* later "archaics," around 130,000 to 40,000 B.P. (before present).

CANDELABRAS AND HATRACKS

Throughout the twentieth century, two basic variants of the story have vied for acceptance in the scientific community. The "candelabra" view recognizes only one major branching of the human line. After the initial dispersal of humans to the three major Old World continents, beginning as early as 1.1 million years ago with the species *Homo erectus,* the populations of each region evolved in parallel fashion into modern humans. Some migration or gene flow between the regions ensured that new characteristics appearing in one region would eventually spread to all. In this theory, most of the immediate ancestors of the modern humans of Africa are found in Africa, while the immediate ancestors of the Chinese are found in China, and so forth.

Also according to this view, the immediate ancestors of Europeans are their predecessors on that continent—namely, the Neandertals. The current version of the "candelabra" theory is referred to as "multiregional evolution" (MRE), because it allows more migration from region to region than earlier versions.

In a contrasting view, known as the "hatrack" theory, a single main stem or center pole leads to modern humans, with branches at intervals through time representing evolutionary dead ends. According to this theory, the Neandertals of western Europe are one such dead end; the "Peking Man" or *Homo erectus* fossils of East Asia are another. Until recently, the central stem was always given a European or Near Eastern identity, through such fossils as "Piltdown" (a now-discredited forgery), Swanscombe (a large English skullcap without a face, dating to a period just before the earliest Neandertals), or the Skhul fossils from Israel. The central role of Europe in human evolution was attributed by some to the

THE "CANDELABRA" VS. THE "HATRACK" THEORY

influence of a colder climate, a limited growing season, and more reliance on both hunting and food storage, all of which would have promoted intelligence and growth of the brain.

In the current version of the "hatrack" theory, however, the central stem is African, and all the earlier fossils of other continents constitute the dead ends of human evolution. Since, in this view, all anatomically modern humans derive from recent African ancestors, the modern theory is called the "out-of-Africa" hypothesis.

How can two such disparate views continue to coexist? Why do the data not exclusively support one or the other? And why has the "hatrack" school shifted its focus from Europe to Africa? Three new D's—new dates, new data (fossil and archaeological), and new DNA studies—have combined to heighten the debate surrounding modern human origins.

DATING THE DATA

By 35,000 years ago, the shift to modern humans was virtually complete throughout Europe, Asia, Africa, and even Australia. The most accurate dating technique for the later periods of archaeology, radiocarbon dating, gives good results back to about 35,000 years ago, but not much older. Some dates of 38,000 to 40,000 are acceptable, but dates in the range of 40,000 or older are decidedly dubious. Most of the story of modern human origins lies beyond 40,000 years ago. Until recently, there were no reliable ways to determine the age of anything between 40,000 and 200,000 years ago, beyond which potassium-argon dating is useful.

A range of new techniques has come into general use for exactly the period when modern humans must have emerged, between 200,000 and 40,000 years ago. These techniques include: (1) measuring the accumulation of "radiation damage" from soil radiation in buried crystalline materials such as flints or quartz sands (thermoluminescence); (2) measuring the decay of uranium that soaks into buried bones and teeth from groundwater (uranium series), or radiation damage in the crystals of tooth enamel (electron spin resonance); and (3) studying the decay of the proteins encapsulated in hard tissues of fossil animals such as mollusc shells, bones, teeth, and ostrich eggshells (amino acid racemization).

Unlike radiocarbon, none of these techniques is entirely independent of the burial environment. Thermoluminescence and electron spin resonance dates can be thrown off by inaccurate measurement of the soil radiation or by heating or reexposure of the sample before the archaeologist finds it. Protein decay rates are dependent on temperature, which is difficult to estimate for 40,000 to 200,000 years ago. And the uranium that soaks into bones and teeth can also wash out again. Using two different techniques to date the same site can help avoid these problems, at least when the two sets of results agree.

The effect of the new dating techniques has been to make many sites and fossils in Africa earlier than was previously thought. The European dates did not change quite as much, because the ebb and flow of ice ages had provided a chronology that tied most of the sites together, even in the absence of exact numbers.

Once the chronology of Africa was worked out on the basis of its own internal sequence of dates, comparative faunal extinctions, and climate changes, it became obvious that the earliest fossils in Africa with "chins" and small teeth were much older than the Cro-Magnons of Europe. In a 1992 discussion of ostrich eggshell dates, I and my colleagues suggested that several of the most important early African sites with modern humans (Klasies River Mouth and Border Cave) date as far back as 105,000 years ago or older. Modern human teeth at Mumba shelter in Tanzania were dated to about 130,000 years by uranium series.

Meanwhile new dates for Zhoukoudian (Peking Man sites) and other sites from China and Java suggest that East Asia was occupied exclusively by the more primitive species *Homo erectus* until about 300,000 years ago. The new Chinese fossils announced in 1992, which supposedly represent a transition between *erectus* and *sapiens,* do *not* show that this transition happened in China *first,* as several newspaper reports seemed to suggest. That the earliest modern humans were African seems quite well-established, although very few sites have been dated thus far.

In Europe, the new dates have had two principal impacts. First, they demonstrate the great antiquity in Europe of the Neandertal-type long face, large nose, and flattened bulge at the back of the head. The oldest fossil now referred to as Neandertal (Le Biache, France) was discovered in 1976 and is about 190,000 years old, while older fossils (e.g., Arago in the Pyrenees) with some Neandertal characteristics, date to 300,000 years or older. Second, newer, more precise radiocarbon dates from the end of Neandertal times show that, in particular areas, the transition from Neandertal to Cro-Magnon was quite abrupt. A Neandertal from St. Cesaire in France, found in 1979, is about 35,000 years old, while the Cro-Magnon fossils probably date to at least 34,000, on the basis of comparisons with the Pataud site next door. Such an abrupt transition does not leave enough time for evolution to have occurred in place. In addition, the oldest modern human fossils and archaeological sites of the Aurignacian culture of Cro-Magnon are found in eastern Europe just before 40,000 years ago, while Neandertals still lived in the West, which is just what one would expect if modern humans invaded Europe from Africa via the Near East. And in the Near East itself, modern humans from Qafzeh, in Israel, excavated in the 1960s, have been dated to about 92,000 years ago by thermoluminescence on burned flints, and a similar antiquity was suggested for at least some of these fossils by our work on ostrich eggshells. Still unclear in the Near East is the chronological relationship of the Qafzeh modern humans to Neandertals. What might explain Neandertal dominance of this region *after* a brief period of modern human occupation at 92,000 years? One possible answer lies in the tiny bones of birds, rodents, and insectivores found with the human fossils. Earlier modern humans are accompanied by tropical African birds, mice, voles, and so on, while later Neandertals are accompanied by cold-adapted animals from Eurasia.

If Neandertals were the cold-adapted archaics, and the earliest modern humans were tropical, this shifting pattern implies that the distribution of the two populations was originally limited by ecological considerations, and that the Near East represented a boundary zone that shifted as the world's climate changed. By 40,000 years ago, when modern humans returned to dominate the region, they seem to have invented a way to get around this ecological limitation. The animals found at the modern human sites dating later than 40,000 years ago remain primarily cold-adapted.

THE "AFRICAN EVE" HYPOTHESIS

That humans were "modern" in appearance in the tropics long before these characteristics appear in Europe seems confirmed by the new dates and data. But what is the relationship of the first modern humans in Africa to the later ones who occupied Europe after 35,000 years ago? This relationship is the hottest part of the current controversy.

In 1987 geneticist Rebecca Cann and her colleagues proposed that a recent migration out of Africa within the last 200,000 years had completely replaced all other human populations. None of the "archaic" East Asians or the Neandertals of Europe had left any descendants at all. All modern humans share a recent African ancestor. The data used to support this hypothesis did not come from the fossil record or from the dating lab, but from analysis of genetic differences among people living today.

The most common and abundant genetic material (DNA), which occurs in the nucleus of a cell, changes too slowly to measure recently evolved differences—even comparing humans to chimpanzees reveals a less than 1 percent difference between the two species. But mitochondria, small organelles within cells that are important in converting food to energy, contain a more rapidly changing form of DNA. Since sperm consist almost entirely of nuclear DNA and lack mitochondria, an individual's mitochondria derive entirely from the mother via the ovum. A family tree of human genetic similarities, based on mitochondrial DNA (mtDNA), reflects only female ancestry, hence the "Eve" in the hypothesis.

This last common ancestor of all humans is thought to have been African because Africans are more variable in their DNA than the peoples of other continents, which suggests that they have been in place the longest. Furthermore, some genetic variants are unique to Africa, while all the variants on other continents are found in Africa as well. If Neandertals from Europe or *Homo erectus* from China contributed to our ancestry, where is their unique DNA?

What about "Adam"? A similar study was done on the genetics of the Y-chromosome, which appears to determine maleness but little else. Family trees based on similarities in the genetic makeup of the Y-chromosome reflect only male ancestry, since women do not have one. The same pattern was observed: greater variability and unique patterns in African populations, but no unique patterns outside that continent. The most variable DNA in both studies belonged to the small isolated populations of hunter-gatherers in the Kalahari Desert (!Kung) and forest basin of the Democratic Republic of the Congo (Mbuti, Aka, Efe).

At first, the major debate was over possible errors or omissions in the sample (use of African Americans instead of Africans, assuming little admixture in the maternal line) and the timing of the dispersal from Africa. Using as a guide the degree of differentiation developed within Australia and New Guinea (first colonized about 50,000 to 40,000 years ago) or among the populations of the Americas, it was estimated that human mtDNA diversifies from a common ancestor at a rate of 2 to 4 percent per million years. Since the total amount of difference observed in modern populations was only about 0.57 percent, this implies a time scale of 140,000 to 290,000 years since all humans last shared a common ancestor.

More recently, the family tree itself has been questioned on statistical grounds. Given enough time and repeated tries, the computer program used to generate the published family tree can also generate alternative trees in which Africa plays a diminished role. The genetic basis for total replacement of all previous human populations by the descendants of "African Eve" appears to be in doubt, although this does not negate the importance of the early *fossil* evidence from Africa.

ANCIENT AFRICANS, WHOSE ANCESTORS?

What was the relationship between the Neandertals or other archaics of regions outside Africa and their successors? Is there any evidence of population movement from Africa to Europe or East Asia? Did the invaders interbreed with the older populations of these areas, or did they simply wipe them out? Much of the argument hinges on current analyses of the fossils themselves. Three issues are central: (1) Who were the Neandertals (and what "explains" their robust body form)? (2) Are there any intermediate fossils between Neandertals (or archaics) and modern humans? and (3) Are there regional continuities in facial shape or teeth that continue across the transition from archaic/Neandertal to modern?

Up through the early 1970s, many scholars tended to lump Neandertals with other archaics as having modern brains and large primitive faces (and teeth). Western European Neandertals, whose faces were longer and more projecting, and whose elongated heads appeared to have an "occipital bun" of bone at the back, were simply more extreme than others. It was widely suggested that "if you gave a Neandertal a shave and a haircut (and a shopping trip to J. C. Penney), you wouldn't recognize him on the New York subway."

In the 1970s Erik Trinkaus began a lengthy study of Neandertals from a new perspective—below the neck. His analysis strongly suggested that *all* Neandertals, including those from the Near East but *not* the archaics from tropical environments and East Asia, shared a common and very unusual "post-cranial" form. Their bones, even in the fingers and toes, were extremely thick and bore heavy markings for muscle attachments that could not be found in modern samples of skeletons. The joint surfaces were sometimes twice as large as the modern human average. Discovery of a pelvis from Kebara, Israel, suggested that the way the body was carried was quite different, as the spinal column was more deeply indented into the back than in ourselves. Yet, from the same site, a hyoid bone, which attaches to the voice box, suggested that the movement of the throat, tongue, and voice box in producing speech was similar to ours, despite the greater distance in Neandertals between the neck and the back of the throat.

In addition, Neandertals, like other cold-adapted animals, had very large deep chests and short lower arms and legs, to better conserve body heat. New studies of the face suggest that the very long projecting face and huge, broad nose were distinctive; other large-faced archaics from Africa or East Asia had shorter, flatter faces, with more angulated cheek bones. The distinctions between Neandertals and other archaics appeared quite striking and led most scholars to exclude fossils formerly grouped as "Neandertaloids" from this category. Neandertal morphology was peculiar: you would definitely notice it even on the New York subway!

Are there any transitional fossils? In Africa, several fossils are intermediate between archaics and moderns. According to Trinkaus, even the early moderns themselves at Klasies River Mouth, for example, are more robust in their limbs than Cro-Magnons of Europe. In Europe, the argument is very heated. Those who argue for interbreeding between Cro-Magnons and Neandertals (such as Milford Wolpoff and F. H. Smith), or even for an indigenous evolution from Neandertals to Cro-Magnons (C. Loring Brace), point to the less extreme characteristics of some later Neandertals, or to the presence of significant brow ridges and large rugged faces along with definite chins at modern human sites in central Europe.

Transitional or even archaic *Homo sapiens* fossils from Asia are quite

CHEWING STRESS AND BROWRIDGES

rare; most of the best specimens from China have not been documented in an accessible form. Regional continuities in Asia, however, are striking to proponents of the multiregional evolution theory (Milford Wolpoff, Wu Xinzhi, A. G. Thorne, and G. G. Pope). If the earliest modern Asians came from Africa, why do the earliest ones we find already have the flat upper faces, and dental characteristics of Asians today? Why are the earlier archaic Asians also flat-faced? "Out of Africa" theorists (such as Christopher Stringer) argue that the flat faces and other features are either primitive features retained in that population, or simply adaptations to the cold dry Asian climate that are favored each time a new human population reaches the area.

REVOLUTION OR EVOLUTION?

In his 1992 book, *The Last Chimpanzee,* Jared Diamond argues that modern humans became fully modern in their behavior rather suddenly about 40,000 years ago. This "great leap forward" or "human revolution" is largely based on the perspective from Europe, where major changes in technology (blade and bone tools), economic strategies (ambush hunting, fishing), size of social networks, and symbolic activities (art) occurred over a few thousand years as the Cro-Magnons replaced the Neandertals.

The recovery of new sites, fossils, and other materials dating to between 250,000 and 40,000 has accelerated since the 1960s. Even with the limited exploration of Africa to date, it seems that, like modern human facial shape, some of the modern behaviors associated with the "human revolution" appear well before 40,000 years ago in Africa. While the later Neandertals ran down their prey and stabbed it with sharpened sticks or an occasional stone-tipped spear, central and eastern Africans hafted small delicate stone points onto spear or even arrow shafts; made stone blades, backed triangles, or crescents, barbed bone points, and other bone tools; engaged in regular fishing and ambush hunting; ground their food (and some pigments) with grindstones; scratched designs on ostrich eggshell fragments; and traded precious raw materials such as obsidian over more than 500 miles. The early modern humans also buried their dead with grave goods, unlike most Neandertals.

New data show that by 50,000 to 40,000 years ago Africans wore beads of ostrich eggshell and engaged in organized mining of precious raw materials. Elsewhere, modern humans had used boats to reach Australia, New Guinea, and New Caledonia, where rock art has been dated to 32,000 years ago. Outside of Europe, the "great leap forward" began earlier and was more like a slow jog, with occasional detours and backward movements.

BUT WERE THE CRO-MAGNONS AFRICAN?

Although modern humans appear to have developed earlier in Africa, physical anthropology and archaeology do *not* demonstrate migration of modern humans to Europe. Despite earlier claims for the fossils from Grimaldi, Italy, African characteristics such as nose shape and width, wide distance between the eyes, and forward projection of the mouth do not occur in the early Europeans. Grimaldi itself is not only not "African" but is considerably later in time than the earliest modern Europeans—new dates suggest an age of less than 28,000 years. According to recent dates on archaeological sites, the Aurignacian culture of the Cro-Magnons appears *first* in central and southeastern Europe, just before 40,000 B.P., spreading to an area near Barcelona, Spain, by about 38,000 and finally to France and Germany by 34,000. Southern Spain, near the Straits of Gibraltar, is one of the *last* areas to make the transition from the Mousterian culture of Neandertals—archaeology does not suggest an invasion via this route. The big blades, thick scrapers, and bone points of the Aurignacian are quite unlike anything from the preceding Mousterian culture of Neandertals, so it was assumed that it came into Europe from outside. Yet there is nothing "outside" in this time range, either in the Near East or in North Africa, from which the Aurignacian can be derived. In much of Africa and the Near East at about 40,000, the stone industries were characterized by finely made small blades, many with narrow points created by blunting or battering the sides, or by small points with a tang or projection for hafting. The Aurignacian does show up in the Near East, but recent dates suggest that this is only *after* it was well-established in Europe, at about 34,000. The Near East may have been a migration corridor, but it was open in both directions.

CAN THIS CONTROVERSY BE RESOLVED?

The controversy over modern human origins is particularly heated because it concerns ourselves and our most recent history. The argument has been widely featured in the public media: *Time, Newsweek, The New York Times,* and at least two television specials produced by the Public Broadcasting Service. Unlike the controversy over earlier phases of human evolution, many of the voices expressed in these pieces are the voices of nonscientists, who argue that up to now Eurocentric bias has suppressed recognition of our "true" heritage. While the discoveries of the past two decades have gone far toward demonstrating the priority of continents other than Europe in the evolution of modern humans, the data also suggest that this was not a simple event of evolution followed by migration in one direction. Replacement of earlier populations may not have been total. More and better dates and data, particularly from regions such as western Asia, Turkey, and the Balkans, as well as Africa, may help clarify the complex interactions involved in this transition.

FURTHER READING

Diamond, Jared M. 1992. *The Third Chimpanzee: The Evolution and Future of the Human Animal.* HarperCollins.

Lewin, Roger. 1993. *Origin of Modern Humans.* W. H. Freeman.

Stringer, Christopher B., and Clive Gamble. 1993. *In Search of the Neanderthals.* Thames and Hudson, 1993.

Trinkaus, Erik, and Pat Shipman. 1993. *The Neandertals: Changing the Image of Mankind.* Knopf.

Wolpoff, M. H. 1996. *Human Paleontology.* McGraw-Hill.

Excellent discussions on this topic can be found in the following journal issues:

Discover, September 1992.

Proceedings of the National Academy of Sciences, January/February 1996.

Scientific American, April 1992, October 1991, December 1990.

Science, February 7, April 3, May 29, June 12, 1992; August 23, 1991; March 11, 1988.

U.S. News and World Report, September 16, 1991, May 20, 1996.

5 MAN THE SCAVENGER

Kathleen D. Gordon

For several decades now, long enough to have influenced generations of students, the most familiar picture of early man has been that of the hunter, whose very instincts, social behavior, and mating patterns were all honed by the stringent demands of a predatory existence. This preoccupation with hunting as the "master behavior pattern of the human species" (Laughlin, 1968) has been fueled by many factors: the indisputable evidence of large-scale big-game hunting in Upper Paleolithic Europe; the visible archaeological record, with its emphasis on stone "weapons" and animal bone fragments; and also (perhaps somewhat subliminally) the high value accorded meat and hunting as a leisure activity in Western society.

But is it really true that hunting is the primary human adaptation? Some new research suggests, "Maybe not." Given the widespread influence the "hunting hypothesis" has had in shaping our thoughts about human evolution and psychology, some careful rethinking of the work of the last several decades is in order.

If the hunting proclivities of early hominids were interesting only for the evidence provided about diet and food acquisition, then changes in the portrait of early man would scarcely be noted beyond the ivy-covered walls of academic research. But of course, our interest in what early humans ate and how they obtained it has far wider implications. How any animal makes a living in large part determines many other aspects of its behavior, reproduction, and social organization. The question of human hunting, moreover, invokes larger and more philosophical questions about the very essence of human nature. Since the discoveries of early hominids in South Africa, it has suited those impressed by the evil capabilities of mankind to find the roots for this darker side of human nature in the adaptations of the earliest hominids. It was Raymond Dart, the discoverer of the Taung baby, who in 1953 first characterized *Australopithecus* as a "confirmed killer" who bore the "mark of Cain."

EVIDENCE FROM BONES

The physical evidence Dart used to support this contention, the fragmented animal bones found with hominids in South African cave sites, has since been reexamined, and his claims refuted. Yet the image of early man as a predator who killed his food and occasionally his conspecifics has persisted in popular literature such as *African Genesis* and *The Hunting Hypothesis,* by Robert Ardrey. As a result, human hunting has been equated with innate aggressiveness, and aggression in modern man has often been seen as an unfortunate but probably unavoidable consequence of this earlier reliance on predation.

However, new evidence and theories proposed in the last few years are dramatically altering the way in which paleoanthropologists currently reconstruct early hominid diet and behavior. The strongest evidence comes from finds of flaked stone tools with quantities of animal bones. East Africa has produced many such sites, from as early as 2 million years ago. The tendency among paleoanthropologists has been to assume that these accumulations of bone were the end-product of hominid hunting. Although to most workers it now seems indisputable that early man was involved at some level in transporting or processing animal carcasses, recent studies have challenged the idea that human hunting was responsible for acquiring the animal parts.

A survey of animal bones from hominid-bearing deposits at Olduvai Gorge and Koobi Fora showed that a number of them bore surface markings that looked very much like damage done by stone knives or flakes (Bunn, 1981; Potts and Shipman, 1981). These scratches, or cut marks, could be proof that early hominids were cutting up animal carcasses. The purpose of this is not as obvious as it first looks, however. Potts and Ship-

man's survey of Olduvai bones showed that cut marks frequently occurred in locations where little or no meat is found, such as lower limb bones and feet. They speculated that sinew and hide might have been what the hominids sought, rather than meat. In addition, they found some bones showing the gnawing marks typical of carnivore chewing as well as cut marks from stone edges. The cut marks were often made after the gnaw marks, suggesting that carnivores had first possession of the carcass, and hominid utilization came later.

MODERN SCAVENGERS

The idea that early humans might have obtained meat by scavenging rather than hunting is not a new one. But the recent evidence from cut marks has produced a spate of new studies exploring this idea. Prominent among these is a survey of animal carcass condition, size, and availability on the modern Serengeti savanna by Robert Blumenschine, a graduate student at the University of California at Berkeley. Though the work is still in progress, he has determined that usually very little meat is left for scavengers on the typical lion kill (Bower, 1985). Other edibles, such as marrow, fat, and brains, might be more important, he proposes. These results may support Potts and Shipman's speculations that meat was not the only possible attraction for early hominids. Blumenschine has also discovered that the best opportunities for scavenging today occur in wooded patches near water sources, which is the very same type of geological setting in which most East African hominids, tools, and fossil bone sites have been found.

Whereas Blumenschine has been testing the possibilities of making a living by scavenging on a modern savanna, Shipman (1984) has been exploring the theoretical needs of scavenging as a way of life. By surveying modern scavenging birds and animals, she has found that a successful scavenger has four special qualities: the ability to cover large distances searching for carcasses, a way of improving its vantage point to locate carcasses, a strategy for dealing either with the primary predator or with other competing scavengers in order to gain possession of a carcass, and an adequate fall-back diet for when times are lean. Shipman suggests that bipedal locomotion would have satisfied the first two requirements. Because of their small body size, early hominids probably relied on stealth rather than direct confrontation to get hold of carcasses and ate fruits and insects when they could not. Although the model does not fit everything we now know about early hominids (for instance, some hominids were considerably bigger than her estimates, as the recent find of a 1.6-million-year-old *Homo erectus* from West Turkana shows, and other types of plant food may have been more important than either fruits or meat), Shipman's scenario provides paleoanthropologists with an important new hypothesis to test.

In sum, evidence is accumulating that scavenging was at least a feasible strategy for early hominids. It may have been from gleaning bits of meat and other animal protein from carrion that humans first acquired a taste for meat and later developed the means to obtain it more regularly.

LESSONS FROM LIONS

Although this revision of early man's food habits is bound to distress some, it should be pointed out that the lion, an animal we often endow with humanlike qualities and refer to as the "greatest hunter" and the "king of beasts," has also been revealed recently as somewhat less "noble" than was thought before. Ironically, lions in East Africa scavenge or steal other hunters' kills at least as often as they kill themselves, and by such behavior they fall into Shipman's "bully-scavenger" category.

Perhaps it is time to demythify hunting and its purported influence on human psychology, and recognize that just as there is more than one way to skin a cat, so are there several ways to bring home the bacon. Hunting is merely a somewhat more reliable way of acquiring the bacon in the first

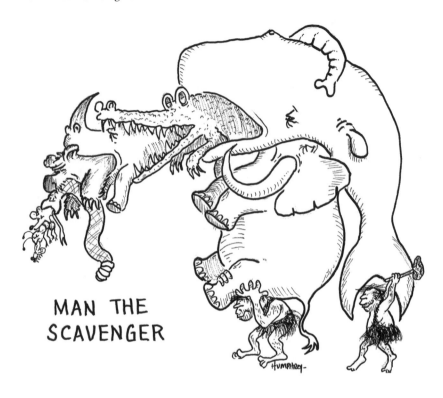

MAN THE
SCAVENGER

place, and although armed hunting certainly represents a quantum leap in terms of foresight and strategy, it does not necessarily imply a major change in human psychology or aggression.

UPDATE

In the decade since this chapter was written, scientists have uncovered much new information about early hominid diet. The dialogue between those who see early hominids as successful hunters and those who say the record shows only signs of a kind of marginal, scrounging-scavenging feeding strategy continues today, but the argument has sparked many new studies that are refining our views about what early humans ate and how they obtained it.

Research on how modern African carnivores obtain their food has shown that for most species, hunting and scavenging are complementary, not mutually exclusive strategies, and that many animals simply do what they have to do to get by, scavenging when they must, hunting when they can. On the other hand, these same behavioral studies of modern predators have revealed some scavenging opportunities that were not known earlier, and that may have been available to Plio-Pleistocene hominids as well. For instance, Blumenschine and his students have proposed that leopard kills could have provided a possible source of scavenged meat for early hominids. Leopards are solitary hunters and often drag their kills high up into trees to hide them from other predators. They leave these carcasses for many hours at a time and return to them sporadically. Opportunistic and observant hominids might have raided the leopard's "pantry" for more than a few meals.

Studies of what happens to an ungulate carcass as it is consumed and picked over—often by a succession of predators—have also helped us to better interpret the bone debris at early hominid sites. It turns out that prey body size is an important factor when considering whether a given animal's carcass might be a candidate for hominid scavenging. Small ungulates, like the ubiquitous savanna gazelles, are consumed very quickly by lions and hyenas, leaving literally nothing behind for other predators to scavenge. Large-bodied prey, on the other hand, usually are not consumed so quickly, and subsequent challengers or visitors to the carcass may well find something left to eat. Now, when bones of small bovids such as gazelles are found in hominid sites, we tend to see them as possible evidence of hominid hunting, since they were unlikely to have been scavenged from another animal. Bones from larger animals are more ambiguous: they could have been either hunted or scavenged by hominids.

We have also learned that different parts of a carcass have different values as food, and carnivores show a consistent order of consumption that reflects this. Viscera are consumed first, followed by flesh, and finally by long bone marrow and skull contents. When carcasses are disarticulated, the forelimb tends to be the first part to be taken away by a predator, then the hind limb, and last to be transported will be items from the axial skeleton (skull, ribs, and vertebrae). Viscera leave no fossil signal, of course, but meat is attached to bones, which do. From these patterns it is possible to "read" a bone assemblage to determine when the bone collector—or collectors—got access to a particular animal carcass. Early access—either by hunting or scavenging an intact dead animal—provided hominids with the meatiest parts: the upper portions of the limbs, and the early disappearing forelimb in particular. In contrast, a hominid coming upon the same carcass much later missed all the fleshy parts, and perhaps had access only to marrow and brains by cracking open limb bones and skull.

When all these indicators were applied to the assemblages at Olduvai Gorge in a comprehensive study by Potts (1988), a complex picture emerged. While a specialized scavenging niche, like that proposed by Blumenschine, should result in a fairly narrow spectrum of prey animals, the Olduvai remains show that hominids obtained parts from a wide variety of prey species from diverse habitats. Furthermore, the bones present show that hominids sometimes had early access to carcasses, but sometimes did not, and then they brought back what was available. The hominids at Olduvai probably did hunt sometimes, while they apparently scavenged as well. Neither of the extreme positions, either predominant hunter or marginal scavenger, can be supported by the Olduvai evidence. For most researchers, the Man the Hunter/Man the Scavenger dialogue has resolved in an awareness that the hominid fossil record often records *both* activities.

Since 1985 some other new discoveries or interpretations have added provocative clues to the effort to understand early hominid diet.

Chipped stone artifacts are now known from as early as 2.6 million years ago, from sites in Ethiopia and the Democratic Republic of the Congo. Of course, we do not really know how the earliest toolmakers used the tools they made, but if it was food related—as we usually assume—then they were already engaged in these activities by more than 2.5 million years ago. Coincidentally—or not—this is also about the time when the genus *Homo* first appears in the fossil record in East Africa.

Studies of the biochemistry of fossil bones (especially trace elements and nitrogen and carbon isotope ratios) from the South African site of Swartkrans suggest that the "robust" australopithecine *Paranthropus,* long assumed to have been a vegetarian, may have been more of an omnivore than previously thought, and apparently included some animal protein in its diet.

"Lucy" (*Australopithecus afarensis*), however, probably was not an omnivore, according to a new study comparing gut size, brain size, and dietary specialization. Big brains are the "gas-guzzlers" of the human body: they are very expensive to support and it turns out that in evolutionary terms, they probably had to compete with other organ systems, especially the digestive system, for energy. An innovative study by Aiello and Wheeler (1995) has shown that humans have very short digestive tracts for their body size, and that this is a trait shared with other carnivores in general, and with primates that have higher-quality diets (those that eat more animal protein, lipids, and simple sugars, and relatively less of the bulky structural carbohydrates). They suggest that the early hominids with small brains and long guts contrast with later hominids who had to sacrifice gut tissue in order to "afford" an increase in brain size. A change to a higher-quality, more easily digested diet (probably including more animal protein) could compensate for a reduced digestive system and still support a bigger brain. The brain of *A. afarensis* is small, and Lucy's ribs are quite flared, indicating that *A. afarensis* still had a voluminous digestive system and probably ate a basic primate diet higher in bulky plant foods and lower in its protein-fat-sugar component.

FURTHER READING

Aiello, Leslie C., and Peter Wheeler. 1995. "The Expensive-Tissue Hypothesis." *Current Anthropology* 36:199–221.

Ardrey, Robert. 1961. *African Genesis*. Collins.

Ardrey, Robert. 1976. *The Hunting Hypothesis*. Atheneum.

Blumenschine, R. J. 1987. "Characteristics of an Early Hominid Scavenging Niche." *Current Anthropology* 28:383–407.

Bower, Bruce. 1985. "Hunting Ancient Scavengers." *Science News* 127:155–57.

Bunn, Henry T. 1981. "Archaeological Evidence for Meat-eating by Plio-Pleistocene Hominids from Koobi Fora and Olduvai Gorge." *Nature* 291:574–77.

Cavallo, J. A., and R. J. Blumenschine. 1989. "Tree-Stored Leopard Kills: Expanding the Hominid Scavenging Niche." *Journal of Human Evolution* 18:393–99.

Dart, Raymond A. 1925. "*Australopithecus Africanus*: The Man-Ape of South Africa." *Nature* 115:195–99.

Dart, Raymond A. 1953. "The Predatory Transition from Ape to Man." *International Anthropological and Linguistic Review* 1:201–18.

Laughlin, William S. 1968. "Hunting: An Integrating Biobehavior System and Its Evolutionary Importance." In Richard B. Lee and Irven DeVore, eds., *Man the Hunter*. Aldine.

Potts, Rick. 1988. *Early Hominid Activities at Olduvai*. Aldine de Gruyter.

Potts, Rick, and Pat Shipman. 1981. "Cut Marks Made by Stone Tools on Bones from Olduvai Gorge, Tanzania." *Nature* 291:577–80.

Shipman, Pat. 1984. "Scavenger Hunt." *Natural History* 93(4):20–27.

6 THE REAL FLINTSTONES?

What Are Artists' Depictions of Human Ancestors Telling Us?

Diane Gifford-Gonzalez

You have probably seen her, frequenting the diorama scene at your local museum or in that coffee table book on human evolution. It is likely that you have not given her a second glance, she is so much a part of the scenery.

THE DRUDGE

She is the Drudge-on-the-Hide; the woman on her hands and knees scraping away at the skin of a large animal, on the margins of the home camp scene. The men are usually center stage foreground, doing something interesting, while she's over there, hiding out. You usually cannot see her face; she is looking down, and the artist may not have bothered to sketch in her brows or mouth. She is not talking to anyone; no one is talking to her.

Even in the high-tech Upper Paleolithic, she never manages to get that skin up on a stretching frame and to work it sitting or standing, as do documented hide workers. The men may be down in the cave, trancing, dancing, and doing art, but she's scraping away, on all fours, same as back in *Homo erectus* times (Eugène Dubois was obviously not thinking of her when he named the species).

Conventionalized representations such as the drudge repeat themselves

THE ASCENT OF THE DRUDGE

through the works of various artists, their postures and actions suggesting that artists have drawn from their own fine arts traditions, rather than from ethnographically informed suggestions from their scientist collaborators. The "Drudge-on-a-Hide," for example, mimics the scullery maid scrubbing the floor in the background of eighteenth-century evocations of bourgeois success.

THE GUY-WITH-A-ROCK

Another common motif, the "Guy-with-a-Rock" about to hurl a huge rock into a pit containing a large and unhappy beast (mammoth, mastodon, woolly rhino, or cave bear), suggests herculean figures in portrayals of classical myths. Though his hunting mates sport the latest ballistic weapons, this stone-age conservative has a hefty rock as his weapon of choice from 2 million B.C. to Holocene bison hunts in Dakota. One can imagine the dialogue:

"Dammit, Og, we told you to leave the rock at home and bring a spear-thrower!" "Right, Og, remember last time, when the mammoth threw the rock back and broke Morg's leg?" "Hey! This rock has been in my family for a million years!"

THE DEER-ON-A-STICK

The homecoming from a successful hunt incorporates the "Deer-on-a-Stick" motif. The massive prey portrayed in most hunt scenes shrinks to a readily transported package, hefted on a pole between two extraordinarily tidy hunters. They are never shown bringing home dismembered animal parts, nor besmirched with gore. If anyone is portrayed close to such nastiness, it is Woman, crouched on a bloody hide. Faced with the lack of fit between ethnographic data on animal butchery and these scenes, one's mind readily wanders down Freudian, rather than archaeological, corridors.

"Man-the-Toolmaker," in fact the most common stereotypic portrayal of men at work, pounds stone on stone in a technique more suitable to smithing than to stone percussion, echoing mythical and quotidian blacksmiths in classic oil paintings. Depending upon where his anvil lies, the Toolmaker risks either blinding or genital mutilation, in which art he often appears jovially inclined to instruct the young.

MADONNA-WITH-CHILD

The other common female motif besides the abject Drudge is the "Madonna-with-Child," a youthful woman standing with a baby in her arms and doing absolutely nothing. Cumulatively, illustrations of paleolithic women present a contrast to the busy lives of ethnographically documented mothers in hunter-gatherer societies. Stone Age woman's life seems to have begun with a placid but immobile young motherhood, rooted decoratively to the spot as camp life swirled about her, followed by dull and dumpy middle age, hiding out on the margins of the fun stuff (still not a whit of social interaction), followed by aged and inactive sitting and watching, waiting for the paleolithic version of the Grim Reaper to work his way up the valley. It is a wonder women learned to talk at all.

Once you really consider them, paleolithic figures such as the Drudge and her companions do seem hackneyed and ethnographically uninformed. Anyone with experience of rural life nearly anywhere on the planet can see that they portray the Stone Age through a Western—suburban—lens, two steps from the Flintstones.

Archaeologists can readily testify to the difficulties of assigning gender or maturational stage to most of the activities portrayed, in view of humanity's global diversity in cultural practices. Yet the graphic story reaching out from the museum halls and pages of the book on the coffee table treats men's and women's—and youngsters' and oldsters'—estate as foregone conclusions. When viewed cumulatively, as we would see them in our lifetimes of museum-going and reading, the vast majority of existing portrayals give us a narrow and repetitious view of prehistoric human life.

THE VISUAL/INFORMATION GAP

Given this repetitiveness, it is easy to fault the artists for a lack of imagination in their mechanical reproduction of earlier motifs. However, the fault is really in the shared vision of artists and experts, archaeologists and paleoanthropologists such as myself. Our vision in the literal sense has been faulty because we have not seen these stereotypes for what they are and challenged their perpetuation. In the more abstract sense, our vision has failed, because we experts have not offered artists who seek our expertise better-informed and more imaginative alternatives. Ironically, the texts accompanying such illustrations, usually drafted by science writers, often offer up-to-date, ethnographically informed perspectives. This emphasizes the great information gap between many of the artists and the text-based workers, a gap not bridged by scientific experts.

Many scientific experts may literally overlook visual depictions in museums or popular books simply because they are for the general public. Experts are trained to think of scientific communication as written text, and graphics such as illustrations of specimens, maps, and graphs as subsidiary material. Speculative reconstructions of prehistoric life are dismissed by many as "museum stuff" for the general public, and unsuitable for real scientists to use or even to help create.

This is a profoundly mistaken and potentially dangerous perspective. Portrayals of human ancestors present a parallel, visually based narrative of the human past. This visual narrative, because of its pervasiveness and communicative potency, must be taken seriously. Widely used in museums and popular literature, it represents much of the knowledge that laypersons have of the prehistoric past. In the face of Barney Rubble and other enduring icons of pop prehistoricity, museums and educational books strive to impress and convince the viewer of "the real facts" through the power of visual arts. The style in which these portrayals are executed is central to their plausibility and power and merits a closer look.

For Western viewers, naturalistic representation is read as objective reporting, and rigorous naturalism characterizes science illustration. Historian of science Barbara Stafford (1991) argues that this stylistic convention developed over the seventeenth and eighteenth centuries, as scientists and explorers strove to present convincing images of newly discovered worlds within the human body and around the globe. Given our cultural conditioning, the realistic graphic style itself advances claims for the plausibility of what it depicts. It is therefore the style of choice for science fiction graphics and Disneyland, as well as for prehistoric representations in your local museum or coffee table book.

As portrayed in artists' representations, the prehistoric past is enticingly "real" and accessible. Natural details of landscape, vegetation, animal life, and the painstakingly reconstructed hominid bodies themselves render the scenes plausible. These people, or near-people, have hands, eyes, facial expressions, and they draw us in toward them. Yet the "naturalness" of the human bodies, their expressions, and gestures serves to subtly support another argument for plausibility that we overlook at our peril: that their social world as depicted was also real. These bodies are gendered, they display the marks of age, and they exist in the scenes as socially identified actors. If their realistic style and context are arguments for their credibility, then what primordial human conditions are conveyed, so powerfully and plausibly?

GENDER/AGE DISCRIMINATION
IN VISUAL REPRESENTATIONS

To further explore this question, I recently analyzed 136 pictures of early modern humans ("Cro-Magnons") of the last Ice Age in books readily available to lay readers in North America, Great Britain, and France (Gifford-Gonzalez, 1993). I documented the types of persons and activities portrayed and commonly repeated motifs, such as the Drudge, looking for the cumulative pattern of artistic choices in portraying different ages and genders. As a whole, the portrayals consistently exclude children and older people from active, useful roles. They represent women's work in patronizing ways, if at all, implying that the real early human story consisted of a suite of male activities, which are themselves really rather limited, too.

Who and what most often fills the frame of these portraits of the past reveals the assumptions of both makers and viewers. Of the 136 pictures, about 85 percent include young to middle-aged men; only half include women; children appear in slightly more than 40 percent of the scenes, and elders in less than a fifth. Although scenes depicting men exclusively are common, only 3 of 136 portray women only, and no pictures show only elders or children, or any combination of women, elders, and children without men. Of the 1,076 individual human figures in these pictures, about 49 percent are men, 22 percent are women, 23 percent are children, and about 6 percent are older persons.

Critics of Western art and advertisements have shown that men's and women's bodies are differentially represented in dynamic motion, with women's bodies being placed in lower positions and shown in more static poses than those of men, and that active, "important" activities are in the hands of men (e.g., Berger, 1972; Goffman, 1976). It should come as no surprise that these portrayals of Cro-Magnon men show upright walking and running more frequently than would be predicted from their proportion in the sample, while the opposite is true of women. Males are also disproportionately depicted with arms in dynamic motion, as when making and wielding tools or lifting loads. Women are less often shown in such dynamic poses, and children, never. Elders are almost never represented upright, much less in motion or doing anything active. Only men of a certain age participate in hunts, carry game home, and conduct rituals. It is mostly men who construct, create art, make tools. Only women scrape hides, hold babies, or touch children.

THE QUESTION OF RACE

This discussion does not permit an extended treatment of the equally important question of which racial groups are recruited to visually depict stages of hominid evolution. I invite the reader to engage in a brief examination of magazine covers concerning human evolution, to see which genders and racial features "sell." For example, U.S. magazine representations of "The Way We Were" (*Newsweek, 1986*) show "our" ancestral modern human as white, male, and in his prime. Discussions of the "African Eve" hypothesis for modern human origins in *Time* and *U.S. News & World Report* offered a diluted Africanity in the faces they presented, and "Eve" naturally required a male companion for inclusion on a cover.

Ruth Mathis (1991), a graduate student in archaeology at the University of Massachusetts, Amherst, wrote a compelling indictment of traditional visual narratives of human evolution from an African American viewpoint. Specifically, she pointed to the common practice of present-ing *dark-skinned* australopithecines and *light-skinned* modern humans as opposite ends of the evolutionary spectrum. One can make biologically based arguments for portraying the earliest African hominids with heavily pigmented skin, but Mathis notes there is no compelling scientific basis for consistently choosing white people to represent the most advanced species, since non-European varieties of modern humans populated all continents by the end of the Ice Age. She stresses the alienating impacts of these visual narratives on the children of color who visit museums to learn more about human history and view these narratives with their own con-sciousness of racial stereotypes.

TOWARD MORE EQUITABLE AND
REALISTIC REPRESENTATION

The challenge for illustrators and experts really is not to fashion politi-cally correct portrayals of human ancestors (drawing a Guy-on-a-Hide or a Gal-with-a-Rock), nor to produce accurate but pedestrian ones (daily trips to the waterhole, perhaps). Nor should we throw up our hands and say real scientists should not use such inevitably speculative illustrations anyway. Exciting exceptions to the stereotypic rules of illustration do ex-ist. French illustrator Veronique Ageorges (Ageorges and Saint-Blanquat, 1989) and former Smithsonian artist John Gurche (e.g., in Waters, 1990) have created scenes that reflect a deep appreciation for the rich archaeo-logical and ethnographic resources available. Their human ancestors en-gage in a range of technically believable activities and include strong older persons and capable women and children, interacting with one another in good and ill temper. Women, children, and older persons break the con-fines of their occupational straitjackets, making art, dancing, fabricating tools, and foraging away from camp. Men wear ornaments, smile, and are idle. Significantly, these artists have built on their own expert knowledge, rather than relying on the testimony of other experts, who, for the most part, have seemed little concerned with the social content of these dio-ramic scenes.

As a scientist, I see these artists' representations as science fictions—visually mediating the often complex research tactics of specialists for an interested, educable public. When I call these reconstructions science fic-tions, I mean no slur. In fact, strong philosophical parallels exist between what "real scientists" trying to understand unseeable ancient events do and what a careful artist does in these representations. We each link together points of scientific fact—things we think we know for sure—into narratives of educated guesses and arguments of plausibility. From this perspective, the work of the most thoughtful of my artist colleagues in portraying ancient humans exactly parallels my own struggles to make sense of the evidence actually left behind by them.

Once each acknowledges the social power of the visual assertions about our ancestors that populate our museums and popular books, rich possibilities for collaboration between scientists and artists emerge. As an archaeologist trained in an anthropological view of the past and a citizen of an ethnically and racially diverse nation, I believe we can serve the greater public by expanding the range of possible pasts represented in depictions of prehistoric people. I am not arguing for revising past worlds as they have conventionally been represented using a representational quota system, by which various ages, genders, and races get their fair share of prestige as defined in these works—where women hunt, men scrape hides, old folks run and dance—though all probably did a good deal of these activities. Rather, why not combine scientific rigor and creativity to offer viewers social arrangements different from any known today, or hominid

species with truly different adaptations and behaviors? By picturing unexpected past worlds—inhabited not by mimics or parodies of ourselves
but by those who may have been strong, successful, yet very unlike us—
we might succeed in actually drawing more viewers into the real problems,
possibilities, and pleasures of research on the past.

FURTHER READING

Ageorges, Veronique, and Henri de Saint-Blanquat. 1989. *Lascaux et Son
    Temps*. Casterman.
Berger, John. 1973. *Ways of Seeing*. Viking Press.
Gifford-Gonzalez, Diane. 1993. "You Can Hide, but You Can't Run: Representa-
    tion of Women's Work in Illustrations of Palaeolithic Life." *Visual Anthropol-
    ogy Review* 9:3–21.
Goffman, Erving. 1979. *Gender Advertisements*. Harper Colophon.
"The Way We Were. Our Ice Age Heritage: Language, Art, Fashion, and the
    Family." 1986. *Newsweek* (November 10).
Mathis, Ruth. 1991. "Race and Human Origins Narratives: Whose Past?" Un-
    published manuscript.
Rudwick, Martin, J. S. 1992. *Scenes from Deep Time: Early Pictorial Represen-
    tations of the Prehistoric World*. University of Chicago Press.
Stafford, Barbara M. 1991. *Body Criticism: Imaging the Unseen in Enlighten-
    ment Art and Medicine*. MIT Press.
Waters, Tom. 1990. "Almost Human." *Discover* 11(May):42–44, 53.

7 WHAT BONES TEACH US

Kathleen D. Gordon

Collecting and studying human skeletons in museums and scientific laboratories is at present a complex, controversial activity. The purpose of this chapter is to explore the kinds of information scientists obtain by studying human skeletons, and how that information is used.

A physical anthropologist is trained to determine many facts about an individual from bones alone. For instance, sex identification often can be determined by the differences in the pelvis and skull. Even bone fragments may be sexed; some chemical components of bone differ between men and women. Age at the time of death can be estimated very closely by looking at the teeth and at the fusion between different parts of the same bone, especially for children and young adults. For older people, the estimates are less exact and rely more on changes in joint surfaces, fusion between skull bones, and microscopic details of internal bone structure. Height is estimated by the length of the long bones, especially the leg bones. Ancestry can often be determined by looking at characteristics of the facial skeleton. Statistical studies of tooth, skull, and face shape can even distinguish closely related groups within the same major population.

The skeleton reveals information about lifestyle as well. Well-developed muscles leave their mark on bone and tell of heavy physical activity during life. Habits (such as pipe-smoking) and handedness may leave traces on teeth or in asymmetric bone and muscle development. Health, injuries,

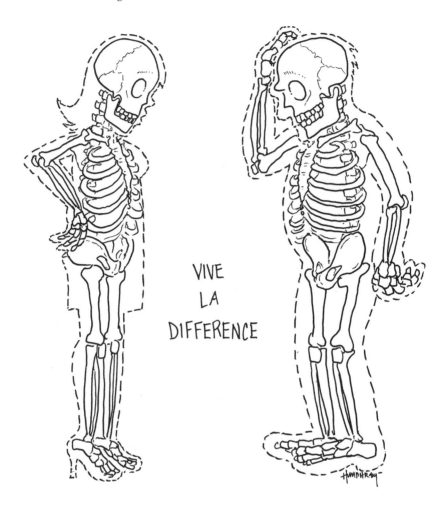

VIVE
LA
DIFFERENCE

and many diseases, such as syphilis, tuberculosis, arthritis, and leprosy, may leave traces on bone. A subfield of physical anthropology, paleopathology, is devoted to the study and diagnosis of diseases in ancient human remains.

From these studies, paleopathologists are often able to provide medical insights into the history and ecology of modern human diseases. For instance, childhood illness or malnutrition can be detected by abnormalities in tooth enamel and bone mineralization. By noting the position of these abnormalities, physical anthropologists, with their knowledge of normal growth patterns of bones and teeth, can often pinpoint at exactly what age the illness or growth disturbances occurred. From this it can be determined whether a child's health problems were caused by a sick or poorly nourished mother, by early weaning, or by later periods of food shortage.

VICTIM IDENTIFICATION

Because of their skill at piecing together an individual's life history from skeletal clues, physical anthropologists are constantly in demand to help identify humans who have been the victims of accidents or foul play. The forensic anthropologist can tell authorities if bones are human, and if disarticulated, whether or not they all come from the same individual. Today, physical anthropologists are helping authorities in Argentina locate and identify skeletons of people kidnaped and murdered by political extremists during the country's period of upheaval in the past decade. Recently, anthropologists helped confirm the identification of a skeleton attributed to Nazi war criminal Josef Mengele. Other scientists use information learned from studying museum skeletons to help provide facial reconstructions of what missing children might look like several years after their disappearance.

BURIAL REMAINS

Why do scientists collect and study more than one skeleton from the same site or cemetery? Isn't one enough? The answer depends on what questions the scientist wants to answer. Although a single skeleton can tell us much about an individual, that person is known only in isolation, and people do not live in isolation. To the anthropologist, much more important information about whole social groups, their history and relationships with neighboring and past cultures, their diet and health, and also their social customs and relationships can be obtained only by studying large numbers of skeletons from the same culture or living site. Such population-wide studies require many specialized analytic techniques that depend on having large numbers of observations in order to be valid.

THE CASE OF THE AINU

Many of these population studies have provided information about past human migrations, declines, and relationships that were unrecorded even in traditional stories and myths. For instance, research by anthropologists on the Ainu of Japan has resolved some long-standing questions about their origins. Traditionally, many Japanese have considered the Ainu to be an ethnic minority of low status whose physical features are somewhat different from the majority population. Although Japanese tradition holds that modern Japanese are descended from the prehistoric Jomon culture found throughout Japan, two studies now show that the Ainu are the true descendants of the Jomon people. According to studies of minute variations in the teeth and skulls of the modern inhabitants of Japan, and of various prehistoric cultures from Japan and other parts of Asia, the modern Japanese are most likely the descendants of invaders from northern China called the Yayoi, who conquered the islands a little over 2,000 years ago. An interesting twist to the story is that many of the medieval Japanese warrior class, the samurai, show physical features that suggest that they were descendants of Jomon mercenary armies recruited by the Yayoi during their military conquest. As the samurai gained power and status, they eventually intermarried with the Yayoi ruling classes and passed on some of their typically "Ainu" facial traits into the modern upper classes of Japan. Today's Ainu are the descendants of unabsorbed Jomon populations who were pushed into increasingly marginal areas by the Yayoi-Japanese and their Jomon-derived samurai.

Similar kinds of studies have been used to provide answers to questions as diverse as how many waves of prehistoric immigrants populated Australia, how much white admixture there is in various American Indian groups, and how much intermarrying there was between Pueblo groups in the Southwest and Europeans during the contact period. Other researchers using the same techniques have been able to chart the progressive distinctiveness of American Indian groups from other Asians and Pacific island populations to estimate when American Indian migrants first entered the Western Hemisphere and when the various tribes became separate.

MOHENJODARO REVISITED

Scientists utilizing new techniques have even been helpful in resolving questions about classical civilizations. The city of Mohenjodaro, the center of Harappan civilization in the Indus Valley, was thought to have been sacked by Aryan warriors invading in 1500 B.C. After studying the human remains from Mohenjodaro, anthropologists have now concluded that no massacre ever occurred because they found no battle injuries on the bones. They also found no evidence of genetic differences between populations before, during, and after the decline of Mohenjodaro, which makes an invasion of foreigners very unlikely. However, the skeletons did show high levels of disease and parasites, which might have been a more important cause of the Harappan decline than any invasion or conquest.

DISEASE, DIET, AND DEMOGRAPHY

Studies of cemeteries show scientists how human groups interact with their environment, and how they in turn are affected by changes in the physical world they occupy. Reconstructions of demography, diet, and growth and disease patterns help physical anthropologists understand the ecology of prehistoric groups and make some surprising discoveries about human adaptations, such as the health costs of agriculture and the origins of some modern human diseases.

Many diseases can be diagnosed from skeletons, and it is sometimes possible to recover fossilized bacteria, and occasionally, amino acids for blood typing directly from bone. One extensive study of Grecian cemeteries from ancient to modern times traced the increase in malaria-resistant anemia (thalassemia, similar to sickle-cell anemia in Africa) in Grecian populations and showed the effects of changes in ecology and social and economic patterns on the health and life span of ancient and recent Greeks. By looking at groupings of skeletons in cemeteries, the scientist was also able to reconstruct families or clans, and to show that anemic groups were more fertile than others.

Studies of skeletons can also tell what people ate, even without having any cultural information. Some techniques measure certain chemical isotopes and trace elements in ground bone. These amounts will differ, depending on the proportion of meat to vegetables in the diet, and on the type of plant foods eaten. Results have shown that in some prehistoric groups men and women had different diets, with men sometimes consuming more meat and women eating more plant foods. Other studies have shown that different diets leave different microscopic scratch patterns on tooth surfaces, and several kinds of prehistoric diets can be distinguished in this way.

Changes in diet often cause changes in health, which can be seen in the skeleton. The shift to a reliance on maize in the prehistoric Southwest diet coincided with an increase in porous bone in skeletons, a sign of iron deficiency anemia. In maize farmers from Dickson Mounds, Illinois, defects in tooth enamel, which are caused by stress during childhood, are more numerous. Infant mortality was also higher, and adult age at death lower than in pre-agricultural groups. Similar studies of Hopewell mounds concluded that the agricultural Hopewell had more chronic health problems, dietary deficiencies, and tuberculosis than pre-agricultural groups. Agriculture is usually thought to bring an improvement in quality of life, but the surprising conclusion that prehistoric agriculture marked a decline in general health in the New World has been confirmed by many other studies (see chapter 9).

RECENT POPULATION STUDIES

Studies of human skeletons can be useful even for recent populations, when written records are limited or have been lost. Several studies have reconstructed the living conditions of African Americans both during and after the end of slavery. Skeletons recovered from an eighteenth-century New Orleans cemetery showed many differences in nutrition and physical stress between urban and rural slaves. Skeletons from a late-nineteenth- to early-twentieth-century cemetery in Arkansas open a window on this period, which is not well documented by other historical sources. Researchers concluded that men commonly left the community (there were few male burials), and that some of the community intermarried with the local Indian population. On the whole, the population was poorly nourished and had low resistance to disease. Many infants died at birth of widespread bacterial infections. Children's skeletons show dietary deficiencies and chronic infections, with many dying at 18 months, the weaning age. Iron deficiency anemias were common, probably because of corn-based diets; high levels of arthritis indicate heavy physical labor; and many signs of injuries on male skeletons may be evidence of high levels of interpersonal violence. Even without written records, the skeletons in this Post-Reconstruction community tell us of continual malnutrition, poor health, and levels of physical stress, which even exceeded those found in some communities during slavery.

ANCIENT DISEASES IN CONTEMPORARY POPULATIONS

Physical anthropologists find many contemporary diseases in earlier human populations. Some show peculiar distributions in the United States today, which can sometimes be tied to disease prevalence in the past. One of these is osteoporosis, a weakening of bone due to a calcium-poor diet and low bone mass resulting from low levels of exercise during life. This condition afflicts primarily elderly white females, leading to spontaneous fractures and spinal deformities. Surprisingly, anthropologists have discovered that osteoporosis is common in living and prehistoric Eskimos of both sexes, and appears at an earlier age when compared to American whites. However, fractures and spinal problems have not been common in Eskimo populations. In spite of the traditional calcium-poor Eskimo diet, vigorous exercise results in heavier bones that protect the individual in old age. Now however, increased life span and alterations in lifestyle may contribute to a rise in osteoporotic bone disorders in Arctic populations in the future.

Evidence of a disease in prehistory is sometimes useful in understanding its cause. Osteoarthritis is often found in prehistoric skeletons. Changes in the locations and numbers of joints affected, and in the proportions of men and women afflicted, have suggested that systemic factors affecting only one sex or the other may be involved in the severity of modern arthritis, an insight that may help focus further research efforts. Studies of prehistoric skeletons have shown that high levels of tooth decay are typical only of agricultural populations. This has led to the observation that sticky carbohydrates common to most agricultural diets have something to do with the epidemic of tooth decay modern populations are experiencing. But mineral deficiencies may also be involved, as some high levels of cavities and periodontal disease have been found in nonagricultural prehistoric Illinois Indians. Since the mineral content of groundwater would affect the disease resistance of tooth enamel, such studies have pointed to mineral supplementation of drinking water as a means of combating tooth decay. Tuberculosis has been found in skeletons as early as 5,000 yrs B.P. in the Old World and by at least A.D. 1000 in the New World. It is associated with keeping livestock and living in sedentary or urban centers. Cemetery studies in Europe have shown a curious relationship between tuberculosis and leprosy, also a very ancient disease. Skeletons rarely show signs of both diseases, and as tuberculosis became more common in Europe in the late Middle Ages, signs of leprosy in European skeletons declined. Medical researchers now speculate that exposure to tuberculosis provides individuals with some immunity to leprosy.

Some health problems are more common in Native Americans than in the general population. One of these is rheumatoid arthritis, which had been thought to be a recent disease possibly caused by an infection. The discovery of rheumatoid-like lesions in prehistoric American Indians has changed the focus of medical research on this disease. Another condition more common than expected in some Native American tribes is the cleft palate/cleft lip complex of congenital bone defects. Clefting of the face has been found in prehistoric skeletons from the same region, though it is not as common as in the modern population. It is not known whether this shows a real increase in the problem, or if burials of prehistoric babies who died from their condition are simply not recovered as often as adults. Some researchers speculate that the increase, if real, might be the result of more inbreeding in tribal populations than would have occurred in the past, after groups were confined on reservations, and traditional migration and marriage patterns were disrupted.

PATTERNS OF SOCIAL ORGANIZATION

It might seem surprising that we can learn much about the patterns of political and social organization of past cultures from a study of bones, but in fact physical anthropologists and archaeologists can discover a great deal about social customs in prehistory through studies of cemeteries. This is only possible, however, with data about age and sex of each burial.

Evidence of status and marriage patterns is often visible in cemetery populations. Anthropologists studying skeletons from the prehistoric North American site of Moundville, Alabama, reconstructed three different status groups in Moundville society. These included individuals whose remains were either used as trophies, or were possibly sacrifices sanctifying the mound-building process, an intermediate group containing both men and women, and a high-status group composed entirely of adult men. By analyzing genetic differences among men and women in the same cemetery, it is often possible to reconstruct marriage and residence patterns. For instance, in one study of prehistoric and historic Pueblo cemeteries, women in each cemetery had very similar genetic markers, while the men in each group were quite variable for those same traits. This indicates that women lived and were buried with their kin groups, while men lived and were buried with unrelated groups. The ancient Pueblo people were matrilocal, just as the modern tribes are today. Some studies have revealed a relationship between an individual's status during life and his or her physical characteristics, such as height. Taller people tend to have higher-status markers in their graves in several prehistoric cultures. This is more often true for men, but in some groups taller women also had higher status. By studying skeletons for indications of growth disturbances and disease, scientists can sometimes tell whether the greater height of high-status people was due to better diet and more resources, or whether they were just genetically predisposed to be taller.

CONCLUSION

The above examples show how anthropologists can learn about many facets of the lives of individuals and communities of past cultures by studying their skeletal materials. The study of modern, historic, and prehistoric skeletons has made it possible for anthropologists to uncover an enormous and diverse array of information about human behavior and morphology past and present. None of these studies could have been accomplished without the thorough study of human skeletons. To obtain this information, scientists commonly use techniques that were unheard of and unanticipated even a generation ago. It is certain that many more new approaches to reconstructing past lives from bones will be discovered in the future. Many collections may be studied and restudied, in the quest for new answers to old questions, or for answers to new questions altogether.

Prehistoric populations left us little of their history and experience from which to learn. By careful study of their skeletons, we gain an understanding of ancient humans that would not otherwise be possible. The late J. Lawrence Angel, a noted Smithsonian physical anthropologist and forensic expert, always kept a sign in his laboratory: *Hic locus est ubi mortui viventes docent* (In this place, the dead teach the living). They teach us about the past, and if we listen carefully, about the future as well.

UPDATE

It is perhaps ironic that just at the time when many human skeletal collections in museums are shrinking because of claims filed under the Native American Graves Protection and Repatriation Act (NAGPRA)—which requires federal institutions and museums to inventory their collections of Native American human remains and funerary objects and repatriate them to culturally affiliated tribes upon request—new advances in molecular biology are providing us with innovative and exciting techniques to learn about the genetics of past human populations directly from bones themselves.

Researchers first discovered that DNA could be recovered from soft tissues of some ancient species in 1984, when mitochondrial DNA sequences were cloned from an old museum skin of the quagga, an extinct zebra-like animal. The following year, Svante Pääbo, then a Swedish graduate student in molecular biology, managed to clone DNA from ancient Egyptian mummies in several museum collections. In the decade since, DNA has been extracted from a variety of fossilized remains: wheat seeds, insects trapped in amber (featured as the source of dinosaur DNA in the movie *Jurassic Park*), 18-million-year-old magnolia leaves, and from human brains preserved in bodies buried in a Florida peat bog more than 7,000 years ago.

But the most exciting result came when it was discovered that DNA could be recovered not just from unusually preserved soft tissues, but from ancient bone itself. Since bone is by far the most prevalent kind of fossil, this has opened up a new arena of research possibilities. One study using this approach was an analysis of the relationships of the moas of New Zealand, an extinct group of flightless birds that disappeared shortly after humans colonized the islands around 1,000 years ago. Researchers were able to determine that the extinct moas were not closely related to the other flightless birds of New Zealand, the kiwis, and that they must have colonized the region before the kiwis, which probably migrated from Australia where their cousins, the emus and cassowaries, still survive. More spectacularly, Brigham Young University researchers claimed in 1995 to have isolated DNA from fossil dinosaur bones some 80 million years old, but so far the sequences recovered have been too short to convince most others that the DNA really derives from dinosaurs. More studies of this material are under way, but the difficulties the Brigham Young researchers have encountered are typical of problems that the field of ancient DNA research has yet to resolve.

The earliest ancient DNA studies relied on the technique of molecular cloning to produce a large enough amount of DNA to analyze. In this method, the extracted ancient DNA is fused to a carrier DNA molecule and introduced into bacteria to multiply the original strand, hopefully into thousands of copies. But molecular cloning is severely hampered by the damage all ancient DNA has undergone—most of which occurs in the first few hours after death. The bacteria often fail to make copies when the sequence is damaged, or the copies they make may reproduce errors caused by degradation of the original fragment. Because the clones resulting from this procedure are so few, it was often hard to reproduce results, and sometimes impossible to perform particular experiments at all.

The prospects for ancient DNA studies improved dramatically in the late 1980s with the invention of PCR, short for "polymerase chain reaction," a test-tube cloning technique that produces many more copies of the target DNA fragment than does molecular cloning, and that is not nearly as affected by any underlying damage in the original. Because of its high rate of multiplication, or amplification, of the original DNA fragment, PCR can be successful even when a sample has only one or a few intact molecules of DNA.

Nonetheless, even when PCR reproduces billions of copies to work with, complete sections of genes are seldom recovered from ancient DNA. Most ancient sequences range from 100 to 500 base pairs of nucleotides in length, whereas intact genes range from 75 base pairs to over 2 million, depending on the complexity of the gene involved. Bone, interestingly enough, seems to provide a more stable environment for the preservation of DNA than soft tissues, because sequences retrieved from bone are longer on average than those that have been derived from soft tissue.

The most difficult challenge in the study of ancient DNA is how to avoid contamination. Scientists may be able to amplify minute amounts of DNA, but sometimes the results show that it must have come from the researchers or excavators themselves! Stringent procedures to reduce contamina-

tion, from the first moment of fossil recovery, through the entire laboratory protocol, are being developed by researchers in order to improve
success. Contamination during fossilization by microbes and fungi is also
a problem, though selecting particular target genes like those on mitochondria or in hemoglobin and collagen may eliminate the problem,
since plants and fungi do not carry these. Although the Brigham Young
researchers have convinced others that they indeed have extracted DNA
from 80-million-year-old bones, the question remains, whose DNA?
While the bones are within the size range of dinosaurs typical of the strata
from which they were recovered, DNA results showed a closer similarity
to whales than to the reptile or bird sequences expected in this comparison. Whether this is an anomaly, a result of contamination, or an indication of more variability within dinosaurs than anticipated cannot yet be
determined.

So, while fossil bone may be plentiful, methodological issues will probably prevent an immediate bonanza of ancient DNA results. However,
human applications have already shown their worth. DNA studies of the
Tyrolean "Iceman," a mummified human body found eroding out of a
melting Alpine glacier in 1991, were instrumental in ruling out the possibility that the body was planted as a hoax. Early skeptics had wondered
if the mummy was not really Egyptian or Peruvian instead of European.
Mitochondrial DNA analysis clearly showed that the 5,000-year-old man
was most likely part of the local central-northern European population,
and not at all similar genetically to either African or American groups.
Studies of New World populations have challenged the current theories
about how the Americas were populated. Linguistic and genetic studies
of modern Native American populations had suggested that colonization
from Asia occurred in two or three waves, and that Amerind, Na-Dene,
and Aleut-Eskimo speakers may have migrated at separate times. However, recent studies of more genetic markers in mitochondrial DNA, from
both contemporary and several prehistoric populations, show that there
are four distinct mitochondrial "lineages" in the New World, and that
most groups studied so far show at least two of these, and often all four.
This implies that there was more likely a single migration, not separate
waves, with all four lineages represented among the initial migrants. Ancient population movements in the Old World may also benefit from
ancient DNA studies. Linguistic and blood group studies have suggested
that modern European populations date from a relatively recent migration
of Neolithic farming peoples from the Middle East, around 10,000 years
ago B.P. Mitochondrial DNA analysis has recently turned up evidence

suggesting instead that modern Europeans show lineages that predate this Neolithic influx, back to at least 30,000 years ago. Further studies are now under way to compare these sequences in Upper Paleolithic and Neolithic humans as well. If the researchers are ultimately able to extend the analysis further backward, to 40,000 to 50,000 years, when modern humans first appeared in Europe, then this could provide important data in the continuing controversy about whether or not the European Neandertals made any genetic contribution to early modern people. The potential for ancient DNA studies to shed light on poorly understood aspects of human history and prehistory is one of the most exciting developments in biological science in the past decade.

FURTHER READING

Bass, William M. 1996. *Human Osteology: A Laboratory and Field Manual.* 4th ed. Missouri Archaeological Society.

Brothwell, D. R. 1981. *Digging Up Bones.* 3d ed. Cornell University Press.

Brown, T. A., and K. A. Brown. 1992. "Ancient DNA and the Archaeologist." *Antiquity* 66:10–23.

Hagelberg, Erika. 1993/1994. "Ancient DNA Studies." *Evolutionary Anthropology* 2(6):199–207.

Krogman, Wilton Marion, and Mehmet Y. Iscan, 1976. *The Human Skeleton in Forensic Medicine.* 2d ed. Charles C. Thomas.

Mann, Robert W., and Sean P. Murphy. 1990. *Regional Atlas of Bone Disease: A Guide to Pathological and Normal Variation in the Human Skeleton.* Charles C. Thomas.

Pääbo, Svante. 1993. "Ancient DNA." *Scientific American* 269(November): 86–92.

Ubelaker, Douglas H. 1989. *Human Skeletal Remains: Excavation, Analysis, and Interpretation.* 2d ed. Taraxacum.

Ubelaker, Douglas H., and Henry Scammell. 1992. *Bones: A Forensic Detective's Casebook.* Harper-Collins.

Wells, Calvin. 1964. *Bones, Bodies, and Disease.* Praeger.

8 DISEASE IN HUMAN EVOLUTION

The Reemergence of Infectious Disease in the Third Epidemiological Transition

George J. Armelagos, Kathleen C. Barnes, and James Lin

For millions of years, humans and their ancestors suffered from diseases—both the kind caused by infectious pathogens (e.g., bacteria, viruses, parasites) and the kind caused as our own bodies degenerate. Over this long period, humans constantly created new ways of living and eating, and actual physical or genetic changes evolved to minimize the effects of these diseases. From the point of view of a bacteria or virus, however, any shift in the physical makeup or behavior of its human host represents not only an obstacle but also a challenge to be overcome. As a result, new diseases emerged with each major change in the human way of life.

For nearly 4 million years, humans lived in small, widely dispersed, nomadic populations that minimized the effect of infectious diseases. With the agricultural revolution about 10,000 years ago, increasing sedentism and larger population groupings resulted in the *first epidemiological transition* in which infectious and nutritional diseases increased. Within the last century, with the advent of public health measures, improved nutrition and medicine, some populations in developed nations underwent a *second epidemiological transition*. During this transition, infectious diseases declined and noninfectious chronic diseases and degenerative conditions increased. Today, we are facing a *third epidemiological transition*, in which there is the emergence of new infectious diseases and a reemergence of infectious diseases once thought to be under control, with pathogens that are antibiotic-resistant and have the potential to be transmitted on a global scale. Populations that experienced and those that never experienced the second epidemiological transition are both experiencing increasing exposure to antibiotic-resistant pathogens.

"Emerging" pathogens are seen as "new" diseases, "discovered" when they have an impact on our adaptation or survival. Even when we take a more holistic ecological perspective, it is often limited to a position that considers "emerging" disease as the result of environmental changes that are only relevant to the present situation as it affects humans here and now. It should be recognized that the emergence of "new" diseases has been the human pattern since the origin of the hominids and that it accelerated with the shift to agriculture 10,000 years ago.

PALEOLITHIC BASELINE

For most of their 4 million years of evolutionary history, human populations lived in small, sparsely settled groups. Population size and density remained low throughout the Paleolithic. Fertility and mortality rates in small gathering-hunting populations would have to have been balanced for the population size to remain small.

Demographic factors creating this stability are still a matter of discussion. Some demographers argue that gatherer-hunters were at their maximum natural fertility, balanced by high mortality. Armelagos, Goodman, and Jacobs (1991) argue, however, that gatherer-hunters maintained a stable population with controlled moderate fertility balanced by moderate mortality.

The demographic changes following the Neolithic may provide insights into the case for population stability controlled by moderate fertility and mortality during the Paleolithic. Following the Neolithic revolution, population size and density increased dramatically. It was thought that the Neolithic economy generated food surpluses that led to a better-nourished and healthier population with a reduced rate of mortality. If populations were at their natural maximum fertility, there would have been a rapid increase in population size.

The empirical evidence suggests an alternative scenario in the shift from gathering and hunting to agriculture. The picture of health is much bleaker. Instead of experiencing improved health, there is evidence of a substantial increase in infectious and nutritional disease (Cohen and Armelagos, 1984). If the traditionally accepted models of Paleolithic fertility and mortality are correct, the question arises: How can a population experiencing maximum fertility during the Paleolithic respond with exponential growth in population when its health is deteriorating?

A consideration of the disease ecology of contemporary gatherer-hunters provides insights into the types of disease that probably affected our gatherer-hunter ancestors. Polgar (1964) suggests that gatherer-hunters had two types of disease to contend with in their adaptation to their environment. One class of disease would be caused by those organisms that had adapted to prehominid ancestors and persisted with them as they evolved into hominids. Head and body lice (*Pediculus humanus*), pinworms, yaws, and possibly malaria would be included in this group. Cockburn (1967) adds to this list most of the internal protozoa found in modern humans and such bacteria as salmonella, typhi, and staphylococci.

The second class are the zoonotic diseases, which have nonhuman animals as their primary host and only incidentally infect humans. Humans can be infected by zoonoses through insect bites, by preparation and consumption of contaminated flesh, and from wounds inflicted by animals. Sleeping sickness, tetanus, scrub typhus, relapsing fever, trichinosis, tularemia, avian or ichthyic tuberculosis, leptospirosis, and schistosomiasis are among the zoonotic diseases that could have afflicted earlier gatherer-hunters (Cockburn 1971).

Although early human populations were too small to support endemic (ever-present) pathogens, they maintained some kind of relationships with the vectors that would later serve to perpetuate such human host-specific diseases as yellow fever and louse-borne relapsing fever. Certain lice were ectoparasites as early as the Oligocene, and the prehumans of the early Pliocene probably suffered from malaria, since the *Anopheles* (mosquito) necessary for transmission of the disease evolved by the Miocene era. Frank Livingstone, an anthropological epidemiologist, dismisses, however, the potential of malaria in early hominids except in isolated incidences because of the small population size and an adaptation to the savanna, an environment that would not have included the mosquitoes that carry the malaria plasmodium.

The range of the earliest hominids was probably restricted to the tropical savanna. This would have limited the pathogens that were potential disease agents. During the course of human evolution, the human habitat expanded gradually into the temperate and eventually the tundra zones. Hominids, according to epidemiologist Frank Lambrecht, would have avoided large areas of the African landscape because of its tsetse flies and thus avoided the trypanosomes they carried. He also argues that the evolution of the human species and its expansion into new ecological niches would have led to a change in the pattern of trypanosome infection. While this list of diseases that may have plagued our gathering-hunting ancestors is informative, those diseases that would have been absent are also of interest. The contagious community diseases such as influenza, measles, mumps, and smallpox would have been missing. There probably would have been few viruses infecting these early hominids, although Cockburn (1967) disagrees and suggests that the viral diseases found in nonhuman primates would have been easily transmitted to hominids.

THE FIRST EPIDEMIOLOGICAL TRANSITION

The first epidemiological transition affected early agricultural populations as well as the early urban settlements of more recent history.

Disease in Agricultural Populations

The reliance on primary food production (agriculture) increased the incidence and the impact of disease. Sedentism, an important feature of agricultural adaptation, conceivably increased parasitic disease spread by contact with human waste. In gathering-hunting groups, the frequent movement of the base camp and frequent forays away from the base camp by men and women would decrease their contact with human wastes. In sedentary populations, the proximity of habitation area and waste deposit sites to the water supply is a source of contamination. While sedentism did occur prior to the Neolithic period in those areas with abundant resources, sedentary living became necessary following the shift to agriculture.

The domestication of animals provided a steady supply of vectors and greater exposure to zoonotic diseases. The zoonotic infections most likely increased because of the close contact with domesticated animals, such as goats, sheep, cattle, pigs, and fowl, as well as the unwanted domestic animals such as rodents and sparrows, which developed (Polgar 1964) permanent habitats in and around human dwellings. Products of domesticated animals such as milk, hair, and skin, as well as the dust raised by the animals, could transmit anthrax, Q fever, brucellosis, and tuberculosis. When breaking the sod during cultivation, workers would become exposed to insect bites and diseases such as scrub typhus. Frank Livingstone showed that slash-and-burn agriculture in west Africa exposed populations to *Anopheles gambiae,* a mosquito that is the vector for *Plasmodium falciparum,* which causes malaria. Agricultural practices also create pools of water exposed to sunlight, expanding the potential breeding sites for mosquitos. The combination of disruptive environmental farming practices and the presence of domestic animals also increased human contact with arthropod (insect) vectors carrying yellow fever, trypanosomiasis, and filariasis, which then developed a preference for human blood. Some disease vectors developed dependent relationships with human habitats, the best example of which is *Aedes aegypti* (vector for yellow fever and dengue), which breeds in stagnant pools of water in open containers. Various agricultural practices increased contact with nonvector parasites. Irrigation brought contact with schistosomal cercariae (from snails), and the use of feces as fertilizer caused infection from intestinal flukes (Cockburn, 1971).

The shift to agriculture led to a change in ecology; this resulted in diseases not frequently encountered by forager populations. The shift from a varied, well-balanced diet to one that contained fewer types of food sometimes resulted in dietary deficiencies. Since food was stored in large quantities and widely distributed, there were probably outbreaks of food poisoning as well. Intensive agricultural practices among the prehistoric Nubians gave rise to iron deficiency anemia, as did the reliance on cereal grain, weaning practices, and parasitic infestation. The combination of a complex society, increasing divisions of class, epidemic disease, and dietary insufficiencies no doubt added mental stress to the list of illnesses.

Disease in Urban Populations

The settlement of urban centers is a recent development in human history. In the Near East, cities with as many as 50,000 people were established by 3000 B.C. In the New World, large urban settlements were in existence by A.D. 600. In settlements of this size it is all the more difficult to remove human wastes and deliver uncontaminated water to the people. Cholera, which is transmitted by contaminated water, was undoubtedly a potential problem in those centers. Diseases such as typhus (carried by lice) and the plague bacillus (transmitted by fleas or by the respiratory route) could be spread from person to person. Viral diseases such as measles, mumps, chicken pox, and smallpox could be spread in a similar fashion. As a result of urbanization, populations were for the first time large enough to maintain disease in an endemic form. Aidan Cockburn, a paleopathologist, has estimated that populations of 1 million would be necessary to maintain

measles as an endemic disease. What was an endemic disease in one population could be the source of a serious epidemic (affecting a large number
of people at the same time) in another group. Cross-continental trade and
travel gave rise to intense epidemics (McNeill, 1976). The Black Death
plague took a serious toll in Europe in the 1300s; that epidemic eliminated
at least a quarter of the population of Europe (approximately 25 million
people).

The period of urban development was also one in which populations
explored and expanded into new areas and thereby introduced novel diseases to groups that had little resistance to them (McNeill, 1976). The
exploration of the New World, for example, may have been the pathway for the treponemal infection (syphilis) that was transmitted to the
Old World. This New World infection was endemic and not sexually
transmitted. When it was introduced into the Old World, the method of
transmission changed to a sexual one, and the pathogen had a new environment in which to develop. This resulted in a more severe and acute
infection. Furthermore, crowding in the urban centers, changes in sexual
practices (such as prostitution), and an increase in sexual promiscuity may
have been factors in the venereal transmission of the pathogen.

The process of industrialization, which began a little over 200 years
ago, led to an even greater environmental and social transformation. City
dwellers were forced to contend with industrial wastes and polluted water
and air. Slums that arose in industrial cities became focal points for poverty and the spread of disease. Epidemics of smallpox, typhus, typhoid,
diphtheria, measles, and yellow fever were well documented in urban settings. Tuberculosis and respiratory diseases such as pneumonia and bron-
chitis were even more serious problems that developed in association with
harsh working situations and crowded living conditions. Urban population centers, with their extremely high mortality, were unable to maintain
their population bases through the reproductive capacity of those living in
the city. Mortality outstripped fertility, and immigration was required to
maintain the size of the population.

THE SECOND EPIDEMIOLOGICAL TRANSITION:
THE RISE OF CHRONIC AND DEGENERATIVE DISEASE

The second epidemiological transition refers to the shift from acute infectious diseases to chronic noninfectious, degenerative diseases. The increasing prevalence of these chronic diseases is related to an increase in longev-

ity. With cultural advances, a larger percentage of individuals live to reach the oldest segment of the population. In addition, the technological advances connected with the second epidemiological transition caused environmental degradation to grow worse. An interesting characteristic of many chronic diseases is their particular prevalence and "epidemic"-like occurrence in transitional societies, or in those populations undergoing the shift from developing to developed modes of production. In developing countries, many of the chronic diseases associated with the epidemiological transition appear first in members of the upper socioeconomic strata, because of their access to Western products and practices.

The accelerating advances in technology, medicine, and science led to the development of the germ theory of disease. Although there is some controversy about the role that medicine has played in the decline of certain infectious diseases, we now have a better understanding of the source of infectious disease and consequently better control over its spread. Immunization, for example, has made it possible to control many infections and recently was the primary factor in the eradication of smallpox. In the developed nations, a number of other communicable diseases have declined in importance. Because of the decrease in infectious disease and the subsequent reduction in infant mortality, life expectancy at birth has risen. In addition, there has been an increase in longevity among adults, with a concomitant increase in chronic and degenerative diseases.

Many of the diseases of the second epidemiological transition share a number of etiological factors related to human adaptation, including diet, activity level, mental stress, behavioral practices, and environmental pollution. For example, the industrialization and commercialization of food often results in malnutrition, especially in societies in "transition" from subsistence forms of food provision to agribusiness. Some segments of the population simply do not have the economic capacity to purchase food that meets basic nutritional requirements. Such food provision may also be responsible for obesity and high intakes of refined carbohydrates, which in turn increase the risk of heart disease and diabetes. Obesity is considered to be a common form of malnutrition in developed countries and is a direct result of an increasingly sedentary lifestyle in conjunction with steady or increasing caloric intakes.

A unique characteristic of chronic diseases is their relatively recent appearance in human history as a major cause of morbidity. This is indicative of a strong environmental factor in disease etiology. While biological factors such as genetics are no doubt important in determining who is most likely to succumb to which disease, genetics alone cannot explain the

rapid increase in chronic disease. Some of our current chronic diseases such as osteoarthritis were certainly prevalent in early human populations, but other more serious degenerative conditions such as cardiovascular disease and carcinoma were much rarer.

THE THIRD EPIDEMIOLOGICAL TRANSITION

Today, human populations are moving into the third epidemiological transition. Infectious diseases are reemerging because of their growing resistance to multiple antibiotics. Furthermore, these diseases could have a global impact. In a sense, the contemporary transition does not eliminate the possible coexistence of infectious diseases typical of the first epidemiological transition (some 10,000 years ago) in our own time; the World Health Organization (WHO) reports that of the 50 million deaths each year, 17.5 million are the result of infectious and parasitic disease. WHO reports that 3 million people die annually of tuberculosis and 30 million people are infected with HIV.

The emergence of infectious disease has been one of the most interesting evolutionary stories of the past decade and has captured the interest of scientists and the public alike. The media have responded to the public's fascination with the possibility that emerging diseases might threaten human survival by releasing books such as *The Hot Zone* and movies such as *Outbreak*. There is also genuine scientific concern about the problem. David Satcher (director of the Centers for Disease Control in Atlanta, Georgia) lists 22 diseases that have emerged in the past 22 years, including Rotovirus, Ebola virus, *Legionella pneumophila* (Legionnaire's Disease), Hantaan Virus (Korean hemorrhagic fever), HTLV I, *Staphylococcus* toxin, *Escherichia coli* 0157:h7, HTLV II, HIV, Human Herpes Virus 6, Hepatitis C, and Hantavirus isolates.

Such diseases have emerged as a result of the interaction of social, demographic, and environmental changes in a global economy and the adaptation and genetics of the microbe, influenced by international commerce and travel, technological change, and the breakdown of public health measures. Ecological changes precipitated by agricultural development projects, dams, deforestation, floods, droughts, and climatic irregularities have allowed diseases such as Argentine hemorrhagic fever, Korean hemorrhagic fever (Hantaan), and Hantavirus pulmonary syndrome to take hold. Human demographic behavior has been a factor in the spread of dengue fever, and the source for the introduction and spread of HIV and other sexually transmitted diseases.

The engine that is driving the reemergence of many of the diseases is ecological change that brings humans into contact with pathogens. Except for the Brazilian purpuric fever, which may represent a new strain of *Haemophilus influenzae,* biotype *aegyptius,* most of the emerging diseases are of cultural origin. The development of antibiotic resistance in any pathogen is the result of medical and agricultural practices. The indiscriminate and inappropriate use of antibiotics in medicine has made hospitals the source of multidrug resistant strains of bacteria that infect a large number of patients. Agricultural use in which animal feed is supplemented with subtherapeutic doses of antibiotics has risen dramatically in the last half century. In 1954, 500,000 pounds of antibiotics were produced in the United States; today, 40 million pounds are produced annually.

CONCLUSION

Recently, much attention has focused on the detrimental effects of industrialization on the international environment, including water, land, and the atmosphere. Massive industrial production of commodities has caused pollution. There is increasing concern about the health implications of contaminated water supplies, overuse of pesticides in commercialized agriculture, atmospheric chemicals, and the future effects of a depleted ozone layer on human health and food production. At no other time in human history have the changes in the environment been more rapid or so extreme. The increasing incidence of cancer among young people and the growth of respiratory disease has been implicated in these environmental changes.

Technology's anthropogenic impact has been evident since Neolithic times. Within the past 300 years, transportation has played a major role in disease patterns by bringing larger groups of humans into contact with the pathogens at an accelerated rate. Disease gained a foothold in the New World when large sailing ships became a major mode of transportation and brought Europeans into contact with other populations. Air travel has made it possible for a pathogen to move between continents within a matter of hours. There now exists a virtual viral superhighway, bringing people into contact with pathogens that affect adaptation. The present pattern reflects an evolutionary trend that can be traced to the beginning of primary food production. The scale has changed. The rates of emerging disease and their impact can now affect large segments of the world population at an ever increasing rate. It is essential to recognize the implications of these changes for today's human populations around the globe.

FURTHER READING

Armelagos, George J. 1991. "Human Evolution and the Evolution of Disease." *Ethnicity and Disease* 1(1):21–25.

Armelagos, George J., A. H. Goodman, and K. H. Jacobs. 1991. "The Origins of Agriculture: Population Growth during a Period of Declining Health." *Population and Environment* 13(1):9–22.

Cockburn, T. A. 1967. "The Evolution of Human Infectious Diseases." In T. A. Cockburn, ed., *Infectious Diseases: Their Evolution and Eradication.* Charles C. Thomas.

Cockburn, T. A. 1971. "Infectious Diseases in Ancient Populations." *Current Anthropology* 12(1):45–62.

Cohen, M. N., and G. J. Armelagos, eds. 1984. *Paleopathology at the Origins of Agriculture.* Academic Press.

Ewald, Paul W. 1994. *Evolution of Infectious Disease.* Oxford University Press.

McNeill, W. H. 1976. *Plagues and Peoples.* Anchor/Doubleday.

Polgar, Steven. 1964. "Evolution and the Ills of Mankind." In Sol Tax, ed., *Horizons of Anthropology.* Aldine.

Swedland, Alan C., and George J. Armelagos, eds. 1990. *Disease in Populations in Transition: Anthropological and Epidemiological Perspectives.* Bergin and Garvey.

ARCHAEOLOGISTS EXAMINE THE PAST

What Do We Know about the Past?
How Do We Learn about the Past?
Why Is Archaeology Relevant Today?

9 HISTORY, PROGRESS, AND THE FACTS OF ANCIENT LIFE

Mark N. Cohen

How many of us consciously or unconsciously assume that human history is largely a tale of progress through time? Can anyone dispute that the development of modern medicine, sanitation facilities, and almost universal education have brought us today to an era of great benefits for all? If we look far back into human history, did it not all begin with the "Neolithic Revolution," the domestication of plants and animals that ushered in sedentary farming, earliest cities, trade networks, large-scale governments, and craft specialization? Did not these, in turn, bring humankind to a new level of well-being from which progress could continue steadily up to today?

Most of our elementary, secondary, and college texts still reflect a deep human belief in the progress wrought by "civilized" life, by the developments growing out of ancient cities. Unfortunately, our sense of human history as steady progress in human well-being does not accord with the actual data at hand. Instead, the facts provide innumerable clues that "civilized" living has been accomplished only at considerable cost to most of the players. We need to revise our thinking, our teaching, and our textbooks to reflect this information.

THREE METHODS OF RECONSTRUCTING PATTERNS OF HEALTH & NUTRITION

RECONSTRUCTING THE PAST

Scientists use three main means of reconstructing patterns of health and nutrition in ancient societies. The first method focuses on small groups (hunter-gatherers) in the modern world to offer clues about our prehistoric ancestors. The !Kung San of the Kalahari (sometimes known as the Bushmen) come to mind most readily, but there are dozens of such groups (among whom the vaunted "affluent" San actually appear somewhat impoverished) scattered across the various continents.

The second method relies on what geologists call "Uniformitarian" reasoning to argue that natural processes—in this case the processes of nutrition and disease—must have operated in the past much as they do today and can therefore be reliably reconstructed. The third and most recently exploited method analyzes the skeletons of prehistoric populations to measure health and disease. Although many skeletons are now being reburied, there were once many thousands available for study. Many prehistoric communities were each represented by several hundred skeletons. There were, for example, 600 representing one Mayan town in my own small college laboratory—a fairly good sample from which conclusions could be drawn about health and disease in an ancient community.

None of these three methods—looking at modern hunters and gatherers, studying modern disease processes, and analyzing ancient skeletal remains—is wholly satisfactory. Contemporary hunting and gathering populations do live in the modern world, after all, so they are not exact prototypes of prehistoric groups. Disease processes involve living organisms that can evolve; thus they may not adhere to uniformitarian principles as reliably as do rocks. And prehistoric skeletons document only a limited sample of human ills. But the three methods taken together gain strength, often supporting one another in the manner of the legs of a tripod.

In any case, these three types of evidence are the only information that we have ever had concerning prehistoric health, or that was available to Hobbes or Rousseau or any of the more recent philosophers, historians, and educators who write the textbooks and the history books we use with our students. Taken together, the three types of evidence paint a picture very different from the one we were shown as children, and it is important to correct the erroneous old images of progress still found in many of our "authoritative" texts.

EVIDENCE ON NUTRITION

The evidence suggests, first, that the quality of human nutrition—the balance of vitamins, fats, minerals, and protein—has for the most part declined through human history except, of course, among the ruling classes. We talk of twentieth-century increases in stature (humans getting taller) as proof of improving nutrition, yet prehistoric hunting and gathering populations were often as tall if not taller than the populations that replaced them, and the predominant trend in human stature since early prehistory has been downward. (The people of Europe of the seventeenth and eighteenth centuries to whom we usually compare ourselves with pride are, in fact, among the shortest people who ever lived.) Eclectic diets of fresh vegetable foods with some meat apparently assure hunting and gathering populations a good balance of vitamins and minerals, and, in fact, such groups generally have access to relatively large amounts of meat and protein, rivaling consumption in the affluent United States and exceeding modern Third World averages by a large margin.

Modern hunter-gatherers rarely display clinical manifestations of protein deficiency, anemia (iron deficiency), or deficiencies of any other vitamin or mineral even when more "sophisticated" farmers nearby are deficient. To the initial surprise of health teams, infantile and childhood malnutrition, marasmus and kwashiorkor, are also quite rare among hunter-gatherers. These diseases are more common among share-croppers or other modern populations forced by poverty to rely on a single food such as rice or maize. The most poorly nourished people turn out to be the poor or lower classes of historic and modern "civilized" states from which modern trade systems withhold or actively withdraw various nutrients.

The most common shortage among modern hunter-gatherers is one of calories. Paradoxically to any American who has ever gone on a diet, modern hunter-gatherers tend to be chronically lean while otherwise well nourished probably as a result of exercising and eating lean animal products and high-roughage vegetable foods. They get no "free" processed calories. In addition, modern hunter-gatherers are making a living in some of the poorest environments on earth, the only environments still left to them after the expansion of modern states.

The skeletons of prehistoric hunter-gatherers generally confirm this sense of good nutrition. They commonly show fewer signs of porotic hyperostosis (the skeletal manifestation of a type of anemia) than the skeletons of later populations. Rickets (bending of bones), a disease of vitamin D deficiency reflecting poor diet and/or lack of exposure to sunlight, is primarily a disease of modern cities and is extremely rare either in modern hunter-gatherers or in ancient skeletons. Teeth of early archaeological populations display relatively little enamel hypoplasia, the scars of infantile illnesses, or periods of malnutrition, which are permanently recorded in the teeth.

Whether the reliability of human food supplies has improved with time is one of the most controversial and most important issues that needs to be resolved in assessing the "march of human progress" through time. There are many anecdotes about hunger or starvation among historic and modern hunter-gatherers. However, these typically occur in the Arctic or in extreme deserts, where more advanced civilizations do not even try to compete, or they occur in contexts where modern states restrict the movement of hunters or limit their activities. To judge by the relative efficiency with which different kinds of wild foods can be obtained, prehistoric hunter-gatherers would have been particularly well off when they lived in environments of their own choosing and before large game (one of the richest food sources) were depleted, as appears to have been the case on every continent occupied by early people. We like to think that modern transportation and storage capabilities have alleviated hunger, and they can; nevertheless, farmed fields may be inherently less stable than naturally selected wild resources. Being mobile may be safer in the face of famine than being sedentary.

Moreover, storage and transportation can fail; governments can and do refuse to help the needy; and in a world of economic specialists and private property, people may be unable to command the price of food even when food is plentiful. We have to remember that any government, the institution that can protect its people, is double-edged, since it is almost always in some way protecting a privileged class. Modern trade networks inevitably move food (both calories and quality nutrients) away from some populations in favor of others.

The archaeological record of skeletons reflects no steady record of improvement. In fact, if the clues in our teeth are used as the measure, one could argue that the frequency of stressful episodes to which the average individual has been exposed generally increases through time in most parts of the world. The historical record of famine in Europe, Russia, or China over the past several centuries also suggests no improvement until perhaps the last 150 years—and, of course, people in the Third World are still not protected from starvation.

DISEASES THROUGH TIME

In addition to the decline in the quality of human nutrition, the second point confirmed by all three types of evidence is that the variety and intensity of human infections and infectious diseases have generally increased through human history. Epidemiological theory predicts that diseases will not be transmitted as readily among small groups of people who change their base camp periodically as they are transmitted when people live in large permanent human settlements.

Diseases transmitted directly from person to person via the air or by touch, such as influenza, operate most efficiently when population density is high and large crowds are gathered (that is one reason why schools and other similar institutions commonly help disease to spread). Diseases that spread through human feces (including cholera, most other diarrhea, and hookworm) will obviously be most dangerous for large permanent populations where feces accumulate. Historic outbreaks of cholera in London occurred amid high-density populations whose wells had been contaminated by latrines. Such conditions also facilitate the spread of diseases such as bubonic plague, which are carried by rats or other parasites on accumulations of human garbage. And as the experiences of American Indians after the arrival of Columbus demonstrate, long-distance travel and large-scale trade can spread diseases with devastating effect (it has been estimated that 90 percent of the Native American population was destroyed by disease). The history of bubonic plague in France, which decimated large port cities but left villages in the interior unharmed, is a good example of the dangers of urban living and conversely the ability of small size and isolated population patterns to provide protection against infectious diseases.

It is, in fact, a fairly commonplace observation that hunting and gathering bands are relatively infection-free and that the rates of many diseases increase when mobile hunters are settled in larger permanent camps. The skeletal record again provides confirmation. Signs of infection in the skeleton become more common as people settle in large-scale cities in essentially every region of the ancient world where the appropriate study has been done. In addition, the low incidence of anemia among ancient hunter-gatherers is thought by many scholars to reflect low rates of parasitic infestation as much or more than diet. Tuberculosis, one of the specific diseases that can often be detected in skeletons, is conspicuously absent or quite scarce in the archaeological record until relatively recent times.

Moreover, many "epidemic" diseases appear to require a critical threshold of population size (either in one place or connected by rapid transport) in order to spread. Measles, mumps, smallpox, influenza, and German measles all appear to need large and rapidly reproducing human populations to survive. The implication is that these diseases did not spread until the recent growth of cities and transportation networks. However, once many Europeans were immunized by constant childhood exposure, these diseases became major vehicles of conquest in the spread of European hegemony. These diseases not only killed many Native Americans but also appeared to provide evidence that Europeans were divinely favored.

Many other diseases that plague modern populations are also rare or absent in modern hunter-gatherers. High blood pressure is generally not found in hunter-gatherers regardless of age, "racial type," or location. Diets naturally low in sodium may be one reason; another may be the lack of the fatty buildup in blood vessels that contributes to widespread high blood pressure, strokes, and heart attacks. Diabetes also seldom occurs among hunter-gatherers, although the same individuals may be prone to diabetes when fed a "modern" diet. Bowel and breast cancer are relatively rare in populations who do not live a "modern" lifestyle. While this is sometimes attributed to a lower life expectancy, in fact the proportion of adults over age 60 in hunting and gathering societies can be comparable to that of our own (see chapter 26).

LIFE EXPECTANCY

The history of human life expectancy is difficult to reconstruct. Life expectancy, the number of years an individual can expect to live, refers to a rough average of age at death in a population, not to how long the oldest individuals live. (A group will have a life expectancy of 40 if half the group lives to 80 and half the group dies at birth). We can observe modern hunter-gatherers and measure their individual life spans, but in most cases the cause of death will be something that was not part of ancient life, such as a tuberculosis epidemic. Most observed deaths are from infectious diseases, and most of those are diseases we consider modern. We can determine the ages of skeletal populations, but they may not be complete. Moreover, while it is relatively easy to establish the age of children from their teeth and unfused bones, determining the age of adults is difficult and inexact. Nevertheless, the combined data suggest that our early ancestors had a life expectancy at birth of about 25 years, a low figure but one that again compares favorably with figures from much of urban Europe as late as the eighteenth or nineteenth century, and from India well into the twentieth.

In particular, hunters and gatherers seem to have been fairly successful in rearing their young. A survey of all of the known modern hunter-gatherer populations suggests that they lose an average of 20 percent of their children as infants and about 45 percent before adulthood, figures that accord reasonably well with the evidence of ancient skeletons. These figures, terrible as they are, compare favorably with most of Europe prior to about 1850 and with many major American cities as late as the turn of the last century.

CONCLUSION

The point of the foregoing remarks is that our models of history—the models that consciously or unconsciously shape our planning for the future—are misleading. They are based too much on the experience of the privileged classes, which mistake their privilege for progress. In the seventeenth century, Thomas Hobbes characterized primitive life as "nasty, brutish, and short" at a time when life for most of his compatriots was apparently shorter and was certainly nastier, at least for all those outside the ruling classes, than it is today.

We do not simply progress. Many aspects of so-called civilization—the

adoption of sedentary farming, cities, trade, social class distinctions—
are mixed blessings for the participants. It is more accurate to see history
as simple population growth and the endless competition between ever
larger political units in which some societies lose and some societies win,
without necessarily generating benefits for all of their citizens.

It is particularly important to be aware of our own biases and our often
unconscious desire to believe in progress, as well as our tendency to forget
the larger frames of reference through which human history develops. The
facts of ancient human life not only inform the understanding of our past
but also help us plan more carefully for the future.

UPDATE

Knowledge continues to grow on many fronts, particularly those concerned with individual diseases and individual historical situations. To
name just a few examples, a conference (as yet unpublished) debating
anew the origin and history of syphilis was held in Germany in 1992.
Articles in the *Annual Review of Anthropology* in 1992 and 1993 reviewed new knowledge of nutritional adaptation, prehistoric arthritis,
and the transfer of diseases from Europe to the Americas after Columbus
(Dobyns, 1993). The latter subject is also the focus of two new books, by
Larsen and Milner (1994) and Verano and Ubelaker (1992). The causes
and effects of the adoption of agriculture are debated in several articles in
Current Anthropology and the *American Anthropologist* for the same
years. A new book by Stuart-Macadam and Kent (1992) debates and refines the meaning of the skeletal pathology known as porotic hyperostosis
(anemia).

A major challenge has also been issued concerning the interpretation of
data from skeletal pathology, which contributed significantly to this chapter and to the books on which it was based. Cohen (1989, and this chapter) used the relative frequency of visible pathology in prehistoric skeletons to represent or at least approximate the relative frequency of disease
in the once-living populations—a common practice among skeletal pathologists. Critics writing in *Current Anthropology* (Wood et al., 1992)
have argued that while this interpretation may be correct, other interpretations are possible. For example, since responses to disease are slow to
develop in the skeleton, an increase in skeletal pathology might not mean
more disease but an increase in the proportion of individuals who survived
the diseases long enough to develop skeletal scars. Increased visible skele-

tal pathology, they argue, *could* paradoxically be a sign of relatively good health or at least greater longevity.

In response, Cohen (1992) has noted that epidemiological and ethnographic studies of living people independently suggest that the various pathological conditions (and diseases) discussed should be expected to have increased during the economic transitions in question—so his argument is supported by two other lines of evidence. What we know about the history of infection and nutrition, he says, suggests that hunter-gatherers were better nourished and freer of background infections than later populations. Since background nutrition and preexisting infections are major determinants in the outcome of disease, later people were probably not more likely to survive episodes of disease. Furthermore, Cohen argues, alternate explanations that might explain changes in pathology in *individual* populations are not able to explain the *worldwide trends* in visible pathology that he has described. For example, improved survivorship cannot explain the visible worldwide trend toward increased skeletal pathology after the adoption of farming. Population growth rates before and after the adoption of farming (the change in the average rate is extremely small) indicate there cannot possibly have been a large enough increase in survivorship on a world scale to account for the large increases in visible skeletal pathology. In fact, since there is some evidence that human *fertility* went up after the adoption of farming (see Cohen, 1989; Wood et al., 1992)—which could easily account for the very slight acceleration in population growth—it is unlikely that survivorship increased at all. In fact, it may well have declined. The debate continues.

It is also important to point out that the overall conclusions about the rise of civilization—and the very meaning of civilization—presented in this chapter have not been challenged. There seems to be a broad sense within anthropology, medicine, and nutrition (represented by a series of reviews of Cohen, 1989) that the data and recent conclusions in the field as a whole are well represented in the chapter and in Cohen's 1989 book, even though the conclusions come as a surprise to nonprofessionals.

FURTHER READING

Cohen, Mark Nathan. 1989. *Health and the Rise of Civilization.* Yale University Press.
Cohen, Mark Nathan. 1992. "The Osteological Paradox Reconsidered." *Current Anthropology* 33:358–59.

Cohen, Mark Nathan. 1997. *Culture of Intolerance: Chauvinism, Class, and Racism in the United States.* Yale University Press.

Dobyns, Henry F. 1993. "Disease Transfer at Contact." *Annual Review of Anthropology* 22:273–91.

Larsen, Clark Spencer, and George R. Milner, eds. 1994. *In the Wake of Contact: Biological Responses to Conquest.* Wiley-Liss.

Stuart-Macadam, Patricia, and Susan Kent, eds. 1992. *Diet, Demography and Disease: Changing Perspectives on Anemia.* Aldine de Gruyter.

Verano, John W., and Douglas H. Ubelaker, eds. 1992. *Disease and Demography in the Americas.* Smithsonian Institution Press.

Wood, James W., George R. Milner, Henry C. Harpending, and Kenneth M. Weiss. 1992. "The Osteological Paradox." *Current Anthropology* 33:343–58.

10 NEW PERSPECTIVES ON AGRICULTURAL ORIGINS IN THE ANCIENT NEAR EAST

Melinda A. Zeder

How can a heap of long buried, extremely fragmented animal bones help us better understand the origins of agriculture, perhaps the most significant turning point in the course of human history?

Agriculture, which anthropologists define as the domestication of both plants and animals, changed forever the evolution of human societies. While agriculture brought about unparalleled productivity and ever improving standards of living, it also led to swelling populations, widespread hunger, and irreversible environmental change. It should be no surprise, then, that the causes and consequences of the origins of agriculture, often called the Neolithic Revolution, are recurring topics of lively debate within the field of archaeology.

What were the preconditions that gave rise to the domestication of plants and animals? Why did people nearly 10,000 years ago begin to experiment with crops and the rearing of livestock? When and why did these practices replace gathering wild resources and hunting game as the primary means of feeding people?

EARLY-TWENTIETH-CENTURY VIEWS

Theories explaining the causes and consequences of agriculture are not only varied but frequently contradictory. In the late nineteenth through the mid-twentieth centuries, many researchers viewed agriculture as a technological breakthrough, forever freeing humankind from a life on the margins: a mean, brutish existence that relied on wits and luck for survival. Agriculture, in this view, brought an era of bounty, with rich harvests of predictable and nutritious plants and animals. The ability to reap these harvests expanded with each new technological refinement—the plow, draft animals, irrigation. Farmers' labor was seasonal, affording people leisure time to invent labor-saving technologies as well as cultural elaborations in the arts and sciences. Early agriculture was the first major watershed, setting the stage for the subsequent grand threshold of human achievement—the development of civilization.

MID-TWENTIETH-CENTURY VIEWS

During the 1960s and 1970s, the world became increasingly concerned about scarcities of primary resources and overpopulation, and people began demanding limits to growth. Within this context a very different picture emerged of the origins of agriculture. The life of the hunter-gatherer, past and present, was no longer described as one of hardship, privation, and ceaseless toil. Rather, anthropologists saw hunter-gatherers as "the original affluent society"—people with modest needs met by occasional hunting forays and sporadic collecting. Agriculture was viewed as a kind of expulsion from Eden, brought about by the inevitable expansion of population beyond the capacity of hunter-gatherer strategies to satisfy basic needs. The price of the pre-Neolithic baby boom, the punishment for taking the first bite of the domesticated apple, was the farmer's life of hardship and toil.

In this view, growing crops and raising animals provided more food, but the food was less nutritious and less palatable than people had previously enjoyed. Agriculture accelerated the rate of population increase, giving rise to more widespread hunger than the world had ever seen. The reduction in biological diversity accompanying the spread of agriculture undermined the stability of natural resources, paving the way for periodic, devastating ecological crises.

These two alternative visions of the origins of agriculture, as blessing or blight, serve as opposite poles of the debate. Researchers are discovering, however, that the story of the development of plant and animal domestication and the resultant food-producing economies is far richer and more complex than either of these two views indicates.

EXPULSION FROM EDEN ?

Earlier interpretations, for example, posited that all peoples throughout the Near East adopted food-producing technologies quickly and completely, never looking back to earlier days of hunting and gathering. The wide array of suitable plant and animal domesticates, the favorable local environmental conditions, and the human population dynamics may well explain a generally rapid embrace of food production as a more reliable subsistence strategy than hunting and gathering. But within the Near East, the domesticates and the timing of their adoption varied, with each region emphasizing different combinations of cereals and animals in varying rates and sequences. The Khabur Basin provides one case study illustrating the variation in human adaptation to the development of farming and herding.

THE KHABUR BASIN OF ANCIENT MESOPOTAMIA

The Khabur Basin is nestled in the far northeastern corner of modern-day Syria, bordered by Turkey to the north and Iraq to the south and east (see map). The northern Khabur Basin is dissected by the Khabur River and a number of streams (or wadis, as they are called in the Near East) fanning out across the basin. These wadis are often dry in the searing summer months. From the late fall through the spring, they carry seasonal rains and runoff from northern upland areas. These seasonal streams converge where the Khabur River begins its journey southward, eventually joining

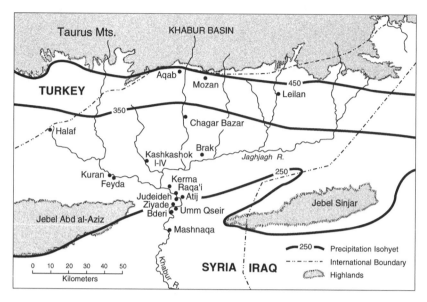

KHABUR BASIN SETTLEMENTS

the Euphrates River. There is a steep north-south gradient of rainfall in the Khabur Basin. Precipitation in the far north is more than enough to support rain-fed, nonirrigation agriculture, but rainfall levels decrease precipitously southward, where rain-fed farming becomes an increasingly risky business.

EARLY SETTLEMENT IN THE KHABUR BASIN

Settlement in the Khabur Basin was sparse until about 6000 B.C. No known sites in the region date to before 14,000 B.C., and only two sites date to between 14,000 and 10,000 B.C. The eighth millennium B.C. (8000 to 7000 B.C.) saw the introduction of farming and herding into the basin. For almost 2,000 years a few small communities, located exclusively in the better-watered northern region, relied primarily on domestic resources: cereal grains, lentils, and pulses (pod-bearing plants such as peas and beans), as well as sheep and goats, and later pigs and cattle. Then the northern steppe witnessed a substantial increase in settlement. A number of farming communities arose in the upper Khabur Basin, all of which produced a distinctive pottery, linking them to a Halafian cultural tradition that spread widely across northern Mesopotamia.

The Halafian Period, named after Tell Halaf in the northern Khabur, is believed to have experienced a remarkable proliferation of rain-fed farm communities, an expansion of far-flung trading networks, and, possibly, the development of more complex social organization. Plant and animal remains recovered from Halafian sites in well-watered areas suggest that these communities relied heavily on domestic crops and livestock, although wild plants and animals were also gathered and hunted in small amounts.

UMM QSEIR

The first indication of population movement out of the northern steppe into the arid southern steppe comes from Halafian levels at the small site of Umm Qseir, situated just below the 10-inch (250-millimeter) rainfall boundary. Umm Qseir is located about 19 miles (30 kilometers) away from the nearest contemporary site and is very small: no more than a quarter of an acre (¹⁄₁₀ hectare) in size. Excavators from Yale University found only ephemeral traces of architecture at Umm Qseir and essentially no tools used in grain harvesting and processing. The entire Halafian occupation of Umm Qseir seems to have lasted no more than 200 years, between 6,000 and 5,000 B.C., and the site was probably never occupied by more than two or three families. We originally thought this tiny Halafian outpost was a seasonal encampment, used by small groups who traveled with their flocks from established villages in the north to take advantage of the abundant southern spring grasses.

ANIMAL BONE ANALYSIS

Through extensive analysis of the plant and animal remains from Umm Qseir, we tested our first hypothesis that the site was a seasonal encampment of mobile herders or pastoralists. Our analysis demonstrated this hypothesis to be dead wrong!

Through the painstaking, sometimes frightfully dull, study of thousands of broken bones and fragments of charred seeds, we uncovered clues to help us reconstruct the daily subsistence of the people living in this tiny community in Mesopotamia between 6000 and 5000 B.C.; the clues told us much about the complexity of these people's yearly strategies to survive.

An average season of archaeological excavation in the Near East can yield upward of 50,000 bones, each of which is of interest to the zooarchaeologist who specializes in studying animal bones. The bone analysis requires an incredible amount of patience and a sharp eye for seeing patterns after thousands of observations have been recorded. Bones first have to be washed and dried, sorted, labeled, and coded for a variety of information: animal species, skeletal element, side, type of breakage, and so on. The zooarchaeologist makes these observations, often using skeletons of modern animals to help identify bone fragments.

The bones and teeth of an animal carry hidden clues to the age and season in which that animal was killed. Long bones (such as the femur or radius) fuse at certain known ages. If you find an unfused distal end of a sheep humerus, you know that that sheep was killed before it reached its first birthday. Like human children, mammals lose their baby teeth, and their adult teeth erupt at known ages. The rate at which teeth wear with use over time also is known for some animals, as are the peak birth months.

Zooarchaeologists use this knowledge when analyzing bones to calculate the age, and, in some cases, the season in which an animal was killed. With a large enough sample of bones, they can construct an age profile of the flock and the primary seasons in which the animals were slaughtered. From this profile, they can draw a range of conclusions about the relationship of humans to the animals with which they lived—both domestic and wild.

THE PUZZLE OF UMM QSEIR

The central question that now began to take shape was whether Umm Qseir was a seasonal settlement for pastoral herders coming down from the north or a year-round settlement.

Pigs Offer the First Clues

Domestic species of the residents of Umm Qseir in the sixth millennium (6000–5000 B.C.) consisted of sheep, goat, and pig, but no domestic cattle. The absence of the full range of Neolithic domesticates (sheep/goat, pig, *and* domestic cattle) at first supported the hypothesis that Umm Qseir was a site for pastoralists taking seasonal advantage of the lush, late winter/early spring pasturage in the region. However, pigs did not fit easily into this scenario. Pigs have neither the legs nor the temperament for long-distance migration, and, though there are some instances of pig drives in the past, swine are not customarily associated with pastoralists in the Near East. In fact, pigs are usually taken as markers of a sedentary lifestyle. It was possible, however, that Halafian Umm Qseirians drove a pig or two down to the area each spring along with their domestic sheep and goats. Information on both the age and, especially, the season of death of the pigs consumed at Umm Qseir was necessary to resolve this question. An examination of pig teeth from Umm Qseir indicated that the slaughter of swine at the site focused on animals 6 to 18 months of age. This is a common culling (slaughter) pattern for *domestic* swine. Yet, although there is an emphasis on young pigs, the kill-off of swine at Umm Qseir was not confined to piglets. There were also older animals, in the range of 3 to 4+ years, which is indicative of the presence of quite elderly swine at Umm Qseir. Not just one or two pigs were brought to the site each season; rather, a viable breeding herd must have been present.

The kill-off of pigs at Halafian Umm Qseir also reflected a strong seasonal pattern. Slaughter of swine seems to have been most common from May to October, particularly from August through October. This period includes the arid summer months and the early rainy season—the leanest resource period in the region. Intensity of swine slaughter slackens in the months between November and April, the period of greatest bounty of plant and animal resources in the middle Khabur.

Sheep and Goats Offer Additional Clues

We tentatively concluded that pigs were present at Umm Qseir throughout the year and that at least some Umm Qseir residents lived here on a permanent basis. But did all the residents live here all year long? Perhaps just a few people resided here year round, eating pigs in the hard times, to be joined by pastoralists in the late winter/early spring, pasturing their sheep and goats. To find the answer, we needed to look carefully at the sheep and goat age and seasonality data.

Sheep and goat age distributions indicate that culling focused on animals in the 1- to 2.5-year range. Once again, the bones told us that both young lambs and kids and older sheep and goats were eaten at the site. Seasonality data indicate relatively low kill-off in the first six months after birth (from February to July), and a peak in slaughter of lambs and kids in the second six months (between August and January). In the following six-month periods, mortality consistently slackens in the late winter/early spring months, and increases in the summer and fall. Once again, it is these months of the hot, dry summer and of the sodden unproductive early rainy season that are the hardest on herds in the region today. This is the most likely season for kill-off of domestic sheep and goats from resident herds. It is, however, the least likely season for pastoralists to be here, since these are the hardest months in this region.

If these animal bones had been the result of nomadic pastoralist culling, they would have reflected a kill-off in the late winter/early spring, when flocks would have been brought to the southern region to feed on the luxuriant spring grasses of the steppe. In addition, there would be a virtual absence of animals in the more stressful dry summer/early winter months, when pastoralists with their herds would have headed north.

Wild Animal Clues

The biggest surprise from this collection of bones did not come from domestic animals, however, but from wild ones. Unlike contemporary and earlier sites on the northern steppe—where domesticated animals are overwhelmingly the most commonly eaten in early farming villages— at Halafian Umm Qseir, bones of domestic animals comprise less that half of the bone sample. Wild species dominate! People were eating gazelle, wild ass, wild cattle, deer, hare, turtles, fish, birds, and freshwater clams—all local wild resources in the area.

Seasonality data for the Umm Qseir gazelle add to our understanding of the subsistence economy. Many gazelles showed an advanced state of wear on the lower deciduous third molar, a tooth that is shed at about 14 months of age. Hence these animals were hunted and killed around the time of their first birthday. Since gazelle in the region give birth in March and April, this means there was special emphasis on spring gazelle hunting. Wild game attracted to the region to feed on the tasty spring grasses would have been easy prey during this time of year.

Final Clues from Plant Remains

Plant remains from Umm Qseir reinforce the picture painted by the faunal (animal) data; the site must have been occupied year-round. Contrary to our initial hypothesis, Halafian occupants of Umm Qseir were not pastoralists, but rather pioneering farmsteaders. People came to this previously uninhabited region, bringing with them their domestic sheep, goats, and pigs, as well as domestic crops—in effect carrying with them the basic elements of the Neolithic Revolution. In this relatively untouched environment with its plentiful wild resources, these early settlers did not march lockstep to the drum of the Neolithic Revolution. They did not settle down to a traditional village life dependent on domestic resources. Nor did they use the area only as a seasonal feedlot for their domestic flocks.

Instead, Halafian Umm Qseirians took full advantage of the natural (wild) riches of this new environment in its seasons of plenty, while relying on their domestic resources to tide them over the lean times. Spring was the most bountiful season at Umm Qseir—a time when crops of emmer, barley, and pulses were harvested, and when wild game feeding on the abundant spring growth of the steppe was easy prey. During the hotter summer months and into the unproductive winter season, when game was in all likelihood more dispersed across the steppe, Umm Qseirians could rely on stored grain, fall fruiting wild shrubs and trees, and their domestic stock of sheep, goat, and pig.

NORTH AND SOUTH KHABUR BASIN COMPARED

Subsequent and ongoing analysis of animal and plant remains from 17 sites in the Khabur Basin demonstrates that Umm Qseir is not unique, but part of an increasingly interesting and unexpected picture of post-Neolithic subsistence in the region. These sites date from the first introduction of domesticated plants and animals into the region (8000–7000 B.C.) through the rise of the first state-level societies (3000–2000 B.C.). Village communities in the better-watered, more densely populated north (today a highly productive dry farming zone) followed the expected post-Neolithic subsistence pattern, with increasingly exclusive reliance on domestic crops and herd animals. Even so, there is evidence that wild animals remained relatively plentiful in the area up through about 3000 B.C.

In contrast, for more than 2,000 years small isolated communities on the drier southern steppe developed highly localized subsistence practices. Residents of the southern steppe mixed and matched selected domesticates with a heavy dependence on a variety of wild resources. People of the more arid, marginal, sparsely populated area apparently compensated for the unpredictability of a high-risk environment by expanding their resource base to include both domestic and wild resources. Significantly, the greatest dietary eclecticism seems to be found not in the fertile heartland but in the more arid frontier. In the more difficult environment, people met the challenge by combining their earlier reliance on wild game with newer domesticated resources.

CONCLUSIONS

There are no more herds of wild animals on today's treeless steppe. The rich diversity of wild plants that once supported these herds has been replaced by monocrop irrigated fields and by highly degraded pasture in outlying areas. The long-term environmental impact of intensive agropastoral economies on wild resources in this region is inarguable.

Our information indicates, however, that the onset of environmental degradation did not immediately follow the introduction of farming and herding. Early inhabitants of this region mixed agriculture and hunting/collecting without significant ill effects on indigenous wild species of plants or animals. Significant ecological change accompanied the urban-based, agricultural economy several thousand years after the establishment of the first farming communities in the region. The small sample of plant remains from sites on the southern steppe dating to the third millennium B.C. indicates that by this time hardwoods had been replaced by fast-growing shrubby plants, and animal dung had become the primary fuel source—the small supply suggests the first fuel crisis in prehistory!

What does this case study of subsistence in the Khabur Basin tell us about the consequences of beginning agriculture in the Near East? Judging from this example, it would seem that the impact of the Neolithic Revolution was not nearly as uniform, nor as irreversible as it is often portrayed. Once people became farmers and herders, many still continued to practice hunting and gathering, mixing old and new strategies. The times after the "revolution" do not conform to theories that see the origin of agriculture as either a technological blessing or an environmental blight that locked people into an economy based solely on domesticated resources. The story of post-Neolithic societies in northern Mesopotamia is far more nuanced than any of these broad-brush models would have it. There is, instead, a complex interplay between the environmental conditions that set the general parameters of possible subsistence strategies in a region, and a web of social and economic factors that shaped the subsistence choices people make at different places and different times. A technology once discovered need not shackle people into its exclusive practice; a social organization or an economy once established need not be an immutable obstacle to cultural flexibility or human ingenuity.

FURTHER READING

Clutton-Brock, Juliet. 1989. *The Walking Larder: Patterns of Domestication, Pastoralism, and Predation.* Unwin Hyman.

Cowan, C. W., and P. J. Watson. 1992. *The Origins of Agriculture: An International Perspective.* Smithsonian Institution Press.

Zeder, Melinda A. 1994. "After the Revolution: Post-Neolithic Subsistence in Northern Mesopotamia." *American Anthropologist* 96(1):97–126.

Zeder, Melinda A. 1991. *Feeding Cities: Specialized Animal Economy in the Ancient Near East.* Smithsonian Institution Press.

11 PYGMIES OF THE ITURI

An Ethnoarchaeological Exploration

John W. Fisher Jr.

T he tall, dark green forest canopy on each side of the dirt road pressed closer and closer together overhead with each passing mile of westward travel. As the emerald-green grasslands of the former Zaire-Uganda border country dwindled behind us, I sat high in the back of our Toyota Hilux pickup on a pile of food, gasoline containers, Toyota spare parts, camp supplies, and shovels and hoes that we always carried to dig the pickup out of deep mud. Our destination: the Ituri Forest Project's field station in a remote area of the Ituri Forest inhabited by the Efe Pygmies. This station—where Helen Strickland, my wife, and I would live for a year—lies along an almost impenetrable narrow track, 1½ days' journey and more than 120 kilometers from the eastern edge of the forest. Here, the villages of the sedentary horticulturists and their wide swaths of cleared and cultivated land are fewer and more widely separated than in the forest margins or on its "main" roads.

INDEPENDENT HUNTER-GATHERERS OR SERFS?

The various groups of Ituri Forest Pygmies, collectively called Mbuti by their village neighbors (or BaMbuti, meaning Mbuti people) are well known to anthropologists through studies by English, Japanese, American, and German scholars. Although they have been cited as a classic example of tropical forest hunter-gatherers, their economic independence from village agriculturists has been much disputed. In the 1920s and 1930s, Paul Schebesta, a German anthropologist, noted in the first comprehensive study of the Mbuti their strong reliance on cultivated foods from the gardens of villagers, to whom Mbuti were bound in a type of master-serf relationship. He expressed doubt that the Pygmies he saw could have survived without such foods. Perhaps the best-known studies, however, are those of the English anthropologist Colin Turnbull (1961), who worked with a group of Mbuti net-hunters about 110 kilometers southwest of our research area. Turnbull argued that the Mbuti were not dependent on their sedentary horticulturist neighbors for basic staples but could live off the wild foods of the forest for extended periods. Although the Mbuti often chose to participate in a symbiotic relationship with the villagers, in which each group provided the other with certain foods (bananas, manioc, game meat) and services (field labor, initiation and funeral rites), Turnbull described Mbuti culture as an independent entity, based on identity with a dependence on the forest.

THE ITURI PROJECT

The Efe are one of the least-studied and most isolated Pygmy groups, and hunt almost entirely with bows and arrows rather than with nets. One of the goals of the Ituri Project, which began in 1980, was to document the subsistence practices of the Efe, as part of a broad study of their adaptation to a forest environment. During the 1960s and early 1970s the project codirector, Irven DeVore, had helped direct the Harvard Kalahari Project, an ecologically oriented study of the !Kung San (Bushmen) of the Kalahari desert in Botswana. The Ituri Project, one of the first comprehensive studies of human ecology, demography, and health and nutrition among tropical forest hunter-gatherers (and horticulturists), was designed to build on and further explore some of the results of the Kalahari study. In particular, the Kalahari project had demonstrated a major reliance on vegetable foods, long birth spacing, low fertility, and a high degree of personal and group mobility among desert hunter-gatherers. These conclusions were further corroborated by other studies of desert hunter-gatherers in Australia. Would these adaptations persist in the more stable environment of the tropical forest? Did the cyclical fluctuation of wet and dry seasons in the forest affect group structure and mobility in the same way as the seasonal changes of the desert? What were the major resource limitations for humans in this environment, where most mammals are small and many dwell in the forest canopy? How independent were the Efe of their village horticulturist neighbors, the Lese?

Since 1980 more than a dozen anthropologists and other researchers have come to the Ituri field station to gain a relatively long-term perspective on the cyclical fluctuations in the forest environment and on the ways in which the Efe and the Lese have adapted to this environment (Bailey and DeVore, 1989). These researchers have observed a symbiotic relationship between the Efe and the Lese. For instance, two-thirds of the calories the Efe consume come from cultivated foods—bananas, manioc, rice, peanuts, sweet potatoes, and other plants—grown mostly in Lese gardens. Efe women, in return for these foods, assist the Lese in planting, caring for, and harvesting the gardens. Efe men help the Lese by clearing patches of forest for gardens and by providing honey, meat, and other forest products. In exchange, the Lese provide the Efe with such items as metal tools and clothing. Efe sometimes plant small gardens, but their mobile lifestyle, moving to a new camp every two or three weeks, is not compatible with the constant care that gardens require in the tropical forest.

Forest foods make up one-third of the calories in the Efe diet. These foods include wild plants such as yams and the olive-sized fruit of the *Canarium* tree, honey, fish, and meat. Several species of duiker (small antelope) and monkey are their primary prey. Less frequently, they hunt animals up to the size of buffalo and elephant. Men, armed with metal-tipped arrows, hunt duiker using a variety of strategies. One method involves a man and dogs working together to flush out game while other men, carefully and quietly positioned, wait for duiker to come within arrow range. On other occasions, a solitary man waits in quiet ambush on a platform built in a tree of ripe fruit. In the early morning and late afternoon duiker will feed on fruit that have dropped to the ground, and, if lucky, the hunter will get a shot at the animal.

Monkeys are hunted with poison-tipped arrows, their wooden shaft carved to an extremely fine point. Poison, made from several forest plants, is applied to the tip and dried over the coals of a fire. To hunt monkeys in the forest trees, solitary hunters stalk their prey quietly and when within range of the animal shoot several arrows.

Despite the hunting skill of the Efe, we and other researchers find it difficult to imagine that the Efe could live in the forest in the absence of cultivated foods, on which they seem to rely quite heavily. Forest ecologists working elsewhere in the Ituri Forest were not able to identify among the wild plants gathered by the Efe year-round abundant sources of carbohydrates comparable to the mongongo nuts and roots collected by the !Kung. If cultivated carbohydrate-rich staples are essential to human existence in the tropical forest, then human occupation of the deep forest may be limited to the last 2,000 to 3,000 years, since the domestication of food crops in Africa.

THE ARCHAEOLOGY OF PRESENT-DAY EFE LIFE

As archaeologists, Helen and I were to document the material remains of Efe life, just as the Harvard Kalahari Project had done for the !Kung (Yellen, 1977). My interest in hunter-gatherers came from my work with the material remains of prehistoric hunter-gatherers of the Great Plains, such as I found at sites in Colorado with bones of bison and mammoth, as well as stone spear tips and other artifacts left by people long ago. The interpretation of these ancient sites, however, requires some insight into hunter-gatherer ecology and behavior. Was this the kind of debris normally deposited near or in the family dwelling, or were these the kinds of bones and stone tools normally left at a kill location? How much and what parts of the skeleton were usually left behind when a mammoth (or elephant) or other animal was butchered? How many people did a mammoth feed, and how often would one have been killed? What kinds of debris did other food-procurement practices generate? Can group size and organization be reconstructed from ancient debris-patterning? How is domestic space organized and used? By carefully observing the Efe, as they carried out routine activities at their campsites, we hoped to learn how to make sense out of the ancient pieces of bone and stone and other clues at archaeological sites, to reconstruct what life was like in the past.

A central question concerns the degree to which the camp design, activity patterns, and disposal practices of hunter-gatherers are universal among all hunter-gatherer groups or are affected by different environments or cultural rules. Archaeologists had often assumed that tools and bones found together related to a single activity, spatially segregated from other activities. The Kalahari research, however, suggested that hunter-gatherer camps were small, closely spaced circles of ephemeral huts. Since most in-camp activities were conducted around the family hearth in front of the hut, debris from many distinct but spatially overlapping activities tended to be concentrated in a ring surrounding an open public space.

Only messy activities were carried out in "special activity areas" on the outskirts of !Kung camps. Since the size of the debris ring was proportional to the number of huts, it could be used to estimate the number of families and hence the population of a !Kung camp. If these patterns and others were also present among tropical and Arctic hunter-gatherers, then perhaps the patterning could be used to understand the hunter-gatherer sites on the Great Plains 11,000 years ago.

The research that Helen and I carried out benefited considerably from the work of other researchers on the project. Their studies give a detailed picture of the Efe subsistence practices and of other aspects of their adaptations to the forest environment. Thus we had a strong foundation from which to focus on material aspects of the Efe life, in particular the spatial organization of their camps. We found that although each campsite is unique in the details of camp layout, all camps conform to a single general pattern (Fisher and Strickland, 1989).

The first step in setting up an Efe camp is to clear away smaller trees and undergrowth. The size of these clearings ranges from 40 square meters to about 550 square meters, depending on the camp population. The number of people living at a camp ranges from about three to thirty-five or forty. Each nuclear family inhabits a dome-shaped hut made of a frame of saplings covered with broad leaves. Huts are situated near the perimeter of the camp in an oval layout. Each hut has one or more fires inside for warmth at night and a fire outside the hut near the door.

Trash heaps, located beside and behind the huts, are a feature of all camps. Initially composed of cleared brush, the Efe trash heaps continue to grow through the life of the camp as its inhabitants discard food remains, ashes from fires, and worn-out or broken implements.

The placement of huts within a camp is strongly influenced by interpersonal relationships and kinship ties. Families that get along particularly well will situate their huts close together, whereas those that are feuding will place themselves a good distance apart.

The location of day-to-day campsite activities—preparing food, eating, making and repairing implements, socializing, and relaxing—conforms to a pattern. Almost all such activities are performed inside the camp perimeter. For safety reasons, applying poison to arrows is usually done outside of camp. Children's play takes place inside the camp and in some cases in a separate area cleared nearby.

The fireplace situated outside the doorway of each hut serves as the focus for many activities. Women sit beside the fire to prepare and to cook food. Men relax and socialize by the fire, and here they also get ready for the hunt, carving new arrow shafts, sharpening metal arrowheads, or strengthening their bow stave over the hot coals. During a rainstorm, these activities are conducted inside the hut. Most of the debris generated by these activities eventually ends up on the trash heaps.

Efe huts vary considerably in size. Floor area ranges from about 1.3 square meters to 13.6 square meters (the average is 5.1 square meters). To our surprise, we discovered that the size of a hut does not correlate with the number of people who live in it. Some large huts had only two or three occupants; conversely, some small huts were the home of five or six people. A partial explanation might be that sleeping arrangements, especially among children, are fairly loose at Efe camps. One night the children may sleep in their parents' hut and the next night in that of their grandparents. Even adults sometimes move around. And if one family moves away to another camp, an incoming family might inhabit the empty hut rather than build its own. This loose fit between hut size and number of occupants is distressing archaeologically; it means that archaeologists cannot estimate accurately the population of a camp on the basis of the floor area of individual huts. However, this loose fit might not be characteristic of other hunter-gatherer societies; further studies might be illuminating in this regard.

The makeup of Efe camps is rather fluid. Families and individuals move in and move away during the life span of a camp. This flexibility seems to be characteristic of most or all hunter-gatherer societies. Sometimes, during the life span of a campsite, one (or more) of the families will abandon their hut and build a new one at the same camp. This behavior could confuse archaeologists into thinking that more families had lived at the camp than was the case, because there would be little archaeological evidence for recognizing that the same family had lived sequentially in two huts. Hence, the archaeologist probably would overestimate the number of families that had lived at the camp.

Efe reoccupation of a recently abandoned camp is another fairly common behavior that could lead archaeologists into overestimating camp population. Some families might reinhabit the hut they had previously lived in. Often, however, one or more families will build a new hut and leave their previous one unoccupied. The reason for returning to an abandoned camp goes back, at least in part, to Efe ties with the Lese. Although Efe move from one camp to another rather frequently, they usually do not move very far. Lese villages and gardens are a fixed point on the landscape

where Efe obtain material sustenance and social interaction. As a consequence, Efe rarely move more than a day's journey away from their affiliate village.

We discovered that when the Efe move camp, they sometimes leave behind a wide variety of possessions such as clay pots, glass bottles, baskets, and sharpening stones. They do this, we think, because of the restricted mobility that is characteristic of their settlement pattern. Clay pots, for example, are heavy and breakable compared with their aluminum pots. During the honey season, when they move deeper into the forest, the Efe might leave clay pots behind, knowing that they eventually will return to the vicinity of their previous camp and retrieve these belongings. It seems unlikely that other hunter-gatherer societies that have a more wide-ranging and less "tethered" settlement pattern would practice this kind of storage to the same extent as the Efe do.

COMPARING THE EFE TO OTHER HUNTER-GATHERERS

The knowledge gained during our year studying the Efe has considerable potential for assisting archaeologists in interpreting prehistoric archaeological sites with respect to questions such as the possible size range of the population that lived at the site, the length of time the site was occupied, the nature of activities carried out at the site, and the practice of storing implements. However, we must recognize that the patterns of the Efe cannot be casually generalized as a model for all prehistoric hunter-gatherer societies.

A comparison of Efe and other present-day hunter-gatherers, including the !Kung and various groups in Australia, reveals that despite many similarities with these peoples, some important differences set the Efe apart. Similarities exist, for example, in the general layout of Efe and !Kung campsites. A !Kung camp consists of a circular arrangement of closely spaced brush huts, each hut the home of a nuclear family. As with the Efe and other Mbuti Pygmy groups, the distance separating huts in a !Kung camp is swayed, in part, by kinship ties and interpersonal relationships. A family fire is situated in front of the hut at a !Kung camp, and a wide variety of domestic tasks are carried out around the fire.

Differences between Efe and !Kung camps emerge in some details of layout and use. Trash heaps are not a feature of all !Kung camps; those occupied for less than two weeks might lack them altogether. !Kung campsites tend to cover a larger area than Efe sites, and the amount of camp space per person is greater among the !Kung. Habitation sites of Western Desert Aborigines in Australia far exceed the Efe and !Kung in both these attributes. And, when !Kung move out of a camp, they leave behind few or no possessions for future reuse other than nut-cracking stones.

One of the great challenges facing archaeologists today is to explain the similarities and the differences among hunter-gatherer groups. Recent studies have suggested that Australian Aborigine campsites are much larger than those of the !Kung because there is little fear of natural predators in Australia. The Kalahari Desert, on the other hand, is home to several dangerous animals, notably lions, leopards, and hyenas. However, this explanation probably does not account for the small size of Efe campsites. We never heard Efe express anxiety about predators—in fact, the greatest danger comes from the falling branches of trees. More likely, they build compact camps to keep within sight and sound of each other, thus maintaining a physical and emotional cohesiveness in the dense forest.

If we could spend another year in the Ituri, what questions would we address? We would like to explore the way material goods move or are exchanged between the Lese and the Efe and among neighboring Efe bands. Which objects are owned individually and which are treated as communal property? What factors influence the size of huts and of domestic space if not the number of occupants? These and other questions will continue to draw archaeologists such as ourselves to the Ituri, the Kalahari, the Arctic, the Australian deserts, Malaysia, and other areas to study living hunter-gatherers.

UPDATE

The spatial organization of hunter-gatherer residential campsites can be studied from an almost limitless variety of research directions. Careful analysis of our maps of Efe campsites reveals, for example, that one can reconstruct the location of dwellings at a campsite by studying the spatial relationships between fireplaces and trash heaps (Fisher and Strickland, 1991). This has considerable importance for archaeologists investigating prehistoric campsites, for although actual dwellings are unlikely to be preserved at most sites, there is a stronger chance of uncovering fireplaces and nonperishable debris discarded onto trash heaps. Reconstruction of the location and number of dwellings at ancient sites provides archaeologists with powerful information for making inferences about the size of those communities, the use of space for living and social arrangements, and so forth.

In an ethnoarchaeological study of Alyawara campsites in Australia, James O'Connell (1987) made a number of interesting and archaeologically important discoveries. For one thing, the distribution within a site of discarded debris is strongly influenced by the size of the discarded item. Larger items tend to be tossed directly onto a nearby trash pile, whereas small items are often dropped right at the activity area where they are used. Moreover, additional sorting by size occurs when activity areas are swept during camp cleanup; the smaller of these items often inadvertently remain behind at the activity area rather than being relocated onto a trash heap. The archaeological significance of size sorting is that items that are used separately and that have no functional relationship to one another could end up lying side by side simply because they have a similar size. At Alyawara camps, small items such as razor blades and soda can pop-tops often lay in close proximity to one another even though these items were not connected by the same activity. Conversely, soda cans and pop-top lids, which are used and discarded as part of a single activity (drinking a can of soda), did not occur together on the ground. The difference in size between cans and lids caused them to become separated at and after discard. This finding reinforces an important lesson: archaeologists investigating ancient sites need to give up the long-cherished belief that close spatial proximity of excavated objects constitutes sufficient evidence, by itself, to signify that those items had been used together in a particular activity.

Changes in the lifeway and values of present-day hunter-gatherers as they give up a nomadic way of life and become progressively sedentary, often as a consequence of external forces, have a substantial effect on the spatial organization of their residential sites. The camps of traditional !Kung in the Kalahari, as discussed earlier in the chapter, were arranged in a compact circle, and hut doorways usually faced into the camp center. Privacy was not an overriding concern, and residents could see into one another's huts. As the !Kung became more sedentary, their camps lost this intimacy. The arrangement of huts became more linear, with greater space separating adjacent huts. In this changing way of life, the increased accumulation of personally owned items, denoting wealth, exacerbated the desire for greater privacy. These changes reflect profound shifts in the economy and value system of these peoples (Yellen, 1990).

Additional changes in site structure resulting from the effects of increased sedentism have been reported among peoples elsewhere in the Kalahari Desert (Hitchcock, 1987). Trash dumps are larger at the sites of sedentary groups, and the distance from hearths and houses (working and living areas) to the trash dumps is much greater at these sites than at the camps of more nomadic groups. These and other differences documented by researchers hint at the great wealth of archaeologically important insights and methodological and theoretical advances that can be obtained through ethnoarchaeological research.

FURTHER READING

Bailey, Robert C., and Irven DeVore. 1989. "Research on the Efe and Lese Populations of the Ituri Forest, Zaire." *American Journal of Physical Anthropology* 78:459–71.

Binford, Lewis R. 1983. *In Pursuit of the Past: Decoding the Archaeological Record*. Thames and Hudson.

Fisher, John W. Jr., and Helen Strickland. 1989. "Ethnoarchaeology among the Efe Pygmies, Zaire: Spatial Organization of Campsites." *American Journal of Physical Anthropology* 78:473–84.

Fisher, John W. Jr., and Helen C. Strickland. 1991. "Dwellings and Fireplaces: Keys to Efe Pygmy Campsite Structure." In C. S. Gamble and W. A. Boismier, eds., *Ethnoarchaeological Approaches to Mobile Campsites: Hunter-gatherer and Pastoralist Case Studies*, pp. 215–36. International Monographs in Prehistory, Ethnoarchaeological Series 1.

Gould, R. A., and J. E. Yellen. 1987. "Man the Hunted: Determinants of Household Spacing in Desert and Tropical Foraging Societies." *Journal of Anthropological Archaeology* 6:77–103.

Hitchcock, Robert K. 1987. "Sedentism and Site Structure: Organizational Changes in Kalahari Basarwa Residential Locations." In Susan Kent, ed.,

Method and Theory for Activity Area Research: An Ethnoarchaeological Approach. Columbia University Press.

Kroll, E. M., and T. D. Price, eds. 1991. *The Interpretation of Archaeological Spatial Patterning.* Plenum Press.

O'Connell, James F. 1987. "Alyawara Site Structure and Its Archaeological Implications." *American Antiquity* 52:74–108.

Turnbull, Colin M. 1961. *The Forest People.* Simon and Schuster.

Turnbull, Colin M. 1975. *Wayward Servants: The Two Worlds of the African Pygmies.* Greenwood Press. Reprint of 1965 ed.

Yellen, John. 1977. *Archaeological Approaches to the Present: Models for Reconstructing the Past.* Academic Press.

Yellen, John. 1990. "The Transformation of the Kalahari !Kung." *Scientific American* 262(4):96–97, 105.

12 WHO GOT TO AMERICA FIRST?

A Very Old Question

Stephen Williams

s most of us know, 1992 was the five hundredth anniversary of Christopher Columbus's famous voyage to the "New World." In recent years, the assertion that Columbus "discovered" America when his trio of ships made a landfall in the Bahamas has been questioned by a number of concerned individuals. Native Americans are understandably disturbed at the suggestion that their status as the "first" Americans is somehow being challenged. Most scholars now insist that the first human settlers of this continent were indeed the ancestors of the contemporary Indian tribes. Their first migration (from Asia via the Bering Strait area) probably occurred more than 15,000 years ago, with several more waves of migrants arriving some thousands of years later.

But if that is the widely held explanation, what is all the argument about? Most of the debate surrounds hypothetical later arrivals in the New World, especially during the past 3,000 years, and purportedly mainly from locations to the east, across the Atlantic. A smaller number of proponents look to trans-Pacific connections during this same period of time. What sort of evidence and how we evaluate it is the subject of concern for many anthropological scholars today. As our review will indicate, these are not new questions, nor are they ones that can be settled for "all time"—the same ones keep reappearing over the centuries.

The century following Columbus's well-documented voyages, none of

" AT THIS RATE IT'LL PROBABLY TAKE THEM 500 YEARS TO SORT IT OUT..."

which actually reached North America, was one of questioning, too. Had Columbus reached Asia or the West Indies? Who were these inhabitants that met him as he stepped ashore? We still refer to them as "Indians" because of the mistaken view that the islands, and later the mainland, were part of the Asian continent, not a "New World" at all. Magellan's circumnavigation of the world in the 1520s would establish the Western Hemisphere as a separate land mass, but then the question arose as to the origin of the inhabitants. Here speculations ran wild. By the end of the century (1590) a Spanish church scholar, Joseph de Acosta, would publish a marvelously well-constructed answer: the inhabitants of the New World came from Asia across a land bridge, arriving as hunters, then developing agriculture and later high civilizations such as he had seen in Peru and Mexico. He specifically discounted possible trans-Atlantic connections to the Lost Tribes of Israel or the mythical sunken continent of Atlantis.

Modern scholars would agree with this Acosta scenario, but just about a decade later another Spanish cleric, Gregorio Garcia, wrote a two-volume work that would open the gates of migration to the Lost Tribes, to refugees from Atlantis, to Carthaginians from North Africa, and many more. He refused to be partial to any on his long list, but they were almost all trans-Atlanteans, bringing seeds of civilization with them. Thus in 1607 the battle was joined: the New World native cultures were either derived from land-based Asian migrants (Acosta) or transplanted from the Old World by trans-Atlantic seafarers (Garcia). The argument has lasted until today.

METHODS OF INQUIRY

The origin of the earth's inhabitants is a central question in anthropology. The answer is also one that requires careful evaluation of all the information available to us each time the question is asked. Acosta and Garcia were limited in the facts they had at hand, although both had lived in several parts of the New World before addressing the problem—no armchair scholars here. But what kind of evidence do anthropologists bring to bear on such questions today?

First, we consider the people themselves: What do they look like? Whom do they resemble? Simple questions in the 1600s: outward appearances were all they had. In today's world of biological anthropology, we turn to sophisticated analysis of genetics and DNA to try to see way back in time as human populations spread across the globe. We can clearly tie Native American origins back to Asia, although we may quibble about exactly at what time and with which Asian groups they are most closely linked genetically.

Second, we consider the cultures of the Native Americans, especially those aspects of culture that will allow a long look back in time. In this case, linguistics, the study of languages, is an important information source. Native American languages represent enormous diversity, much more so than in comparable areas in the Old World, where diversity has decreased over time. This pattern of diversity suggests both internal diversification and repeated migrations from North Asia. According to one scholar, the degree of linguistic diversity in the New World points to a history of "tens of millennia."

Third, when we look at the artifactual content of New World cultures, we conclude that most of these myriad artifacts, covering thousands of years, are definitely of New World origin, although certain aspects of some material cultures do show north Asian connections, especially in the Paleo-Indian period, 7,000 to 10,000 years ago.

Finally, we turn to a rather different category, that of the plants and animals associated with New World cultures. Here, too, just a few specific Asian connections exist: dogs are clearly long-time associates of humankind and quite surely accompanied some of the very first Americans from Siberia. Plants are quite another matter, and here we are discussing agricultural items only. All the major food plants, such as corn, potatoes, and beans, are derived with the help of human intervention from Native American domesticated plants. Only a few questionable items await further study concerning a possible outside origin; these are the bottle gourd and cotton. The sweet potato, another enigma, seems to have gone from South America to Polynesia, just to confuse the issue.

With those basics in place, we can enter the fray of evaluating other sources of evidence for transoceanic connections with one certain understanding: if a hypothesis is bolstered by strong emotional concerns, almost everything can and will be believable to some supporters. Recognizing that each of us has a personal bias that influences our own view of the world does not make us immune to its force, but at least we can consciously try to make our evaluations as bias-free as possible.

MOUNDBUILDERS

Archaeological evidence concerning the question "Who Got Here First?" would necessarily have to await the development of the discipline of archaeology in North America. Thomas Jefferson is very often cited as the "father" of American archaeology, and he certainly attempted one of the first archaeological explanations of the question when he wrote in his famous "Notes on Virginia" (1787) about an Indian mound that he had excavated many years before. However, his strongest evidence to support his belief in an Asian origin (via the Bering Strait) of the Native Americans was from his study of Indian languages. He cited the diversity of these languages as proof that they had been here a long time.

Other scholars joined Jefferson in this well thought-out view. Yet, in the early nineteenth century the westward expansion of settlement into the Ohio Valley produced a great deal more archaeological evidence from Indian mounds. As interpreted by some new voices, the accumulating data supported the supposition that these mounds and the rather elaborate artifacts found in them were made by the exotic "Moundbuilders," purportedly an advanced and extinct culture not connected to Native peoples. The hypothesis spawned some very popular books, such as those by Josiah Priest (1833), that were fanciful in their interpretations and careless in their evaluation of the data.

The voice of reason came from Samuel Haven in a Smithsonian-sponsored volume (1856) that supported the Bering Strait hypothesis and called some of the wilder notions "Vagaries." We now know that much of the Moundbuilder hypothesis was based on fraudulent documents, such as the Grave Creek and Davenport inscriptions, which tried to give support for literate Trans-Atlantean cultures making inroads on the prehistory of the Ohio and Mississippi valleys. It just was not so, and again thanks to the Smithsonian's major research project of Mound Exploration under John Wesley Powell, the Moundbuilder myth was laid to rest by 1900. The mounds, the earthworks, and the artifacts were the handiwork of American Indians, not that of Trans-Atlantean invaders.

VIKINGS IN AMERICA

There was much more than just mounds and Native Americans to argue about. By 1891 a volume entitled *America Not Discovered by Columbus,* by Rasmus B. Anderson, would contain a lengthy bibliography with some 350 sources on the topic. It listed claims of America's discovery by Chinese, Arabs, Welsh, Venetians, Portuguese, and Poles. However, the majority of these references supported the notion of Vikings as the ones who got here first in the race across the Atlantic. This hypothesis came into being more than 150 years ago and really had only the literary evidence from the Norse Sagas to support it.

Not that it was not a worthwhile idea. Few doubted that Vikings in North America could or did happen. There just was no archaeological evidence to prove it. Again frauds came to the rescue; if you can not discover the data you need, just manufacture it! Thus was born the fake Kensington Rune Stone in the 1890s and the "salting" of the Beardmore site in Canada with real Norse artifacts to be used to support a pre-Columbian Norse presence in North America. But good archaeology by Helge Ingstad would finally come to the fore in 1960 with the right answer: Norse ruins at L'Anse aux Meadows on the northern tip of Newfoundland, complete with sod huts and artifacts such as a brass pin, a soapstone spindle whorl, and iron nails, all dated to about A.D. 1000. Was it the home of Leif Erickson? Archaeologists are not sure, but we do know that the Vikings certainly made it to the New World long before Columbus.

OTHER SOURCES OF NEW WORLD INFLUENCES

With an affirmative reply to the Viking presence, one might think that much else might logically follow. What about Chinese voyagers in junks across the Pacific, Lost Tribes from Israel still looking for a homeland, Phoenicians from the Mediterranean, Celts from Ireland or Wales, or

West Africans in Mexico? Well, all of the above and more have been suggested by various writers in the twentieth century alone. Some of the best-known authors among recent long-range diffusionists are Harold Gladwin, Barry Fell, and Ivan Van Sertima.

First, let us consider whether or not such voyages were possible during the past 3,000 years. The answer is a very strong yes. The maritime exploits of the Polynesians during this period are well known and documented by excellent archaeology in the Pacific. They colonized the entire eastern Pacific. Much earlier (50,000 years ago), migrants from Southeast Asia made their way to the great island continent of New Guinea/Australia; part of that trek quite probably included water crossings.

Some of the proposed trans-Atlantic crossings were supposedly made by cultures known to have had maritime skills. Indeed, the fact that Atlantic crossings (especially in summer) in small boats, even in solo attempts, have been successfully made is well known. The Pacific, too, has been conquered in recent times by rafts and small boats, but with a fair number of casualties, although the latter fact is not as well advertised. So we may accept that it can and could have been done with the maritime expertise available from 1000 B.C. on, although the modern successes have benefited from navigational and safety aids not available to all would-be travelers in earlier times.

But what is the basic evidence for this multitude of ocean crossings to the New World that some chroniclers now insist took place in the past? There is certainly no biological evidence that can be used to support any such trips. One would have to admit that additions to the New World gene pool by these shiploads of mariners might be hard to detect; modern studies of prehistoric human skeletal remains in the New World have not shown any identifiable evidence, either, to support the presence of such overseas visitors.

Save for the Norse finds discussed above, no important archaeological discoveries have been made, if one means intrusive sites with buildings, artifacts, and trash heaps attributable to such voyagers. The evidence that has been used to support these hyper-diffusionist claims falls into two major categories: (1) inscriptions found on cliffs, rocks, artifacts, or on crude stone structures where no other pertinent artifacts are found (e.g., Dighton Rock in Massachusetts); and (2) stone sculptures and other figurative pieces of art that are thought to depict foreign visitors or to resemble the artistic work of non–New World cultures, such as the colossal Olmec head (see Grove, 1992).

The inscriptions in a wide variety of purported Old World scripts have been found from one coast to the other, from the Rocky Mountains to the suburbs of Tucson, Arizona; from the Maine coast to the Great Basin of Nevada and Utah. Many of the inscriptions contain mixed texts with symbols of different times and origins. These finds also share another unusual characteristic; none have produced any nearby artifacts or associated living areas. They stand alone as sentinels of the past with no archaeological context—a very strange situation. Who left them? How did the ancient voyagers travel so far without leaving a single trace other than these inscriptions? Why did they do it? Unanswered questions and important to consider. One set of inscriptions *with* accompanying artifacts are the Michigan Relics or Soper Frauds manufactured by James A. Scotford between 1890 and 1920. Although debunked for decades, these pseudo-cuneiform messages are still being deciphered today by some enthusiasts.

The study of stone and ceramic sculptures to prove foreign connections has flourished in Mesoamerica, the area of high culture in Central America. Here these works of art are thought to demonstrate bearded voyagers from abroad, and in the case of the great stone heads from Vera Cruz, Mexico (some are 8 to 10 feet in diameter), they are thought to confirm trans-Atlantic travel from Africa to Mesoamerica and the Olmec at approximately 700 B.C. This hypothesis of African origins has been supported for several decades by Ivan Van Sertima of Rutgers University, and is, in my opinion, based on a mixture of ethnic pride and personal bias. The facial features of these heads, in particular, were thought to represent Africans; however, they are also similar to the features of many Native Americans from the Olmec area. Any resemblance between the peoples of West Africa and Mesoamerica is more likely due to common adaptation to tropical conditions than a closely shared ancestry.

The hypothesis that important cultural transfer from West Africa to Mesoamerica occurred was first put forward by Leo Wiener of Harvard University in several books published between 1920 and 1926. A professor of Slavic languages, Wiener thought that he had discovered important linkages based on "sound-alike" resemblances between the languages of the two areas. He also found what he considered to be other important comparative resemblances in materials as varied as women's hair styles and tobacco pipes.

Wiener's researches were the impetus for Van Sertima's own involvement with this topic, and they now form an important bit of data for Afrocentrist historical arguments. Unfortunately, current archaeological research in Mesoamerica fails to support any of the claims of Wiener and Van Sertima for direct connections between the two areas. Where were

" WELL, I DON'T THINK IT'S SO DANG MYSTERIOUS."

the African landfalls in Mesoamerica, and why are there no African cultural artifacts observable in the well-excavated sites of the Olmec of the Mexican coast? (Furthermore, the new chronology for the development of Olmec culture places its beginnings considerably before 700 B.C.)

Until we have solid archaeological evidence to support other hypotheses, it can be said quite clearly that, No, Columbus was not the first to find America, nor were the Vikings, although they beat Christopher by about 500 years. Instead, it was small bands of Native Americans who first "discovered" the New World via the Bering Strait many thousands of years earlier. At present, although certainly not an impossible hypothesis, there is no credible evidence so far discovered that links any of the oft-cited Trans-Atlanteans with any archaeological discoveries in North America. As far as is now known, the Native Americans were the masters of their own fate. They produced their myriad diverse cultures throughout the New World independent of foreign intervention.

FURTHER READING

Anderson, Rasmus B. 1891. *America Not Discovered by Columbus*. S. C. Griggs.

Fagan, Brian M. 1995. *Ancient North America: The Archaeology of a Continent.* Revised and expanded edition. Thames and Hudson.

Feder, Kenneth L. 1990. *Frauds, Myths, and Mysteries: Science and Pseudoscience in Archaeology*. Mayfield.

Grove, David. 1992. "Updating Olmec Prehistory." *AnthroNotes* 14(2):9–12, 14–15.

Haven, Samuel F. 1856. *Archaeology of the United States*. Smithsonian Institution Press.

Jefferson, Thomas. 1787. *Notes on the State of Virginia*. John Stockdale.

Priest, Josiah. 1833. *American Antiquities, and Discoveries in the West*. Hoffman and White.

Williams, Stephen. 1991. *Fantastic Archaeology: The Wild Side of North American Prehistory*. University of Pennsylvania Press.

13 BONES AND STONES—OR SHEEP?

Studying the First Americans

Ruth Osterweis Selig

If I could find one clearly stratified site with some busted mammoth bones, a couple of crude flake tools, and a single human bone, all in unquestionable association with a charcoal hearth dated 19,500 years ago—I'd have my dream.

Dennis Stanford, February 1983

What keeps a man looking a lifetime for evidence he knows he may never find? What keeps him excavating sites that turn out to be dead ends, hiring research associates to disprove his latest theory, or traveling to South America and China to find a single tantalizing clue? A dream or maybe just a hunch that he might turn out to be right after all. For if Dennis Stanford finds the evidence he has been searching for since 1971 he will unravel one of the major mysteries in North American archaeology: when did the first human beings arrive in the Western Hemisphere?

No serious archaeologist today questions that Native American populations originated from a generalized Mongoloid people that developed in eastern Asia and Siberia during the late Pleistocene. Some time after 50,000 years ago, hunting bands entered the New World following the herds of mammoths and mastodons, camels and horses teeming across the 1,000-mile-wide grassy plain exposed in the Bering Sea when Ice Age glaciers caused a drastic reduction in sea level. But when did the great crossing first take place?

"Recent" history is clear. As of 11,000 years ago, human hunters inhabited virtually all of the Americas. Sophisticated "Clovis" spear points from more than 40 sites in North and South America serve as unmistakable evidence that humans were hunting mainly, or exclusively, mammoths and perhaps bison. But the sudden appearance and rapid spread of Clovis culture remains an archaeological mystery. One thousand years after the first appearance of Clovis spear points, the fluted-point technology has spread across two continents and most of the huge animals that were once hunted have become extinct. Were the Clovis hunters the first Americans? If they were, why have no Clovis points been found in eastern Asia or northern Siberia? If the Clovis technology was invented in America, or as Robert L. Humphrey has suggested, en route to America where it spread among pre-existing populations, when did these earlier migrants first enter the continent? If humans were here before 11,000 years ago—and Dennis Stanford firmly believes that they were—how can archaeologists prove it?

PRE-CLOVIS BONE TECHNOLOGY?

The Yukon Territory's Old Crow Basin yielded a clue in the late 1960s when a caribou bone that had been worked by human hands into a scraping tool was found to be 27,000 years old. The date led archaeologists to propose that pre-Clovis people made use of a bone technology for many tools. Stone was scarce, and bone tools were readily available from butchered carcasses.

In the mid-1970s, Dennis Stanford painstakingly excavated large deposits of broken mammoth bone at two Colorado sites called Dutton and Selby. The animals had died before 11,000 years ago, and their disarticulated broken bones seemed to bear evidence of human activity. "At Dutton in the summer of '76, looking down at a pile of busted camel bone in a 12-foot-deep excavation, with a stone tool found at a level below 16,000 years old, I thought I had found it." Stanford and his colleagues hypothesized that the bones were broken for marrow by humans smashing heavy stone boulders onto them. Today, the stone tool has been mapped as lying at the bottom of a gopher hole and the "busted" bones have been more carefully analyzed. Stanford is no longer sure that Dutton is the dream site he had once thought.

Proposing that pre-Clovis people depended on a bone technology was risky, because broken and polished bones, unlike stone Clovis points, can be produced by natural forces. Though willing to go out on a limb and willing to risk an innovative hypothesis, Stanford was not willing to close his mind to this possibility—even if it meant disproving the bone technology theory. For this attitude, and for his painstakingly meticulous ex-

cavation and analysis, he is esteemed among his colleagues, who watched with interest as Stanford entered a second, highly innovative phase of investigation through experimental archaeology.

ELEPHANT EXPERIMENTS

In order to eliminate nonhuman explanatory factors, Stanford and his associates sought to find out what other natural agencies could produce similar results on bone. At the same time, in order to see if humans could indeed produce and use bone tools, he began to butcher dead elephants and make tools from the bones—of Ginsberg, Maggie, and Tulsa.

These large elephants were dead when Dennis arrived on the scene ready to simulate Pleistocene mammoth butchering. The early, carefully documented results were encouraging: bones broken over stone anvils resembled broken bones at Dutton and Selby; the resulting bone tools worked extremely well in carving up skin and meat; and the wear, polish, and striation matched those on ancient bones. In fact, Stanford remembers, "one flaked bone from Ginsberg looked identical to the 27,000-year-old bone tool from Old Crow."

But many archaeologists remained skeptical, and Stanford was eager to face the skeptics head on. In the mid-1970s Gary Haynes, a graduate student at Catholic University, saw Stanford's evidence for pre-Clovis bone technology and expressed serious skepticism. Stanford encouraged Haynes to try disproving the bone technology theory and supported his plan to feed fresh bones to the Kodiak bears and African lions at the National Zoo. This research, along with studies of captive wolf colonies that were fed whole carcasses of deer and moose, produced for Haynes his first clear evidence that the Ice Age "tools" might instead be the results of gnawing by carnivores that polished and broke the bones.

From those first Zoo experiments there evolved a remarkable professional relationship: Stanford developed hypotheses and Haynes searched to disprove them. Both of them published papers advancing the science of archaeology and taphonomy—the study of what happens to bones after an animal dies in the wild, a subject of increasing importance to archaeologists. For several years, Haynes traveled to the Canadian Northwest Territories to watch bison herds preyed on by wolves in order to document what happens to carcasses in the wild. More recently Haynes has been dispatched to Africa to record the behavior of elephant herds and to describe modern elephant bone accumulations.

What Haynes discovered was exactly what Stanford thought he might find: evidence that natural agencies could produce the spiral fractures, the polish, the wear patterns, and the striations on bone that archaeologists once thought reflected human activity. Wolves chewing on big-game carcasses produce polish as well as tooth marks; bison wallowing in the dust actually fragment and polish previously deposited bone; carnivores break bones to get at marrow just as humans do; and gravel produces the scratches once thought to be clear-cut evidence of human tool use. Broken mammoth bones, previously thought too massive to be broken by natural causes, are explained by Haynes' research, documenting that elephants walk over and break the bones of dead elephants. The resulting broken bones look very much like the broken bones in Dennis Stanford's office that were taken from the Dutton and Selby sites. Even the flaked tusk "tools" have been found in the wild, the result of elephants knocking into one another as they struggle to get to water in the dry season.

At times, Stanford says, he feels "like just walking out, leaving the bones and stones behind, and going to herd sheep." He and Haynes agree that humans and carnivores can produce closely similar evidence for future archaeologists to excavate, and it may be impossible in many cases to differentiate the exact circumstances of bone breakage in the past. But by 1982 Stanford had concluded that the bones at Dutton and Selby did not show *unmistakable* evidence of human activity. Herding sheep, however, was not going to solve the problems.

Instead, Stanford decided to embark on a joint effort that would include research in the High Plains of North America and Northeast Asia, the hypothesized homeland of the Paleo-Indian precursors. With funding provided through the National Geographic Society and Wenner-Gren Foundation, Chinese and American archaeologists worked together during the summer of 1981 at the Lamb Spring site in Colorado excavating a large pile of mammoth bones, many of which had been broken before burial over 1,000 years ago. Lying in the same deposit was a 33-pound boulder that could have been used by pre-Clovis people to break the long bones. Once again Stanford feels he may be on the trail of pre-Clovis hunters, for why would 90 percent of the large long bones be broken while the majority of fragile bones (such as ribs) remain intact?

Haynes's research results on wallowing African elephants cannot neatly explain the modified bones at Lamb Spring. So, in the summer of 1983 Haynes will excavate modern "elephant graveyards" in Africa: these are the waterhole sites where elephant skeletons have accumulated for many decades.

Stanford, meanwhile, went off to another well-stratified site, Blackwater Draw, New Mexico. This site was excavated originally between 1932 and 1937. "Then no one thought there was even a Clovis people, and so no one dug below the Clovis level. Local legend has it that pre-Clovis material has been found there and this summer we hope to find it."

CLUES IN CHINA

After Blackwater Draw, Stanford will return to China, where he spent the fall of 1982. At that time in China, he did not find any evidence of Clovis technology or even tools that look like Clovis's antecedents. But he was able to examine all the Pleistocene collections in the museums, and he traveled to most of the Paleolithic archaeological sites. What he discovered was broken bones, flaked bone, and crude stone artifacts, all very similar to what is found at the sites in North America such as Lamb Spring. Evidence for a highly evolved lithic technology does not appear in China until perhaps as late as about 14,000 years ago, when a microlithic (small tool) technology developed that bears close resemblance to that of the early Eskimo peoples, who are later arrivals on the North American continent.

If the earliest American cultures did not originate in eastern China, where is their source? A new idea tantalizes Stanford. Perhaps the roots of Paleo-Indian culture developed in North Central China. No archaeologist since before World War II has examined the sites west of Manchuria, the first stop on Stanford's planned trip to China in 1984.

He is also continuing his search in America, tracking down the bones and the stones that might give him that unmistakably clear association of human tools with extinct animal remains, that he is sure exists somewhere, if only he knew exactly where to look.

UPDATE

Dennis J. Stanford

Bones and Stones—or Sheep? was written in 1983, and reflects my outlook and the state of our knowledge over a decade ago; it would not be written today. But it demonstrates well how new archaeological evidence changes the stories we tell, making current knowledge only the best we have at any one time.

The major change in my thinking today comes from a shift in a fundamental assumption I held in the 1980s: that the story of the First Americans was, somehow, unilinear. In other words, I believed that if we could find the right evidence, we would find the answer to who came to America before the Clovis people, whose sites we had then dated to about 11,000 years ago. This assumption turned out to be wrong, as the evidence now points to a much more complex story of many different groups of people coming to the New World over successive time periods, with successive migrations and complex environmental factors apparently at work. Some of the earliest peoples seem to be unrelated to one another; possibly we are dealing with two or three different populations, some of whom appear to be related to peoples from the area around the Caspian Sea.

Most important, it now appears that the Clovis complex, marked by distinctive projectile points, was an interesting but short-lived archaeological phenomenon. The technology, apparently highly adaptive to diverse, mosaic environments, arose first perhaps in the American Southeast out of earlier unfluted biface traditions, and spread within a relatively short time span, from about 11,500 to 10,900 years ago, into the Southwest and Plains. After this period, apparently the Pluvial lakes rose and again watered the countryside. The rangelands improved, and the bison populations probably increased dramatically. As in the East, Clovis hunters adapted to new environmental conditions and adjusted their weaponry and settlement pattern accordingly. In the Rocky Mountains and adjacent Plains, Clovis became what we know today as the Folsom bison hunting culture.

The great mystery in North American archaeology remains when, where, and how did the first human beings arrive in the Western Hemisphere? We have much stronger evidence now than a decade ago—genetic, linguistic, and physical anthropological evidence—to support multiple migrations, from various areas of Asia, with northeastern Siberia being only the last stepping point.

We also have evidence to show that the Clovis people were not the sole inhabitants of North America; we now believe there were groups of peoples here, some using Clovis technology, some not, and we have increasing evidence for their existence in South America as well. Furthermore, we no longer believe these earliest inhabitants were simply of Siberian origin or even that they should be called Paleo-Indians; instead, some of the earliest migrants may be from southwestern Siberia or even farther west. There is also evidence that some of the earliest migrants may have originated among people living as far west as the Eastern European Paleolithic. Fifteen years ago I predicted there were earlier occupations of North America before the Clovis peoples, and in that I was correct, but where I was wrong was in the unilinear model of finding a single early Paleo-Indian people predating Clovis. Instead, we probably are dealing with waves of many migrations back and forth across the Bering Land Bridge, peoples originating in Europe and Siberia, only some of whom developed Clovis technology, probably as a response to an increasingly arid environment.

More than a decade ago I investigated a caribou bone "tool" from Old Crow, as well as broken mammoth bones from the Dutton and Selby sites. The hypothesis of a pre-Clovis culture bone and stone technology has gone by the wayside; with new radiocarbon dating techniques, the Old Crow Basin bone tool has been shown to be only about 6,000 years old. The bone tool theory was a popular one in the early 1980s, but my students set out to disprove the theory, and they managed to show the com-

plexities of the issues and disprove many of the "bone tools." What we are now learning is that bone tools are still important evidence, but they have to be in association with lithic materials as well; otherwise, there are just too many other explanations possible. Gary Haynes has continued to do important work, which includes his studies of elephant bones in Zimbabwe, Africa.

Blackwater Draw remains an important site. We found a Clovis level, and, more important, we found a water well that Clovis people dug, at a time when the surface springs were drying up. Unfortunately for the Clovis inhabitants, the well proved to be a dry hole. This find is certainly tantalizing, as it raises the whole question of environmental impact, and the possibility that an increasingly dry environment severely affected the Clovis lifestyle. Lamb Spring has been taken over by the Archaeological Conservancy, which is working with the Denver Museum of Natural History to build an on-site museum there. A planning grant has been received from the state of Colorado. I am the adviser on the project, so work at Lamb Spring will certainly continue.

Although I did not return to China, as planned, I traveled to Siberia in 1990, where strong evidence exists for the origins of the earliest Americans. My other current interests are in northwestern Alaska, where there is a site that appears to be extremely old, with burned lithic remains that can be dated through new thermoluminescence techniques, and in Tennessee and Kentucky, where there is early dated Clovis material, evidence that perhaps Clovis technology developed in the east, and then moved westward. My work over the past fifteen years has clearly shown that the whole story is much more complex than it ever appeared to be in the early 1980s—more complicated, but more interesting as well.

FURTHER READING

Bonnichsen, R., Dennis Stanford, and J. L. Fastook. 1987. "Environmental Change and Developmental History of Human Adaptive Patterns: The Paleo-Indian Case." In W. F. Ruddiman and H. E. Wright Jr., eds., *North America and Adjacent Oceans During the Last Deglaciation: The Geology of North America*, vol. K-3, pp. 403–24. Geological Society of America.

Dixon, E. James. 1993. *Quest for the Origins of the First Americans*. University of New Mexico Press.

Frison, George C., ed. 1996. *The Mill Iron Site*. University of New Mexico Press.

Martin, P. S. 1984. "Prehistoric Overkill: The Global Model." In P. S. Martin and R. G. Klein, eds., *Quaternary Extinctions: A Prehistoric Revolution*, pp. 354–404. University of Arizona Press.

Meltzer, David J. 1995. "Clocking the First Americans." *Annual Review of Anthropology* 24:21–45.

Stanford, Dennis. 1991. "Clovis Origins and Adaptations: An Introductory Perspective." In Robson Bonnichsen and Karen L. Turnmire, eds., *Clovis: Origins and Adaptations*, pp. 1–13. Center for the Study of the First Americans, Oregon State University.

14 THE FIRST SOUTH AMERICANS

Archaeology at Monte Verde

Tom D. Dillehay

When did human beings first set foot in the New World? How did they get here? What lifeways did they follow? How did they adapt to and affect the ancient American ecosystem? These questions have been hotly debated for over 100 years. Scientists now agree only that big-game hunters were in North America by 11,000 years ago.

The earliest possible date for the initial arrival of early humans and other aspects of their culture are disputed, although fieldwork over the last 25 years has yielded more evidence about their economy, technology, and social organization. The biggest surprises have come from South America, where recent work suggests that this continent was occupied by at least 12,000 years ago, and possibly much earlier, by people with very diverse subsistence strategies.

In recent years, the most significant advances in the study of the first Americans have come from innovative data recovery and analysis techniques that have yielded vastly more accurate reconstructions of ancient environments and subsistence strategies. For example, the soil from a house floor at Monte Verde, in Chile, contained amino acids specific to collagen, a protein found in bone, cartilage, and skin. Microscopic analysis of the material suggested that a thick skin, possibly a mastodon hide, had been used in the construction of the shelter. We now know that the earliest peoples—such as the Clovis and Folsom—were not just specialized big-game hunters armed with large bifacially chipped projectile points. Reliable evidence from the Meadowcroft Rockshelter site in Pennsylvania, the Monte Verde site in southern Chile, and others scattered throughout the hemisphere suggests the widespread presence of people who not only hunted large and small game but also collected wild plant food and fished in streams and lakes.

In the early 1970s, evidence about the first South Americans was limited to a small series of stone tools and animal bones, mostly from caves and rockshelters. Dates for these sites were often questionable, and many of the tools were not clearly made by human hands. A significant new body of evidence, mainly retrieved by Latin American archaeologists—including Gonzalo Correal, Gerardo Ardila, José Cruxent, Augusto Cardich, Lautaro Núñez, Gustavo Politis, Nora Flegenheimer, Nièce Guidon, and Pedro Schmitz—has been reported from early radiocarbon-dated stratigraphic contexts in many parts of South America. The Tequendama, Tibito, and El Abra sites in Colombia, the Monte Verde and Quereo sites in Chile, the Los Toldos site in Argentina, and several sites in Uruguay and north central Brazil, including Pedra Furada, all yielded radiocarbon dates of about 11,500 years ago or earlier. As a result of archaeological investigations at these sites, we can now place the minimum time for the first occupation of South America at approximately 12,000 years ago, possibly even 20,000 years ago.

MONTE VERDE DISCOVERED

The Maullin River flows through the cool forested country west of the Andes in South Central Chile. In 1976, while directing the anthropology program at the Southern University of Chile, in Valdivia, a number of Chilean and Argentinean colleagues and I were surveying the river. Buried in the banks of a small tributary creek, we discovered the unusual open-air wetland site of Monte Verde. Layers of peat bog, which only form in cool wet climates where organic materials are water-logged before they have a chance to decay, had preserved organic remains to an extraordinary degree. There we found not only chipped stone tools and the bones of extinct animals but also well-preserved wooden artifacts, dwelling foundations of both earth and wood, and the remains of edible and possibly medicinal plants. What makes Monte Verde especially interesting is the form and arrangement of the architecture and activity areas, which reveal a social and economic organization much more complex and generalized than previously suspected for a late Ice Age culture of the New World. A long sequence of radiocarbon dates on stratigraphic noncultural and cultural deposits place this cultural episode at between 12,000 and 13,000 years ago. In another area of the site, deeper deposits contain stone tools and possibly cultural features that may date to an even older culture.

The majority of late Pleistocene sites so far excavated in the Americas contain stone tools, animal bones, and some plant material. The finds rarely consist of organic remains such as wooden implements, and thus may represent a small portion of the cultural evidence. The preservation, diversity, and complexity of organic and inorganic remains at Monte Verde have been studied by an interdisciplinary research team in an effort to reconstruct the palaeoecology of the site area and to evaluate critically the evidence for human intervention in the site. These specialists include more than 60 scientists from such disciplines as geology, palynology, botany, entomology, animal pathology, paleontology, ecology, forestry engineering, malacology, diatomology, and microbiology.

Collectively, these studies have shown that the area around Monte Verde today has moderately warm, dry summers and cold, rainy winters, with a mean annual temperature fluctuating between 12 and 15 degrees centigrade. The climate that prevailed in the late Pleistocene after the ice sheets receded resembled this setting, although it was probably slightly cooler and more humid. A forest made up of a mixture of deciduous and coniferous trees covers the region today; it supplies numerous varieties of edible tubers, nuts, berries, fruits, and soft and leafy plants abundantly throughout the year. There are also small game, freshwater mollusks, and fish. In late Pleistocene times, mastodonts, saber-tooth tigers, ground sloths, and probably palaeocamelids roamed the area. The nearest point on the Pacific coast lies about 55 kilometers west and 20 kilometers south of the site and offers many edible species of marine organisms. All of these sources of food were available to the early inhabitants of Monte Verde.

LATE PLEISTOCENE SETTLEMENT STRUCTURE

The Monte Verde site is divided into east and west sides. On the east side of the site the remains of 10 or 11 foundations of residential huts have been recovered. The foundations are formed by small timbers, limbs, and roughly shaped planks usually held in place by wooden stakes. Fallen branches and vertical post stubs reveal that the hut frames were made primarily of hardwoods. The side walls were placed about 1 meter apart against a wall foundation and then apparently draped with animal skins, as suggested by the presence of a few small fragments of skin still clinging to the fallen side poles. Preliminary results of microscopic and other studies by microbiologists and pathologists suggest that the skins are most likely from a large animal, probably the mastodont.

A wide variety of plant remains, stone tools, food stains, and small braziers (shallow pits for holding burning coals) was found on the living surface inside each hut. The braziers, which contained ash, specks of charcoal, and the remains of numerous plant foods, were probably used to heat each hut and warm the food. Cooking was evidently a communal effort, as shown by the discovery of two large clay and charcoal hearths centrally located outside the huts. The recovery of three roughly shaped wooden mortars and several grinding stones near the hearths suggest that the preparation of plant food took place next to the hearths.

Who were these ancient South Americans? No human bones have yet been recovered from the excavations at Monte Verde, but there are two indirect indicators of information about the site's inhabitants. One is the imprint of a foot preserved in stored clay around one of the large hearths. The other indirect source of information consists of possible coprolites (fossil excrement) that appear to be of human origin. These were recovered from small pits dug in the ground, also near a hearth.

The west side of the site is characterized by a nonresidential structure and activity area. The central feature is a roughly ovoid-shaped artificial rise of sand and a few gravels. Resting on this rise is an architectural foundation made of sand and gravel compacted to form a peculiar wishbone shape, with a rectangular platform protruding from its exterior base. Fragments of upright wooden stubs were present approximately every few centimeters along both arms of the structure. Presumably these are the remains of a pole frame draped with hides. The same type and size of braziers recorded on the east side of the site were found on the occupation surface both inside and outside the structure. Of particular interest is the association of the hearths with preserved bits of apparent animal hide, of burned seeds and stalks of bulrush reed, and of masticated leaves of plants found in warmer environments and used by the present-day Mapuche for medicinal purposes. The shape, the location, and the artifactual content of the wishbone feature suggest that the structure and this end of the site served a special purpose, rather than being living quarters.

THE ARCHAEOLOGISTS FOUND EVIDENCE OF
SKIN HOUSES, WOODEN TOOLS, FOOTPRINTS
AND COPROLITES AT THE SITE....

STONES AND BONES AT MONTE VERDE

The stone tools from Monte Verde are similar to those from other sites in the Americas, although the use of naturally fractured stones, common at Monte Verde, has not been widely reported from other sites. The Monte Verdeans utilized three different methods for making stone tools: flaking, pecking-grounding, and modification through use on some unflaked stones. The organic remains are more unusual. More than 400 bones, including those of extinct camelids, mastodons, and small game, were recovered from the site. Most of the bone remains are rib fragments of at least seven individual mastodons. Several bones were modified as possible digging sticks, gouging tools, or other implements.

Besides the wooden architecture foundations, several types of artifacts made of wood were excavated, including a sharply pointed lancelike implement, three crude wooden mortars, two tool hafts or handles, five digging sticks, and more than 300 pieces of wood exhibiting cut or planed facets, burned areas, cut marks, and/or smoothed and thinned surfaces. Several bones were sharpened and burned. Their association with underground plant parts (tubers) and with grooved wooden slats with horizontal grooves suggest that they might have been used as digging sticks and gouging tools.

INTERPRETATIONS

What did the ancient Monte Verdeans capture with their assortment of stone, bone, and wooden tools? From the array of inorganic and organic remains, we can determine that they were exploiting resources from distant reaches of the Maullin Valley. Most of the differing environmental zones were aquatic areas: swamps, bogs, river bottoms, marshes, estuaries, and lagoons. How many people lived at the site? Ten or 11 residential structures and 1 unique structure have been excavated. Among the modern Mapuche, similar huts are occupied by 2 to 3 individuals. By analogy, we estimate that at least 25 to 35 individuals lived at Monte Verde during the Late Pleistocene.

If wood had not been preserved, we would have recovered only stone tools, postholes, stains, and perhaps bones and mollusk shells. Evidence of plant foods and most of the residential characteristics that tell us this was a village would have been lost. In fact, the site might well have been interpreted as a kill site with a temporary residential component, like most of the North American Paleo-Indian sites.

CONCLUSION

The preservation of the perishable materials at Monte Verde and the diversity of the social, technological, and economic activities represented there make this site exceedingly important and scientifically unique at this time. Monte Verde cautions us to keep an open mind toward the possible diversity of lifeways of the first Americans and of the various ways these lifeways might be expressed and preserved in a local archaeological record.

This very early dated occupation site comes from the southern end of South America and hence reminds us that we will probably discover and verify yet earlier sites in North America in the future.

As was the case in the past 25 years, the next few years will certainly produce more information on these problems and on other types of sites and will provide additional evidence about the entry date of the first Americans and about their environment, technology, and life ways. I doubt, however, that the most emotionally charged question of when people first arrived on this continent will ever be settled to everyone's satisfaction. The first human site in the New World may never be found, and even if it were, we probably would never recognize it as such.

UPDATE

Over the past seven years, the interdisciplinary research team investigating Monte Verde completed its second and lengthy archaeological report on the site. This report has been published by the Smithsonian Institution Press.

In January 1997 a team of expert archaeologists visited the University of Kentucky to examine many of the artifacts from the Monte Verde site. Afterward, the group traveled to Chile to inspect the site stratigraphy and to study additional artifacts housed at the Universidad Austral de Chile, Valdivia. The team concluded that Monte Verde is indeed a valid archaeological site and that it dates to approximately 12,500 years ago.

Together, the detailed published report on Monte Verde and the confirmation of the site's validity by leading scientists have profound implications for everything archaeologists have thought about the peopling of the Americas. The findings from Monte Verde, coupled with those from several potentially older sites in North America (e.g., Meadowcroft Shelter in Pennsylvania, Blue Fish Cave in the Canadian Yukon), tell us that we should expect to find in Alaska sites of older age. Furthermore, given that Monte Verde is some 10,000 miles south of the Bering land bridge between Siberia and Alaska, then early human entry into the New World had to have occurred at least 15,000 to 20,000 years ago. Archaeologists now must reconsider the ways in which the first Americans successfully adapted to the many different landscapes of the Americas during earlier millennia of the late Ice Age.

FURTHER READING

Bryan, A. L., ed. 1986. *New Evidence for the Pleistocene Peopling of the Americas*. Center for the Study of Early Man, University of Maine.

Dillehay, Tom D. 1984. "A Late Ice-Age Settlement in Southern Chile." *Scientific American* 251(October): 106–17.

Dillehay, Tom D. 1989–. *Monte Verde: A Late Pleistocene Settlement in Chile*. Vol. 1: *A Palaeoenvironment and Site Context*. Smithsonian Institution Press.

Dillehay, Tom D. 1997. *Monte Verde: A Late Pleistocene Settlement in Chile*. Vol. 2: *The Archaeological Context and Interpretation*. Smithsonian Institution Press.

Dillehay, Tom D., G. A. Ardila, Gustavo Politis, and M. C. C. Beltrao. 1992. "Earliest Hunters and Gatherers of South America." *Journal of World Prehistory* 6(2): 145–204.

Fagan, Brian M. 1987. *The Great Journey: The Peopling of Ancient America*. Thames and Hudson.

Meltzer, David J. 1993. *Search for the First Americans*. Smithsonian Institution Press.

15 THE MOCHE

Profile of an Ancient Peruvian People

John W. Verano

A recent discovery of a royal tomb at Sipán has focused public attention on the Moche, an ancient but little-known Peruvian culture (see Alva, 1988, 1990; Donnan, 1988, 1990). Numbering as many as 50,000, the Moche were an agricultural people who resided along the northern coast of Peru as early as 1,200 years before the Inca. In one of the world's driest deserts, they diverted streams from the adjacent Andes into a large network of irrigation canals to grow corn, beans, squash, peanuts, peppers, potatoes, and manioc, as well as avocados and other fruit. They kept guinea pigs and ducks, herded llamas for wool and meat, raised crawfish in the irrigation canals, and fished and hunted sea lions from boats. Their territory stretched over 220 miles along the coast and included towns of up to 10,000 inhabitants: warriors, priests, nobles, artisans, traders, servants, farmers, and fishermen. To house their dead they built platforms topped with pyramids, today called *huacas*. Moche art and technology were comparable in sophistication to that of the Maya, their contemporaries. Beautiful gold and copper metalwork, inlays and beads of turquoise, shell and coral, woven materials, and richly decorated ceramics depicting everyday scenes, warfare, and ritual have been uncovered in the tombs. Unlike the Maya, however, the Moche did not develop a writing or glyph system.

Ongoing excavations at the site of Sipán, directed by Peruvian archaeologist Walter Alva, are revealing a wealth of new information about the ancient Moche civilization. Over the past several years, I have had the good fortune to be able to work with him in Peru, helping to analyze the skeletal remains from the Sipán tombs and other sites.

ANCIENT PEOPLES OF THE COAST

The Moche are one of several ancient civilizations that developed in the coastal valleys of northern Peru. The Moche Kingdom dominated the north coast from about A.D. 100 to A.D. 750. Their culture disappeared some 700 years before the Inca Empire began expanding out of the southern highlands. Best known for their beautiful ceramics and expressive art style, the Moche also left evidence of their relatively brief florescence in the form of numerous mud-brick pyramids, which still dot the river valleys of the north coast today.

Human occupation of the coast of Peru goes back many thousands of years. Survival in the otherwise inhospitable coastal desert of Peru is made possible by a series of seasonal rivers and streams that carry water down from the western slopes of the Andes Mountains. These rivers turn the narrow coastal valley floors into green oases, a stark contrast to the surrounding barren desert. Ancient peoples of the coast learned several thousand years ago to draw water off these rivers into irrigation canals, turning desert into productive agricultural land. Over the centuries many technological advances were made in canal building, eventually leading to complex irrigation networks, which linked several valleys of the north coast and provided productive agricultural land for thousands of coastal inhabitants.

When the Spanish conquistadors first passed through the northern coastal valleys in the 1530s, they marveled at the size and sophistication of the irrigation networks. Strangely, however, these first European visitors found many valleys only sparsely populated, and numerous agricultural fields abandoned. What the Spanish did not know at the time was that a devastating disease, probably smallpox, had spread through the Inca Empire some ten years earlier, taking thousands of victims with it. Smallpox, which had swept like wildfire through the Caribbean, Mexico, Central America, and then down through Ecuador and Peru, was one of the most deadly of the many infectious diseases brought from Europe to the New World in the sixteenth century. New World peoples, who had no immunity to the disease, died by the thousands. The epidemic that swept through Peru in the 1520s killed the Inca emperor and his legitimate heir and led to a bitter civil war between contenders for the throne. It was this divided and traumatized empire that Francisco Pizarro and his soldiers boldly conquered in 1532.

CONQUISTADORS AND *HUAQUEROS*

By the end of the sixteenth century, disease, conquest, and social disruption had forever changed the face of the north coast of Peru. The last of its great civilizations had collapsed, and much of its rich past was lost before it could be recorded by historians. Conquistadors who had sacked the last of the gold and silver from the storehouses and temples of the Inca then turned to the pyramids and burial places of the Inca's ancestors. Hoping to find the buried treasure of former kings, they plundered pyramids and ancient burial grounds up and down the coast of Peru. Historians have recently found early colonial documents requesting formal permits from the Spanish crown to "mine" pyramids for gold. And mine them they did—teams of hundreds of forced laborers were used to tunnel into these structures. The scars of sixteenth- and seventeenth-century looting can still be seen at many coastal sites today. In the Moche Valley on the north coast of Peru, a particularly determined group of "miners" in search of gold even diverted a river to cut into the center of a large pyramid.

The tradition of grave robbing, which began during the early colonial period, unfortunately has continued for centuries in Peru. *Huaqueros,* as they are commonly known today, are professional grave robbers, many of whom make a lifetime career of digging up ancient graves and selling the artifacts. Although the looting and destruction of archaeological sites is strictly prohibited by law in Peru, the limited resources of police and local government officials are simply not sufficient to control the activity. Realizing the importance of preserving and studying its rich pre-Columbian heritage, the Peruvian government actively supports archaeological research, both by Peruvian and foreign scholars. Such research is gradually bringing to light a long and fascinating sequence of pre-Columbian cultural development.

RECONSTRUCTING THE PAST

Peruvian archaeology traces its roots to the late nineteenth century, when archaeologists began making the first systematic attempts to reconstruct

the prehistory of the region. Many of these early excavations focused on coastal Peruvian sites because of the exceptional preservation of perishable materials. The coast of Peru is one of the driest deserts in the world, receiving measurable rainfall only on rare occasions. Such dry conditions make for excellent preservation of plant remains, textiles, and wooden objects—things rarely encountered by archaeologists working in other areas of the world. Bodies buried in the hot, dry sand become naturally mummified, providing physical anthropologists with rare glimpses of details such as ancient hair styles and body decoration (a number of tattooed mummies are known from coastal Peru). I will never forget a naturally mummified dog I helped excavate at an archaeological site on the north coast several years ago. Some time around A.D. 1300, the dog's owner had carefully wrapped the pet in a cloth shroud and buried it outside the wall of a desert city. Seven hundred years later when we unwrapped the shroud, the dog was perfectly preserved, with ears standing straight up and lips drawn back in a permanent snarl.

Despite the destruction of many pre-Columbian cemeteries by artifact hunters, physical anthropologists have been able to make some important discoveries about the physical characteristics of ancient Peruvians, both by studying skeletal material left behind by grave robbers, and increasingly in recent years, by working side by side with archaeologists conducting scientific excavations. Over the past seven years, I have been fortunate to participate in the excavation of several important Moche sites along Peru's north coast. Previous skeletal studies have characteristically focused on only a few isolated sites. Through my study of the skeletal remains, it has been possible to acquire large collections that permit us for the first time to make observations of Moche health, diseases, and demography on a population level.

PHYSICAL ANTHROPOLOGY OF THE MOCHE

Until recently, the physical characteristics of the Moche people were known to us primarily through the way they depicted themselves in ceramic sculpture and painted murals. Their physical remains had received surprisingly little attention by physical anthropologists. Part of my recent research has concentrated on the study of Moche skeletal remains recovered over the past five years from excavations and surface collections at the site of Pacatnamú (pronounced Pah-caht-nah-moo), a major pre-Columbian ceremonial center. These collections, which are now housed in a research facility in Trujillo, Peru, constitute the largest sample of well-documented human skeletal remains ever recovered from the Peruvian north coast and are, therefore, a valuable resource both for the study of physical variation among prehistoric coastal populations, and for understanding patterns of health and disease among ancient Andean peoples.

THE PACATNAMÚ SKELETONS

Most of the Moche skeletal collections from Pacatnamú pertain to the final phase of the Moche Kingdom (Moche V) and date to approximately A.D. 500–750. The skeletal sample we have recovered comprises 65 burials excavated from a single cemetery, 26 burials encountered in other parts of the site, and surface collections (approximately 590 specimens) made from three large Moche cemeteries recently damaged by looters.

LIFE EXPECTANCY IN MOCHE TIMES

In both the large surface-collected sample and the smaller number of individuals recovered from Moche tombs at Pacatnamú, males and females were present in about equal numbers. Although individuals of all ages, from children to people over 50, were represented, skeletal remains of infants and young children were rare in the surface collections and infants were underrepresented in the excavated burials. Remains of children are more fragile and preserve less well than bones of adults, although it is possible that not all infants and children were buried in cemetery areas.

In the cemetery, which we excavated completely, the remains of 67 individuals were recovered. Almost a third of these (20) were under 5 years old, while only 4 individuals were represented in the child and adolescent age range (ages 5–19). This age distribution is consistent with the U-shaped mortality curve commonly observed in living human populations, where probability of death is highest during the first year of life, declines during early childhood and adolescence, and climbs sharply again in the adult years. Of the individuals who died after childhood, about one-third lived to a mature middle age, dying between 35 and 49 years. But a significantly larger proportion of males (12 out of 23) died as adolescents (15–19 years) and young adults (20–34 years), while the majority of females (12 out of 23) fall into the old adult age class (50+). If this sample is representative of the Moche population at Pacatnamú as a whole, these differences suggest that Moche women had a substantially greater probability of reaching old age than did men. Was this due to greater violence or more hazardous activities among men or to greater susceptibility of males to disease? We do know that the Moche frequently depicted scenes of warfare and the capture and sacrifice of prisoners. However, we have found very little skeletal evidence of fractures or other injuries in the Moche sample from Pacatnamú, which makes it difficult to attribute earlier mortality in males to warfare.

PHYSICAL CHARACTERISTICS OF THE MOCHE PEOPLE

Based on his early studies of ancient Peruvian skeletons, Aleš Hrdlička of the United States National Museum (at present the National Museum of Natural History) described prehistoric peoples of the Peruvian coast as broadheaded (brachycephalic) and of relatively short stature. The Moche population at Pacatnamú conforms well to this description. Living stature calculated from Moche skeletons for both males (average 5'3") and females (average 4'11") is very similar to that of present-day north coast people of Indian origin. The Moche had wide faces and prominent, relatively narrow noses. Approximately half of the Moche skulls we studied show artificial cranial modification. This modification varies from a mild to pronounced flattening of the back of the skull, with flattening of the forehead region occasionally visible as well. Broadening of the cranial vault and slight broadening of the cheeks are noticeable in most modified skulls, although I believe the modification we see was probably the unintentional result of infant cradle-boarding rather than a conscious attempt by the Moche to alter the shape of the head. No depictions of infants in cradleboards are known from Moche art, nor have physical remains of cradleboards been found in a Moche context, perhaps because of poor organic preservation. However, well-preserved cradles and cloth bands that were used to fix an infant's head to the cradleboard have been recovered from later coastal cemeteries, along with skulls showing the same form of modification or reshaping observed among the Moche at Pacatnamú.

FAMILY CEMETERIES

One preliminary but intriguing finding on Moche mortuary practices has come out of my study of skeletons at Pacatnamú. Here, I expected to find one large cemetery where the local population buried their dead, as I had found at other sites in this area. I found, instead, numerous small cemeteries throughout the site and began to investigate why so many cemeteries were in use during a single time period.

Variation in the morphology of the facial skeleton is known to be a sensitive indicator of population differences and has been used successfully by physical anthropologists to differentiate ancient populations as well as to identify the population affiliation of recent forensic cases. By applying some of these techniques to Moche skulls at Pacatnamú, I was able to determine that individuals buried in the same cemetery resembled one another (in their facial morphology) more closely than they did individuals buried in other cemeteries of the same time period. Since greater resemblance implies closer genetic relationship, I interpreted the results as suggesting that the Moche buried their dead by family group. This conforms with the findings of the sixteenth-century Spanish chronicler, Cieza de Leon, who on his travels in 1547 through the valley where Pacatnamú is located, learned that native people buried their dead by kinship group in the hills and bluffs above the valley floor. This, along with the results of my research at Pacatnamú, suggest that burial by family group was a very ancient practice in the valley.

HEALTH AND DISEASE

All the Moche skeletal material excavated or surface collected at Pacatnamú was examined for evidence of disease or nutritional deficiency. Infants and children showed little sign of nutritional stresses due to low protein or insufficient calories (something that I found in some later burials at the site), and adults were relatively robust. All the older individuals and several younger adults had some degree of arthritis in the joints, particularly in the hips, knees, shoulders, and elbows. In the older adults, arthritis of the temporomandibular (jaw) joint was also common. The Moche also suffered from tooth decay and loss; middle-aged adults (35 – 49) had lost an average of 4.9 teeth and had cavities in an average of 3.6 of the remaining teeth, while old adults over 50 had lost an average of 17.2 teeth. Remaining teeth were frequently affected by periodontal disease. This is consistent with a growing body of data on dental disease among prehistoric agriculturalists, indicating that people who eat diets rich in soft foods and carbohydrates frequently have a high incidence of cavities and other dental disease, even in the absence of refined sugars.

UNDERSTANDING THE MOCHE:
ONGOING RESEARCH AND FUTURE PROSPECTS

Recent archaeological excavations at sites such as Sipán are rapidly increasing our knowledge about ancient Moche culture. The study of their skeletal remains is providing additional information about their physical characteristics, health, and mortality patterns. The high-status tombs found at Sipán pose some new research questions, which we are currently working to answer. For example: Are there differences in the health, stature, or other physical characteristics of the Moche elite that might reflect a lifestyle and diet different from that of Moche commoners? Do the skeletons of the elite show any rare or unusual skeletal traits that might suggest a lineage of hereditary Moche rulers? Do the skeletons that surround the central occupants of elaborate tombs at Sipán represent retainers or relatives of the deceased?

Ongoing research may provide answers to these and other questions about the population responsible for this remarkable prehistoric South American culture. It may well be that the next generation of school children will be as familiar with the Moche as with the Inca, who dominated the coast of Peru 1200 years later.

UPDATE

Since the publication of the foregoing discussion on the Moche, many new and exciting discoveries have come to light at Moche archaeological sites.

Two more royal tombs were found at Sipán, along with many other discoveries, such as rooms filled with dedicatory offerings of ceramics, metal objects, and human and animal bones. In 1993 objects from the Sipán tombs began a tour of the United States in the exhibition "Royal Tombs of Sipán," which opened at the Fowler Museum of Cultural History at the University of California, Los Angeles, in the fall of that year. The exhibition made its final appearance at the Smithsonian's National Museum of Natural History in June of 1995, before returning to Peru to be permanently installed in the Brüning Archaeological Museum, a small regional museum near Sipán that is directed by archaeologist Walter Alva.

Over the past several years, I have made numerous visits to the Sipán excavations, to continue my study of the human skeletal remains from the tombs. Much of this work has involved assisting Walter Alva and his team to determine the age at death, sex, and physical characteristics of the individuals buried in the royal tombs. The sex of an individual, as well as the age at which he or she died, can be important in interpreting the offerings found with them in the grave. Evidence of disease or injury can provide further details about the daily lives of these people.

Unfortunately, the Sipán skeletons are not well preserved, and many have been crushed over the centuries by the overburden of artifacts, tomb fill, and later construction at the ceremonial center. Nevertheless, it has been possible to determine sex and approximate age at death, and to identify health problems such as arthritis, dental cavities, dental abscesses, and tooth loss. I found evidence of cultural behavior recorded in the skeletons, as well. The high-status male buried in Chamber Tomb 1, known popularly as the Lord of Sipán, showed flattening of the back of his skull identical to the cradle-board deformation that I found in Moche burials of low-status individuals at Pacatnamú. This flattening indicates that the Lord of Sipán was strapped to a cradle-board during the first years of his life, like any other Moche child, and may indicate that he rose to his position of power through his own accomplishments in life, rather than simply because he was born into a hereditary line of rulers.

The new discoveries at Sipán over the past several years have been joined by important finds at other Moche sites. Another mortuary complex similar to Sipán, Huaca San José de Moro in the Jequetepeque Valley near Pacatnamú, was the focus of excavations by Christopher Donnan and Luis Jaime Castillo of the University of California, Los Angeles, in 1990 and 1991. The site is very important in that it has yielded the first tombs of high-status Moche women ever found by archaeologists. Based on the elaborate funerary masks and other grave goods buried with them, Chris Donnan believes that these women served as priestesses in important religious ceremonies related to warfare and human sacrifice.

Other important Moche discoveries in the last few years have been made in two valleys further south. Multicolor painted murals of Moche deities and warriors have been found at two major Moche ceremonial centers: at the Pyramid of the Moon, in the Moche River Valley, and at Huaca El Brujo in the neighboring Chicama River Valley. These murals are some of the finest examples of Moche polychrome mural painting ever found and provide a wealth of new information about Moche monumental art and iconography.

In the summers of 1991 and 1992, I traveled up and down the north coast of Peru with a close friend, Julio Vizcarra, a video producer for the Pan American Health Organization, and a native of Peru. Julio had been wanting to make an educational video on the Moche for some time, and he and I agreed to work together on the project. We filmed the excavations in progress at Sipán, San José de Moro, Huaca de la Luna, and Huaca El Brujo and interviewed Walter Alva, Christopher Donnan, and other archaeologists conducting the excavations. Editing of the video was completed during the summer of 1993, and the program, entitled "Secrets of the Moche," aired on the Learning Channel (Discovery Communications) in September 1993. As a final note, I am pleased that my *AnthroNotes* report on the Moche was translated into Spanish by the director of the Archaeological Museum of the University of Trujillo, Enrique Vergara Montera, who published it in his museum's journal in Peru.

FURTHER READING

Alva, Walter. 1988. "Discovering the New World's Richest Unlooted Tomb." *National Geographic* 174:510–49.

Alva, Walter. 1990. "New Tomb of Royal Splendor." *National Geographic* 177(6):2–15.

Alva, Walter, and Christopher B. Donnan. 1993. *Royal Tombs of Sipán.* Fowler Museum of Cultural History, University of California, Los Angeles.

Donnan, Christopher B. 1978. *Moche Art of Peru: Pre-Columbian Symbolic Communication.* Fowler Museum of Cultural History, University of California, Los Angeles.

Donnan, Christopher B. 1988. "Iconography of the Moche: Unraveling the Mystery of the Warrior-Priest." *National Geographic* 174:550–55.

Donnan, Christopher B. 1990. "Masterworks of Art Reveal a Remarkable Pre-Inca World." *National Geographic* 177(6):16–33.

Donnan, Christopher B., and Luis Jaime Castillo. 1992. "Finding the Tomb of a Moche Priestess." *Archaeology* 45(6):38–42.

Lumbreras, Luis G. 1974. *The Peoples and Cultures of Ancient Peru*. Smithsonian Institution Press. Translated by Betty J. Meggers.

Verano, John. 1991a. "Moche: Perfil de un antiguo pueblo Peruano." *Revista del Museo de Arqueología* (Trujillo, Peru) 2:104–113.

Verano, John. 1991b. "Physical Characteristics and Skeletal Biology of the Moche Population at Pacatnamú." In Christopher B. Donnan and Guillermo A. Cock, eds., *The Pacatnamú Papers*, vol. 2: *The Moche Occupation*, pp. 189–214. Fowler Museum of Cultural History, University of California, Los Angeles.

Verano, John. 1997. "Human Skeletal Remains from Tomb 1, Sipán (Lambayeque River Valley, Peru) and Their Social Implications." *Antiquity* 71: 670–82.

16 A QUIET REVOLUTION

Origins of Agriculture in Eastern North America

Ruth Osterweis Selig

> Long before the introduction of maize, farming economies and an agrarian way of life had been established in eastern North America. . . . Documenting the origins of agriculture in North America emerged from revolutionary improvements in collecting ancient seeds combined with the application of new, sophisticated technologies—and the puzzle's missing pieces finally fell into place.
>
> —Bruce D. Smith

Plant domestication can be defined as the human creation for human purposes of a new form of plant—one that is clearly distinguishable from its wild ancestors and its wild relatives living today, and one that is dependent on human intervention—harvesting and planting—for survival. Today we take the domestication of plants and animals for granted, but the grains, vegetables, fruits, milk products, and meats we eat every day come from long ago human intervention in the life cycles of wild plants and animals. Plant domestication is not simply a physical change. It is a revolutionary alteration of the relationship between human societies and plants brought under their control, enabling relatively few people to create food for large human populations, freeing most people to pursue other activities.

Many textbooks today still assert that agriculture in the New World originated in Mesoamerica, and that maize and squash spread from Mexico to eastern North America around A.D. 800. At that time, textbooks explain, Native Americans learned to cultivate not only maize and squash but also beans and a few indigenous seed crops such as sunflower. The growing of corn, squash, and beans thus enabled eastern North Americans to build larger settlements and more complex societies that depended on maize agriculture imported from Mesoamerica, where larger-scale societies had also developed.

New research shows that contrary to this long-held belief, eastern North America now can be unequivocally identified as a fourth major independent center of plant domestication, along with the Near East, China, and Mesoamerica (Smith, 1989:1566). In fact, eastern North America provides the most detailed record available of agricultural origins anywhere in the world, providing new understanding of the processes involved in this key transformation in human history.

The beginning of agriculture marks a clear watershed and defines one of the major ecological changes in the history of the planet. However, revolutionary changes producing dramatic transformations may not be particularly dramatic in their origins or swift in their impact, or even easy to pinpoint and document.

PUZZLE PIECES

What were the domesticated food crops that Native American farmers grew in eastern North America? When and how did their domestication occur? Why has it taken so long to discover and recognize the contribution Native North Americans made to the origins of agriculture in the history of humankind? The understanding of Native American domestication in eastern North America is a story that can be visualized as a puzzle, with some pieces in place long before the full picture emerged.

Some pieces were discovered in the nineteenth century: Ebenezer Andrews excavated the first cache of stored indigenous seeds in Ash Cave, Ohio, in 1876. Many pieces emerged in the 1930s and 1950s, but several key pieces came together only in the late 1980s and early 1990s as new evidence—seeds and gourds—came to light and new technologies for dating and analysis were applied.

The "quiet revolution" is a story of several transformations: of native North Americans slowly changing their own way of life from foraging to farming; of a new generation of archaeologists transforming their discipline with new discoveries, questions, and sophisticated technologies; and of one particular scientist, Smithsonian archaeologist Bruce Smith, working to put some of the final puzzle pieces in place. A scientist who relishes puzzles, theoretical challenges, and the opportunity to turn conventional wisdom on its head, Smith found the pieces in some unlikely places: in an

THE TRANSITION FROM HUNTING AND GATHERING TO DOMESTICATION

old cigar box containing thousands of tiny ancient seeds, and along an Arkansas river valley where a bunch of small, wild, lemon-sized gourds grew.

EARLY NATIVE AMERICAN FARMERS

These facts now are indisputable. By 2000 B.C. in the eastern Woodlands, Native Americans deliberately planted and harvested at least four indigenous seed plants independently of outside influences. This activity marked the beginning of their transition from foragers to farmers. Maize arrived from Mexico about A.D. 200, but for six hundred years thereafter, corn was not a major food source. Why corn did not become widespread until after A.D. 800 remains a mystery; at first it may have been used only for religious and ceremonial purposes. After A.D. 800, intensive maize agriculture spread quickly and widely throughout the eastern Woodlands as corn became a major staple of the diet.

With new tools, archaeologists have documented three major episodes in native North American domestication, as discussed below.

PHASE ONE: 3000 TO 2000 B.C.

Native Americans discovered that wild seed plants growing along river floodplains could be controlled, that plants could be harvested and used as food, with seeds stored and replanted in prepared garden plots the next year. Four indigenous plants underwent this transition to full domesticates, with clear morphological changes taking place in their seeds; three additional cultigens appear as food crops as Native Americans encouraged and harvested these previously wild sources of food. The highly nutritious seeds from these seven plants could be variously boiled into cereals, ground into flours, or eaten directly.

Each of the seven indigenous plants involved—chenopod, marshelder, squash, sunflower, erect knotweed, little barley, and maygrass—had its own particular course of development. Most began as wild plants growing along river floodplains that Native North Americans first gathered and utilized, then gradually brought under their control as they harvested them and planted their seeds in prepared fields the following year, sometimes quite far from their original habitats. There is evidence of indigenous crop domestication occurring over a broad geographical area by 2000 B.C., on lands today known as Tennessee, Arkansas, Illinois, Kentucky, Ohio, Missouri, and Alabama. After a slow beginning for each crop, the overall shift occurred rather abruptly, and in groups, with several spring and fall crops introduced together, some high in oil and some in starch. As Bruce Smith wryly comments:

> If domestication occurred in some other part of the world, and involved grains such as wheats or barleys, such an abrupt, broad scale, and highly visible transition to an increased economic presence of seven domesticated and cultivated plants would quickly be acknowledged as marking a major shift toward farming economies. But in eastern North America . . . where the indigenous crops in question have little name recognition, this transition is still often brushed aside as involving minor crops of little economic import, in all likelihood grown only in small garden plots. (Smith, 1992b:14)

PHASE TWO: 250 B.C. TO A.D. 200

In this phase, food production economies emerged. Much greater amounts of seed appear in the diet, and seed crops become the focus of more intensive cultivation, as farmers plant crops away from their original habitats. Maize first appears in small amounts.

New information pinpoints the emergence of indigenous crop economies, not maize, as parallel in time with Hopewellian cultures. Ohio,

Illinois, and states farther south are dotted with the remains of farming communities that existed between 250 B.C. and A.D. 200, many of them marked by Hopewellian features such as large geometric earthworks, conical burial grounds, elaborate mortuary decorations, and beautifully molded pipes, bowls, icons, and other objects.

Members of Hopewell farming societies lived in single-household settlements of perhaps a dozen individuals. They settled in river valleys—ideal locations for small fields—and crafted hoes and other tools suited for small-scale land clearing. Studies of modern wild stands of the crop plants grown by these farmers indicate that the plants have high potential harvest rates and yields. For example, a square field, 200 feet on a side, planted equally with marsh elder and chenopod, could have been harvested by five people in little more than a week. Even more impressive, nutritional analyses indicate that a field of this size and content would have provided half the caloric requirements of a household of 10 for a period of six months.

PHASE THREE: A.D. 800 TO 1100

Because of the earlier emergence of agriculture, which served as a preadaptation, a rapid and broad-scale shift to large field, maize-centered agriculture emerges.

Food-producing economies based on indigenous crops flourished from about A.D. 200 until about A.D. 800, when a new, nonindigenous crop plant—maize—came to dominate the fields and diets of ancient North American farmers extending from what is now northern Florida to Ontario in Canada, from the Atlantic Coast to the Great Plains. Archaeologists now know that maize appeared in Native American villages more than 2,000 years after indigenous plants were domesticated and well after the rise of Hopewell societies. Even more dramatic and interesting is the coincident emergence of a second major episode of social transformation known as the Mississippian chiefdoms. From A.D. 800 until about A.D. 1000, the river valleys of the Southeast and the Midwest became dominated by the fortified villages of Mississippian chiefdoms. These societies exhibited considerable social inequality and organizational complexity reflected in raised mounds surrounding central plazas occupied by privileged individuals who enjoyed more ceremonial burials than the general populace.

RESISTANCE TO NEW THEORIES

If Native Americans domesticated indigenous seed plants deliberately and independently between 3000 B.C. and 2000 B.C. in the Eastern Woodlands, why has it taken so long for their enormous contribution to be recognized? Perhaps it is because the domesticated seed crops themselves are so little known, since they did not survive as domesticates, in contrast to maize and beans. Only squash and sunflower are used today. In addition, they come from plants with difficult-to-pronounce names and obscure identities and use. They include *Cucurbita pepo* (squash), *Iva annua* (marshelder or sumpweed), *Helianthus annuus* (sunflower), and *Chenopodium berlandieri* (chenopod or goosefoot), as well as three cultigens whose seeds do not reflect the same distinct morphological changes that would enable archaeologists to call them full domesticates—erect knotweed, little barley, and maygrass.

The obscurity of most of these seed crops in today's world, and the rich descriptions early settlers left of Indians growing corn, beans, and squash, go far toward explaining why it is so difficult to change people's conceptions of the origins of Native American agriculture:

> School children across America learn that Indians of the East grew maize, beans, and squash . . . southeastern tribes made more than ninety different dishes from corn. More importantly, maize [or corn] is an ever-present dietary element in modern America. We consume corn oil and margarine, corn on the cob, creamed corn, popcorn, caramel corn, corn nuts, corn flakes, corn fritters, and corn. . . . We know what we eat. (Smith, 1992b: 5–6)

SCIENTISTS AS DETECTIVES

In the early 1980s Smith was increasingly convinced that it was eastern Native Americans who discovered farming, and that seed crops other than maize explained the appearance of Hopewell societies. But how could he find evidence to strengthen this idea and convince those who still did not believe it, that Native North Americans independently discovered agriculture?

Smith knew the answer must lie within ancient plant remains. In the 1960s and 1970s, several investigators had documented two local domesticates—sunflower and marsh elder—and had proposed various plants as likely candidates for early domestication, among them a chenopod that was found in such abundance in archaeological sites that it seemed unlikely to have been merely gathered in the wild. To Smith, *Chenopodium* seemed a particularly good potential domesticate to study because he could compare any ancient seeds he found with seeds from the modern Mexican domesticate, *Chenopodium berlandieri,* and also compare the ancient seeds with modern wild chenopods in the eastern United States. These comparisons would show whether or not the ancient seeds carried the clear markers of domestication.

Smith reasoned he would have a chance to find the "linchpin" evidence if he could find one good-sized collection of whole, well-preserved chenopod seeds clearly stored by ancient farmers. The seeds had to come from an undisturbed site with good temporal context; and they had to date to a time before maize was first introduced to eastern North America. If Smith could find one such collection, and if all the seeds showed the telltale thin, somewhat rectangular coat of domestication when examined in a scanning electron microscope, then he would have added another local domesticate to the list and put one of the final key puzzle pieces in place.

RUSSELL CAVE

Smith began to search old archaeological reports for references to seeds excavated from storage contexts. One collection seemed particularly promising: Russell Cave, Alabama. Fortuitously, Russell Cave had been excavated in 1956 by Carl Miller, then with the River Basin Surveys of the Smithsonian Institution. Smith knew that the large amounts of uncataloged material from these surveys were down the hall from his office in the National Museum of Natural History, and that if seeds still existed, he might have some chance of rediscovering them.

Smith read everything Miller wrote about his excavation but found only a brief paragraph describing a spectacular seed discovery:

> During the first season's work in Russell Cave, the charred remains of a small hemispherically-shaped basket were found filled with equally charred *Chenopodium seeds.* The seeds were later identified by experts in the US Department of Agriculture as belonging to this plant family. Their presence on the Early Woodland horizon, about 5,000 years ago, indicate that *these people knew the potential of these wild uncultivated seeds as a single food*

source, harvested them by means of seed beaters and baskets and converted them to food. (Quoted in Smith, 1993:117; emphasis added)

Could these "wild seeds" be, in fact, from domesticated plants? Could this basket be the "needle in the haystack" that Smith was trying to find? First, of course, he had to find the seeds. Unfortunately, there had been a tragic loss of the original storage basket during the excavation:

> At about seven feet we came across the basket . . . made of coiled strands of grass fiber . . . (the basket was) filled with small seeds, probably some wild grain the cave men gathered and ate. . . . Since it was late in the evening when we found the basket, I decided to wait until morning before trying to dig it out . . . but when we entered the cave the next morning, we were dismayed to find it gone . . . someone had vandalized the cave. (Quoted in Smith, 1992b: 117)

Despite the basket's destruction, Smith decided to search through the 38 drawers of unaccessioned Russell Cave materials at the National Museum of Natural History. Toward the end of several days of endlessly sorting through lithic materials, Smith found an old cigar box (*Tampa Nugget Sublimes*) bearing the longhand inscription "Basket F.S. [field specimen] 23." He opened the box but found only an old, crumbled brown paper bag inside; but it, too, was labeled "F.S. 23." This bag could be the way Miller stored the seeds that had spilled out from the missing basket. With both apprehension and anticipation, Smith unfolded the paper bag and found exactly what he had hoped for: a bunch of very old, very dark, and very charred seeds! In fact, as he examined the plant remains Smith estimated there to be perhaps 50,000 carbonized *Chenopodium* seeds! This spectacular discovery was exactly what he needed!

ARCHAEOBOTANY

Smith next turned to the new tools that were revolutionizing the field of archaeology and strengthening the subdiscipline of archaeobotany. By dating and then analyzing the size, shape, and structure of the Russell Cave chenopod seeds as well as modern domesticated *Chenopodium* and modern wild species, Smith could begin to pinpoint the exact time of chenopod domestication.

Smith's research included innovative applications of recent developments in scientific technology. Most of his discoveries, in fact, are attributable to four new technological advances, serving to underscore the important role instrumentation plays in guiding and stimulating scientific research:

1. *Water flotation technology* dramatically improves the recovery of small carbonized seeds and other plant parts from the archaeological context. The principle is simple: huge amounts of excavated soil are mixed with water, allowing seeds, charcoal, and other light materials to float to the top.
2. *Accelerator mass spectrometry (AMS)* allows radiocarbon dating of individual seeds and other tiny samples.
3. *Scanning electron microscopy (SEM),* like AMS dating, revolutionized the field of archaeobotany in the 1980s, since the SEM can magnify small objects many thousands of times greater than conventional microscopes. Only with the SEM can the seed coat thickness indicating domestication be measured.
4. *Stable carbon isotope analysis* of human bone allows scientists to document the consumption of maize. Maize, a tropical grass, has less carbon [13] than food plants of temperate North America; this deficiency in carbon [13] shows up in the bones of the people in North America who began to eat large quantities of corn after A.D. 900.

Using these new tools, Smith demonstrated without a doubt that the Russell Cave cache of *Chenopodium* was a very early collection of stored *domesticated* seeds, put aside for planting by early Native American farmers at least 2,000 years ago, well before maize entered North America.

A NORTH AMERICAN SQUASH?

The diffusionists, however, still had one "ace in the hole" to prove their theory of Mesoamerican origins for North American agriculture. Mexico was clearly the hearth from which sprang all of today's New World pumpkins, squashes, and gourds, members of the large species *Cucurbita pepo*. In the late 1960s and early 1970s, a number of archaeological discoveries of domesticated *Cucurbita pepo* seeds in Mexico were dated to nearly 8000 B.C., strengthening the belief that Mexico was the primary source of New World domestication. In addition, there were no documented wild *Cucurbita pepo* in North America at all, so it was logically assumed that all the prehistoric remains of *C. pepo* found in eastern North America, including some recently discovered charred rind fragments that were dated as early as 7,000 years ago, must represent domesticated squash that had been introduced from Mexico.

Smith and his colleagues, however, were not convinced. They wondered if the 7,000-year-old fragments of burned *Cucurbita pepo* rind could have come, in fact, from wild gourds. If Smith could prove that the tiny 7,000-year-old rind fragments were from wild and not domesticated gourd plants, and if he could locate closely related present-day wild gourds in eastern North America, the puzzle might at last be complete and the diffusionist theory overturned.

Smith and his colleagues raised some interesting questions. If domesticated gourds were introduced 7,000 years ago in the East, and eastern hunters and gatherers turned to farming, why was this the only crop they grew for the next 3,000 years? More important, if the gourd had been domesticated for 3,000 years, why was it morphologically identical to wild gourds—with its small size, thin rind, and small seeds? Even more curiously, why would *Curcubita pepo* materials from eastern North America that were 4,000 years old exhibit clear morphological changes indicating domestication, when materials 3,000 years older did not show such signs? Smith noted, with satisfaction, that the morphological signs of domestication for *Curcubita* squash (larger seeds, thicker rind) appeared just at the same time that similar changes signaled the domestication of three Eastern North American seed plants—sunflower, marsh elder, and chenopodium.

To Smith and his colleagues this fact suggested the real possibility that the 7,000- to 4,000-year-old *C. pepo* rinds in the East resulted not from an introduced domesticate, but from an indigenous wild *C. pepo* gourd that was domesticated along with the other three eastern plants about 4,000 years ago. But if this were true, why were there no wild gourds left in eastern North America today?

At this point in time a stunning piece of evidence came out of the blue—from a 1986 doctoral dissertation written by botanist Deena Decker—providing the first modern evolutionary and taxonomic analysis of the species *C. pepo*. Decker's research proved through isozyme chemical analysis that the *C. pepo* domesticates fall into two separate genetic groups: the orange-skinned pumpkins (known to have originated in Mexico) in one developmental lineage, and the green and yellow squashes and acorns in a genetically quite different group, suggesting two distinct developmental histories and origins. Hence it was very possible that Native Americans in eastern North America had domesticated indigenous wild gourds about 4,000 years ago. But if they did, there should be modern wild gourds still existing today.

IN SEARCH OF THE WILD EASTERN GOURD

The existence of modern wild gourds could prove once and for all that the second lineage—the summer squashes and acorns—came from indigenous plants, since the 7,000-year-old rind fragments showed no definite signs of domestication and hence easily could have come from wild plants. Not knowing much about gourds but willing to look for them, Smith and his colleague, C. Wesley Cowan from the Cincinnati Museum of Natural History, set out to find them in 1990. In initial response to their questions about wild gourds in eastern North American, several gourd experts told them there were none, nor had there ever been wild gourds in the region. Following the lead of earlier researchers, however, Smith and Cowan began to ask around, and much to their surprise, they heard of free-living gourds in Arkansas, Kentucky, Missouri, Alabama, Illinois, Tennessee, and Louisiana—a number-one weed problem, they were told. They went back to the gourd experts for confirmation. "Oh, *those gourds*," Smith and Cowan were told by the gourd experts. "We know all about those gourds. They are not 'wild' but feral gourds that were derived from domesticated, ornamental gourds which had once 'escaped' from cultivation and since World War II have become agricultural weeds."

Realizing they might just be on the trail of wild gourds, Cowan and Smith decided next to turn to herbaria to find out how long these "escaped" gourds had been around in the United States. To their delight, a survey of herbaria yielded reams of new data, herbaria sheets showing gourds collected from across eleven states, from Texas north into Illinois and east along the Gulf coast to Florida. Even more interesting, the history of collecting this free-living gourd extended long before World War II, well back into the nineteenth century, with a number of specimen sheets from the St. Louis area dating to the 1850s and 1860s. Smith and Cowan then questioned where these nineteenth-century gourds could have come from and were told that early settlers were growing gourds, and some had "escaped" back even in the nineteenth century. But where did the early settlers get these gourds if there were no wild gourds? The answer again came quickly back: from seed catalogs.

Beltsville, Maryland, is home to the National Agricultural Library, which houses the largest collection of seed catalogs in the country. Browsing through reams of seed catalogs in search of an obscure Ozark gourd, Cowan and Smith discovered that with few exceptions *C. pepo* gourds did not begin to grace the pages of seed catalogs until well into the 1870s, several decades after gourds had been collected in St. Louis as evidenced in the old herbaria sheets.

Smith and Cowan next turned to the Ozark River floodplains. They chose the Buffalo River, unsettled until the 1850s, never much of a farming community, and since the 1950s a national scenic river—with virtually no cultivation of any kind carried out in its watershed for four decades. Much to their delight, the Ozark gourds were all over the place. As Smith explains, "in almost every stream or river we investigated, we found wild gourd vines climbing up into trees and bushes or stretching across gravel bars. These gourds had been hiding in plain sight for 150 years!"

THE PUZZLE COMPLETED

The two archaeologists found literally hundreds of wild gourds, each about the size of a hardball or even smaller, ivory colored with occasional green stripes. Each gourd contained from 100 to 200 seeds; these were an excellent food source because they were 25 percent protein. Not surprisingly, Smith and Cowan turned their cache of gourds over to Deena Decker, authority on *Curcurbita* taxonomy, genetics, and evolution. She and Terrence Walters compared the isozyme profile of the Ozark wild gourd with other wild gourds and with a wide range of domesticated pumpkins and squashes belonging to the species *Cucurbita pepo*. They concluded that the Ozark wild gourd exhibited a unique genetic profile, confirmed it as a wild plant and not a "garden escape," and established it as the likely wild ancestor of the eastern North American domesticated squashes, a lineage with a history quite separate from the pumpkins of Mexico!

Still surviving today in the Ozarks, it was this wild gourd that Native Americans living in eastern North America developed into different varieties of domesticated squashes about 4,000 to 3,000 years ago, at the

same time that they domesticated sunflower, marshelder, and chenopod.

The puzzle finally was complete. The old diffusionist theory had been toppled, and the textbooks should now read:

> Native American women and men domesticated local plants, including the wild gourd squash and several highly nutritious seed crops, long before any domesticated plants were introduced from Mesoamerica. This revolutionary contribution of Native North Americans makes eastern North America one of the world's four major independent centers of plant domestication: the Middle East, China, Mesoamerica, and Eastern North America!

UPDATE

Bruce D. Smith

There was clearly no one "prehistoric genius" who discovered how to plant and harvest seeds, no prime mover of domestication. Similarly, no one scholar alone could have unraveled the entire story of the independent origin of agriculture in eastern North America. Although much of the discussion in this chapter is based on my writings, interviews, and unpublished materials, numerous colleagues have also been working on the puzzle of domestication in North America, particularly David and Nancy Asch, Wesley Cowan, Gary Crites, Deena Decker, Richard Ford, Gayle Fritz, Kristin Grimillion, Fran King, Patty Jo Watson, and Richard Yarnell.

Since this chapter was written, research on the origins of agriculture in eastern North America continues at a rapid pace, as scholars both fill in missing pieces of the existing puzzle and identify and begin to work on a number of new puzzles. Flotation recovery and direct accelerator mass spectrometry (AMS) radiocarbon dating of seeds of early eastern domesticates is filling gaps in our understanding of when and where different crop plants were first domesticated. Gary Crites of the University of Tennessee, for example, recently pushed back the earliest evidence of sunflower domestication in the East to 2300 B.C. following his discovery and direct AMS dating of domesticated sunflower seeds at the Hayes site in Tennessee. Other researchers, including Gayle Fritz of Washington University and Kristin Grimillion of Ohio State University, are investigating regional differences in premaize farming economies that existed in different parts of the Midwest and Southeast. They are finding not only that the relative importance of different indigenous eastern crops varied considerably from region to region, but also that the crops themselves differed regionally, as indicated by microscopic comparison of seeds. Fritz and Grimillion, along with other scholars, are also comparing the long and sometimes quite different developmental histories of farming economies in various parts of the East. Fritz, for example, is looking at why the shift over to maize agriculture appears to have taken place much later in Louisiana than in other regions.

In recent years, parallel research on how and when the shift over to farming took place has also intensified in other adjacent parts of North America. Mary Dunn, University of Kansas, has been studying the ways in which Indian societies of the eastern grasslands added crop plants into their way of life. Similarly, Gary Crawford, University of Toronto, John Hart, New York State Museum, and a number of other researchers are documenting when and why different crop plants, particularly maize, were selectively added to local economies by Indian societies in different parts of southern Ontario and across the northeast.

There is also continuing interest in the relative dietary importance of indigenous eastern seed plants during the first 2,000 years after they were domesticated (2500–500 B.C.). Settlements of this time period have yielded relatively few seeds of the eastern crop plants; hence some scholars have concluded that plant cultivation played a relatively minor role in overall economies prior to about 500 B.C. Other researchers, however, have pointed to a unique archaeological collection as providing evidence that crop plants gained dietary importance much earlier in time. Deep within Mammoth and Salts caves, Kentucky, scattered along the passageways, hundreds of human paleofeces have been found, and direct AMS radiocarbon dating indicates many were deposited between 1000 and 500 B.C. by miners searching for mineral deposits. Providing direct evidence of what these early cavers were eating, the human coprolites (feces) contain large numbers of seeds of eastern crop plants. Are these paleofeces representative of the general diet of the times, and do they indicate that crop plants were important much earlier than previously thought? Or do they represent a special "trail mix" diet carried into the caves by these early miners? Although not conclusive, recent analysis of hormone traces in the coprolites by Kristin Grimillion and Kristin Sobolik indicates that they were exclusively male in origin, which adds support to the specialized trail-mix interpretation.

Finally, well-preserved dung of another kind has also provided strong supporting evidence for the deep time depth of wild *Cucurbita* gourds in eastern North America. Mammoth dung deposits from the Page-Ladson site in Florida, recently analyzed by Lee Newsom of Southern Illinois University, Carbondale, dated to 12,500 years ago, contained dozens of seeds of wild *Cucurbita* gourds, providing another key puzzle piece in proving that squash was independently domesticated in eastern North America.

FURTHER READING

Decker, Deena. 1986. "A Biosystematic Study of *Cucurbita pepo*." Unpublished Ph.D. dissertation. Department of Biology, Texas A&M University, College Station.

Smith, Bruce D. 1989. "Origins of Agriculture in Eastern North America." *Science* 246:1566–71.

Smith, Bruce D. 1991. "Harvest of Prehistory." *The Sciences* 31(May/June): 30–35.

Smith, Bruce D. 1992a. "Prehistoric Plant Husbandry in Eastern North America." In C. Wesley Cowan and Patty Jo Watson, eds., *The Origins of Agriculture: An International Perspective*. Smithsonian Institution Press.

Smith, Bruce D. 1992b. *Rivers of Change: Essays on Early Agriculture in Eastern North America*. Smithsonian Institution Press.

Smith, Bruce D. 1995. *The Emergence of Agriculture*. W. H. Freeman.

Smith, Bruce D. 1995. "The Origins of Agriculture in the Americas." *Evolutionary Anthropology* 3:174–84.

17 GLOBAL CULTURE CHANGE

New Views of Circumpolar Lands and Peoples

William W. Fitzhugh

For many years anthropologists believed that Eskimos were the isolated descendants of Ice Age hunters, marginal refugees whose Paleolithic cultures had been preserved for thousands of years in a kind of cultural deep freeze.

In recent years, a quite different view of Arctic cultures has emerged, challenging this "relic of the past" theory with a new view of circumpolar history as a unique and dynamic adaptation to a relatively "friendly" Arctic—if you know how to live there. The cultural similarities among native peoples on either side of the Pacific Basin, from Siberia to Alaska and the Columbia River, and across the North American Arctic to Canada and Greenland, demonstrate a long and complex history of culture contact, migrations, and exchange in Arctic regions, and provide a new perspective on the question of the "independent" history of the Americas. Seen from a global, circumpolar perspective, Arctic and Subarctic regions and their adjacent coasts are increasingly perceived as long-standing "highways" rather than as barriers to the flow of plants and animals, peoples and cultures. Today we recognize Siberian influence in several early Alaskan cultures, and Bering Strait sources are known for many features of Eskimo cultures found across the Arctic.

FIRST CONTACT

Slightly more than 1,000 years ago, Norsemen from Scandinavia crossed the North Atlantic and discovered Greenland and North America. They found these new lands cold and bleak and were surprised to discover them inhabited by "skraelings," whom they described as semihuman creatures with one leg and screeching voices. Five hundred years later, Englishman Martin Frobisher reached Greenland and Baffin Island (1576–78) while searching for the Northwest Passage. Frobisher, too, met native Inuit, but despite their skin clothes and animal-like sod house dwellings, he noted they were shrewd traders and crafty warriors, not afraid to die for their homes or their freedom. Frobisher managed to capture several Inuit, bringing them home to present to Queen Elizabeth I as "tokens of possession" of new lands claimed for England. Lacking resistance to European diseases, these people soon died, but their Asian features and metal tools suggested Frobisher had, indeed, discovered the threshold of the fabled Northwest Passage to Asia.

Early descriptions of Arctic peoples also were recorded in the European Arctic. According to an Old English text, Ohthere, an intrepid Norse chieftain of the late ninth century, described the Saami (Lapp) peoples of northern Scandinavia in fearsome terms. He and other travelers reported meeting Russian Arctic peoples with powerful sled dogs and boats made from the skins of seals.

Today we know these northern peoples as Inuit (Eskimos) in North America and the western side of Bering Strait; Chukchi, Yukaghir, Dolgans, and Nenets inhabiting Siberia; and Saami (Lapps) living in Scandinavia. Occupying similar Arctic lands for thousands of years, these various peoples developed similar cultures, using skin and feather clothing, harpoons, dog and reindeer sleds, oil lamps, underground houses, and skin boats. Many of these people shared shamanistic beliefs and nearly identical folktales of Raven and the aurora borealis.

Who were these Arctic peoples who so fascinated European explorers and travelers? What was their origin and history? Did they come from a single people who spread eastward from northern Europe around the northern rim of the globe, or did they undergo convergent development following independent origins in different areas of the North?

Early anthropologists explored these questions in two ways. First, they tried to connect the cultures of living Arctic peoples to the early hunting cultures of Paleolithic Europe; second, they explored similarities and differences among living Arctic peoples, in the hope of identifying living traces of the earliest "original" Arctic people.

ESKIMO ORIGINS

The search for Eskimo origins began with Martin Frobisher and Europe's introduction to Frobisher's Inuit. Northern lands were indeed hostile to inexperienced Arctic navigators like Frobisher, and they were decidedly so for Sir John Franklin, who lost his life, his ships, and his crew exploring the Northwest Passage in Arctic Canada in the 1840s. Such events influenced how Euroamericans imagined Arctic lands—as hostile to human life—and the history of its peoples as remote from the centers of developing civilizations. Generations of scholars came to view the Arctic as a refuge, where Ice Age peoples with their cultures had migrated and then survived down to the present, in a kind of cultural and biological deep freeze.

Encouragement for this view came from the mid-nineteenth-century discovery of European Paleolithic sites containing harpoons for hunting sea mammals, throwing sticks for hurling spears, ivory figurines, pictographic art, and shaft-straighteners—all nearly identical to tools known from historic Eskimo cultures and their Thule-culture archaeological ancestors in Greenland, Canada, and Alaska. It seemed logical to archaeologists that the Eskimos, for whom these similarities were most striking, were the direct descendants of European Paleolithic reindeer hunters who had retreated north, following the melting ice and the northward movement of animals at the end of the Ice Age. The discovery of cave paintings depicting Ice Age hunters whose prey included reindeer and other Arctic animals only confirmed this view. The Eskimos, it was believed, had preserved the remnants of an ancient Ice Age culture even to the modern day, hunting sea mammals, caribou, musk-ox, polar bears, and other Arctic game. But not all Arctic peoples lived this way.

The peoples of the Russian Arctic in historical times were reindeer herders, not sea mammal hunters, and they practiced a northern variant of animal domestication. Even though their reindeer were not completely tame and could easily be lost if a herder was not attentive, reindeer herding provided a margin of safety for Eurasian Arctic peoples that was missing in the North American Arctic. The implications of this new economy were enormous. A careful herding family did not need to worry where their next meal would come from, and it could devote its energies to other activities, such as trading furs for European or Chinese goods, metalworking, and exchanges with far-flung tribes. In time the reindeer-herding culture expanded from central Eurasia west into Scandinavia and east to Bering Strait, transforming cultures in its path, exterminating wild reindeer (caribou), and imposing a near monoculture economic system throughout much of the Eurasian Arctic.

Interestingly, reindeer herding reached Bering Strait about 1,000 years ago but never entered Alaska. Some Eskimo peoples on the Siberian side adopted reindeer breeding, while others continued to live as sea mammal hunters. In this instance, Bering Strait was both a geographic and ethnic barrier, for none of the American Eskimos adopted reindeer breeding. The rich maritime economy of Bering Strait offered a hearty subsistence for Eskimo peoples who lived there, and when reindeer fur was needed for clothing it could be obtained from the Siberian Chukchi. The spread of reindeer herding peoples and the revolution of reindeer herding that spread through the Eurasian Arctic never entered the New World, and the Eskimo and northern Indian peoples there continued to hunt wild animals as they had for thousands of years. It is only in this sense that North American Arctic peoples can be said to have preserved an ancient hunting tradition and religious beliefs whose roots can indeed be traced to Ice Age times.

Today, archaeological methods have replaced ethnographic parallels in determining the history of Arctic peoples, including Eskimos. At the same time, archaeological interpretations of the evidence of extinct cultures are influenced by the description and analyses of ethnographic (both historical and modern) cultures around the world, as knowledge of known cultural systems help fill in the inevitable gaps in archaeological evidence. After nearly one hundred years, archaeologists are confident that the Bering Sea region was the birthplace of Eskimo culture. But beyond this, there is disagreement as to exactly where this culture first developed; eastern

Siberia, Kodiak Island, the Alaska Peninsula, and Western Alaska are all still in the running. Resolving this question will not be easy because post-glacial submergence, tidal waves, and earthquakes have destroyed much of the coastal zones inhabited by these early cultures, making archaeological investigation of many key areas impossible.

NORTH PACIFIC RIM PEOPLES

The distinction across the North Atlantic between the herding Eurasian and the hunting North American Arctic peoples stands in marked contrast to the cultural and economic similarities among the peoples living along both shores of the North Pacific Rim. The North Pacific Rim peoples, furthermore, provide a fascinating case study of culture contact and change through time. Ironically, it was along the Pacific Rim, where native peoples had been in contact for millennia before Europeans arrived, that the recent twentieth-century history of political antagonisms masked the very real and very long continuities of cultures. Early ethnographic collections made by nineteenth-century Russian exploring expeditions to Russian America (Alaska) ended up in museums in St. Petersburg, Russia, while eastern Siberian collections made by Franz Boas's Jesup Expedition of 1897–1902 ended up in New York, at the American Museum of Natural History. Fortunately, now there are few physical or political barriers to the exchange of information, peoples, and materials across the Bering Strait, and joint exhibition projects such as the Smithsonian's 1988 "Crossroads of Continents" could reassemble these collections from their places of origin.

The Smithsonian's "Crossroads" exhibition combined cultural materials from northeastern Siberia and northwestern North America into a single traveling exhibition seen by peoples on both sides of the Bering Strait. A smaller version of the "Crossroads" exhibit, with strong local education components and many miniature artifacts made originally as toys and models, toured villages throughout Alaska in 1993–95, and a Russian-language version is now traveling in the Russian Far East.

PEOPLING THE NEW WORLD

Archaeologists investigating the history of cultures around Bering Strait have found clear evidence of the movement of Asian peoples into northeastern Siberia and their subsequent migration into Alaska and the Americas. Dates from stratified cave sites along the Aldan River, a tributary of the Lena, in the Sakha Republic (formerly Yakutia) begin as early as 35,000 years ago. Comparable dates are known from sites in northern Japan. Confirmation of the northeastern movement of peoples and acquisition of Arctic adaptation is seen in the trend of archaeological dates upward toward 12,000 B.P. as one approaches Bering Strait. At about this time, settled riverside fishing villages also appear on the lower Amur River and in Kamchatka. In both cases data indicate seasonally settled villages, and sites on the Amur contain some of the earliest ceramics in the world—fired clay animal figurines and grit-tempered pottery have been recovered.

At about this time, around 12,000 years ago, the first well-dated stratified sites appear in Alaska on the Nenana River and in a number of other locations, both in the interior and on the coast. Almost instantaneously, sites of this age also appear at many locations in North and South America. This pattern indicates a very rapid southward movement of peoples from Alaska. Although pottery and pithouse villages have not been found in the earliest Alaskan sites, the presence of sites at both coastal and interior locations document adaptation to a wide range of environments.

The cultures of these earliest Siberian and Alaskan peoples were very similar. Although the early fluted (Clovis-like) points known from northwestern Alaska have not been found in Siberia, these early Siberian-American Paleo-Arctic peoples employed similar bifacial and microblade (core and blade) technologies and clearly shared a cultural tradition. Unlike the earliest Siberian ancestors, who followed a more nomadic hunting way of life, post-12,000 B.P. coastal peoples had already begun to turn their attention to the more abundant and stable resources of the sea.

By 10,000 years ago this maritime-focused economy was present along both the Siberian and American sides of the North Pacific from Japan to Alaska, and to British Columbia and Washington State, in a giant arc connecting the two continents. The northernmost section of this North Pacific culture area was occupied by the ancestors of present-day Yupik Eskimos and Aleuts in Western Alaska and of several Native nations in northeastern Siberia: Koryak, Itelmen, Chukchi, Nivkh, and Asiatic or Siberian Eskimos. Ancestral cultures leading to these ethnographic peoples have been documented throughout this region. Although details of this development are best known from North American sites, a comparable sequence is emerging as archaeological work expands in Siberia. Throughout the region, the trend in coastal regions was toward increasing sedentism and intensive exploitation of marine resources and reached its peak in the early historical period.

These North Pacific developments also appear to have stimulated adaptation of peoples to the icy coasts and Arctic interior regions north of Bering Strait. One prominent theory holds that early Eskimo-like cultures, originating as maritime-based cultures in Kodiak and the Aleutian Islands, spread north along the Alaskan coast as the land bridge was inundated after 11,000 years ago, and became adapted to Arctic regions. About 4,500 years ago the North Alaska hunting peoples received impulses from Siberian Neolithic cultures, which gave rise to the Alaskan Denbigh and Arctic Small Tool Tradition cultures. These groups, in turn, expanded eastward into the recently ice-freed Canadian Arctic, reaching Greenland and Labrador by 4,000 years ago, making this the last major area of the New World to be colonized permanently by humans.

As Igor Krupnik (1995) has noted, the historic Siberian Eskimo and Chukchi inhabitants of the Bering Strait region shared a number of cultural adaptations growing out of an economy based on hunting for sea mammals, either from boats or on ice, hunting for land mammals and birds, and fishing. They mastered the art of dog-sled driving and built sophisticated boats of skin and wood propelled by paddles and sails. When they settled on the coast they gathered in permanent villages, consisting of sod houses or dugouts in winter, skin or birch-bark tents and wooden plank houses in summer. Evidence of ancient origins for their elaborate rituals and community festivals, which included decorated fur and gutskin clothing, skin drums, wooden masks, and ivory carvings, has been found in the Old Bering Sea cultures of this region dating to as early as 2,000 years ago.

In Siberia, about 2,000 years ago, those peoples who did not move to the coast preserved their original nomadic lifestyle of hunting and fishing and developed a distinct cultural pattern focusing on the domesticated reindeer. "Mastering reindeer herding was the second most important economic revolution for Siberian Native people, after mastering the resources of the sea" (Krupnik, 1993:23). As should be clear by now, cultural similarities abound on either side of the Pacific Basin. Sites from both Siberia and Alaska contain early forms of microblade technology. Sites from later times show similarities in Neolithic microblades, ceramics, and architecture. Many of these similarities, such as whalebone-semisubterranean housing, can be traced eastward into Canada and Greenland. Others, such as the distinctive Old Bering Sea, Okvik, and Ipiutak art styles, remain rooted in the Bering Strait region. What is less clear is whether these similarities developed from deep cultural strata accumulated from the cultural residues of shared history before the peopling of the New World, or whether they are instead the result of more recent contact and exchange.

Detailed archaeological comparisons and dating have revealed that many of these similarities resulted from historical contacts. As noted above, we can trace the eastward spread of Paleolithic core and blade technology into Alaska from Siberia about 12,000 years ago. There appears to have been a similar dispersal of Siberian Neolithic blade industry into Western Alaska, Canada, and Greenland at 4500 B.P., and of Asian ceramics into Alaska about 2,000 years ago. But, are the advent of intensive maritime adaptation and the use of seasonal pithouse villages local adaptations or introduced phenomena? And what can be said of Old Bering Sea burial ritual and art? While many of these developments reflect local adaptations and trends, external impulses often had dramatic effects, as seen by dramatic Siberian shamanistic influences in Ipiutak burial ritual at Point Hope, Alaska, about A.D. 500.

GLOBAL ASPECTS OF CULTURE CONTACT AND EXCHANGE

Exploration of culture contact and exchange in Arctic regions provides a new and different perspective on the question of the "independent" history of the Americas. As new data begin to emerge from these relatively unknown northern lands (especially from Northeast Asia), evidence for a continuing history of Beringian exchange is mounting.

The circumpolar region can be seen as a natural pathway for the movement of peoples and ideas between Asia and the Americas. Before A.D. 1000–1500, it was the only conduit we can document through which Asian and American populations interacted. Whether such interaction was initiated by historical and cultural forces of evolution, technological development, population growth, or from the indirect influence of climatic change or animal movements, the circumpolar region with its Bering Sea zone has been the sole point of contact and transmission between the New and Old Worlds. In this sense northern regions have played a unique role as buffer and transmitter of transcontinental historical forces. Most of these seem to have flowed from the centers of more complex cultural development in Asia into the New World. Few, if any, traces of American cultures seem to have influenced Siberian or East Asian culture history.

THE LATITUDINAL/LONGITUDINAL PERSPECTIVE

The circumpolar distribution of clothing styles, blubber lamps, harpoons, skin boats, shamanism, bear ceremonialism, and mythology are striking reminders of common elements in the ethnographic cultures of northern peoples. A comparable suite of common features has been identified in archaeological cultures of this region: persistence of early core and blade industries; ground slate technology; wrench-like shaft straighteners; hunting art employing skeletal and joint-mark art, and others. Mechanisms of culture contact and exchange are visibly recognizable; migration and diffusion in the sparsely populated expanses of northern regions are well documented in historical literature, in ethnographic and linguistic continuities, and in archaeological evidence. The Eskimo peoples and cultures rapidly expanded into the Canadian Arctic, first about 4,000 years ago, and later with the whale-hunting Thule migration at A.D. 1000. Reindeer breeding and herding occurred throughout the Eurasian Arctic and boreal regions during the past 1,500 years. Cultural features—including art styles, iron technology, glass beads, and tobacco—moved rapidly from Siberia into North America. All of these exemplify the existence of latitudinal global conduits and channels for forces of culture contact and change.

Contrasting the circumpolar latitudinal homogeneity is the longitudinal, environmental, and cultural diversity that occurs in both Eurasia and North America on the north-south axis. Throughout history we have seen the increasing divergence in levels of cultural development and complexity between the tropical and temperate regions, on the one hand, and boreal and Arctic regions, on the other. State development processes and the formation of civilizations have been at work in southern Eurasia and Central America for thousands of years, always expanding northward, transforming northern peoples. In the North, environmental conditions and a "big-game hunting" tradition helped Paleolithic and Mesolithic hunting traditions and technology persist into the twentieth century.

One of the more remarkable features of this persistence is the recent discovery that dwarf mammoths existed in some regions of the Eurasian Arctic nearly 5,000 years longer than anywhere else in the world. Paleon-

tological remains of a miniature type of mammoth on Wrangel Island, 100 miles north of the Chukotka coast, demonstrate a Pleistocene "refugium" until 4,500 years ago, or even later. The discovery by Russians of archaeological sites at Chertov Ovrag (Devil's Gorge) on Wrangel dating to 4,000 years ago raises questions of possible human intervention in the ultimate demise of this great Ice Age mammal.

IMPACT OF THE MODERN WORLD

Several dramatic changes have taken place in the Arctic in recent years. Indigenous populations have expanded, but while growing rapidly, they are now a minority in their homelands in all but a few locations. Native subsistence economies have changed under the pressure of modernization, commercial exploitation, and governmental policies. A number of ethnic groups described by nineteenth-century anthropologists, including the Sadlermiut of Hudson Bay, the Eyak of southeast Alaska, and the Aliutor of Kamchatka, have become extinct. Of the eight North American Eskimo languages known historically, only three—Greenlandic, Inuktitut, and Yupik—will survive into the mid-twenty-first century. The cultural diversity and integrity of much of the region is equally threatened.

As the world approaches the end of the twentieth century and faces a new millennium, scholars and the public alike are concerned about the dramatic outcomes of the past century and the legacy it will leave to future generations. Environmental degradation, pollution, and loss of species and ecosystem integrity are issues of major concern. A similar set of concerns is expressed by both the general public and social scientists regarding human cultural diversity and the rights of indigenous people. Paternalistic governmental policies, industrialization, and the spread of consumerist values have damaged indigenous subsistence and languages and distorted their cultural continuity and ethnic diversity.

During this century thousands of Siberian, Alaskan, and Northwest Coast Natives abandoned their traditional lifestyles and joined the modern workforce in increasingly industrialized urban settings. Huge numbers of outsiders immigrated into their territories, bringing demographic, social, and political change. Entrepreneurism, business interests, and military policies have made major impacts on both human and natural environments. While many groups continue to live in their homelands, most have lost their native languages, adopted imported religious beliefs, and rely on modern technology.

Equally dramatic changes have taken place in Siberia. State-controlled hierarchies have dictated policy; floods of recruited and imprisoned outsiders have arrived; and some native groups have been deprived of traditional livelihoods, while others involved in state-owned reindeer herding, peltfarming, and fishing have been artificially subsidized. Official policies of "russification" and relocation have reduced the viability of native life and economy. State-controlled industrial development has had a devastating impact on land and resources over which native people have had little control.

Despite differences in political systems, in many respects the results of twentieth-century developments in Siberia and northwest North America have produced surprisingly similar results. In both areas native people have lost much of their ability to direct their own futures; languages have been weakened or lost; poverty has increased; subsistence economies have been weakened; and alcoholism and social disorders have become serious problems. In both areas cultural and language survival, native rights, education policy, and economic and political issues loom as major problems for the future.

CONCLUSION

After five centuries of a dominant "Atlantic" perspective on world history and politics, we are entering an era in which Pacific resources and relations are assuming an ever more important role in world affairs. Viewing the globe from a circumpolar perspective becomes ever more important, while understanding the lands, peoples, and cultures of the North Pacific Rim can provide immense benefits to northern peoples, and to public and scientific understanding of a little-known but increasingly important part of the world. As our understanding increases through scientific research and public dissemination, new perspectives on the Circumpolar Arctic in general, and the North Pacific Rim specifically, should help prepare younger generations to live in an increasingly global world. Arctic regions and peoples are part of that world. In fact, they may be the most "global" of all!

FURTHER READING

Chaussonnet, Valerie, ed. 1995. *Crossroads Alaska: Native Cultures of Alaska and Siberia*. Arctic Studies Center, National Museum of Natural History, Smithsonian Institution.

Fitzhugh, William W., and Valerie Chaussonnet, eds. 1994. *Anthropology of the North Pacific Rim*. Smithsonian Institution Press.

Fitzhugh, William W., and Aron Crowell, eds. 1988. *Crossroads of Continents: Cultures of Siberia and Alaska*. Smithsonian Institution Press.

Fitzhugh, William W., and Susan A. Kaplan. 1982. *Inua: Spirit World of the Bering Sea Eskimo*. Smithsonian Institution Press.

Krupnik, Igor. I. 1993. *Arctic Adaptations: Native Whalers and Reindeer Herders of Northern Eurasia*. University Press of New England.

Krupnik, Igor I. 1995. "Native Peoples of the Russian Far East." In Valerie Chaussonnet, ed., *Crossroads Alaska: Native Cultures of Alaska and Siberia*. Arctic Studies Center, National Museum of Natural History, Smithsonian Institution.

18 THE ARCHAEOLOGY OF AFRICAN AMERICAN LIFE

Theresa A. Singleton

Excavations of slave cabins in the late 1960s marked the beginning of a new and important field known as African American archaeology. African American archaeology studies the daily lives of past African American communities through the analysis of the tangible material remains recovered from the places where members of these communities once lived and worked. From the careful study of broken pottery, mortar, food bone, tools, buttons, beads, and other objects, archaeologists are able to piece together information on the ways African Americans built their houses, prepared their food, and crafted household equipment and personal possessions.

Archaeologists engaged in this research are ultimately seeking answers to questions such as: How was an African heritage transplanted, replaced, or reinterpreted in America? In what ways are the recovered artifacts from African American sites the reflection of cultural patterns or of social conditions—poverty and restricted access to material goods? What are the differences in the material lives of slaves, free blacks, and tenant farmers and of African Americans living in urban versus rural communities? How did African Americans survive the rigors of everyday life?

Archaeologists first began to study African Americans as part of a growing scholarly interest emphasizing the history of people who created or left behind few written documents. Enslaved African Americans were generally denied the opportunity to learn reading and writing skills. Even after emancipation, many former slaves, lacking other alternatives, were forced to return to plantations as wage laborers and land renters, where they remained poor and illiterate. Thus most of the written records used to examine the 500-year history of African Americans are the products of European Americans whose understanding of African American culture was often flawed. In addition, these records are one-sided in that they contain only information of interest to the author. For example, slaveowners and plantation managers generally recorded information on slave health, his or her capacity to perform work, and behavior considered deviant. These documents rarely contain descriptions of objects slaves made and used or of other cultural expressions.

The archaeological record is also biased. The archaeologist can only interpret abandoned, discarded, or lost objects preserved in buried deposits. This leaves out any object that may have been kept through the years and handed down from generation to generation or any object made of materials that do not preserve well underground. Moreover, artifacts provide the basis for inferences about particular aspects of behavior, not direct evidence of behavior. Therefore, the interpretation of the material record requires archaeologists to incorporate historical and ethnographic descriptions of behavior derived from written sources and oral tradition.

THE SEARCH FOR AN AFRICAN HERITAGE: CERAMICS, MUD HOUSES, AND RITUAL ITEMS

In the archaeological study of African American sites, archaeologists are particularly interested in artifacts suggestive of either an African heritage or of newly created African American traditions. Although the evidence thus far uncovered is fragmentary, and interpretations are tentative, these finds supply empirical data for the widely held view that enslaved Africans and their descendants nurtured and sustained cultural traditions in spite of the oppressive, dehumanizing conditions of slavery. Some of the most convincing evidence that supports the persistence of African heritage includes slave-made ceramics recovered from plantations in South Carolina and Virginia; the building of African-style mud-wall houses on eighteenth-century plantations in South Carolina; and ritual paraphernalia of a traditional healer recovered from a cabin in Texas occupied during and after slavery.

The most frequently recovered artifacts produced by African Americans are ceramics used for preparing, serving, and storing food. So far, ceramics produced by African Americans have been recovered from numerous

sites in South Carolina, Virginia, and several islands in the Caribbean. In the southern United States, these ceramics called "colonoware" are low-fired, unglazed earthenware that resemble traditional pottery produced by Native Americans. Until the past decade, archaeologists thought that only Native Americans had produced colonoware, and it still seems likely that Indians created certain European-styled vessels such as shallow plates and bowls with ring feet that English settlers would have valued. But now most scholars agree that African slaves produced a special variety of this hand-built pottery, particularly the rounded forms, because much of it has been found at sites that date long after the demise of local Indians.

In South Carolina, the first real clue that African Americans made their own pottery came when fragments turned up that appeared to have been fired on the premises of Drayton Hall, a plantation located west of Charleston, South Carolina. Colonoware often makes up 80 to 90 percent of the ceramics found at sites occupied by slaves in the 1700s. Further research by Leland Ferguson, a historical archaeologist at the University of South Carolina, has shown that some of the South Carolina forms resemble pottery still made in parts of West Africa today. More recently, he has identified markings on some pottery fragments that are similar to the cosmograms used in the traditional rituals of peoples in the Congo-Angolan region of Africa. Cosmograms symbolize the way a society perceives the universe. The markings consist of a cross enclosed in a circle, which represents the daily course of the sun and the continuity of life: birth, death, and rebirth.

Why is evidence of pottery making among enslaved African Americans important? The use of this pottery suggests that enslaved African Americans prepared food to suit their own taste, perhaps incorporating aspects of traditional African cuisines. In addition, slaves also used these ceramics to prepare food for their masters, as colonoware accounts for a significant portion—sometimes more than half—of the ceramics used in planter households. This suggests that culinary techniques used by slaves influenced local southern white cuisine as well.

Excavations at the sites of Curriboo and Yaughan, two former indigo plantations in Berkeley County, South Carolina, revealed what may have been rectangular African-style houses designed and built by slaves. These slave quarters consisted of mud walls, presumably covered with thatched palmetto leaves, similar to thatched roof houses in many parts of Africa. Although no standing walls exist, archaeologists have found wall trenches containing a mortar-like clay. The presence of numerous pits, apparently used to extract clay, found throughout the sites, further suggests the use of clay as the primary construction material.

Since this discovery, a careful examination of written records has revealed several scattered references to slave-built, mud-walled structures. Indeed, previously unnoticed written descriptions seem to suggest that these African-style houses may have been commonplace. W. E. B. DuBois offered a description of palmetto-leaf construction in his 1908 survey of African and African American houses: "The dwellings of slaves were palmetto huts built by themselves of stakes and poles, with the palmetto leaf. The door, when they had any, was generally of the same materials, sometimes boards found on the beach. They had no floors, no separate apartments."

The mud houses at Curriboo and Yaughan plantation were built and occupied between 1740 and 1790. They were abandoned and replaced with European American style framed dwellings in the early 1800s. This change in housing styles coincided with a period when many European Americans came to view anything African as backward and inferior, and in the case of housing, as unhealthy. As a result, many slaveholders began to impose their standards of appropriate housing upon slaves.

At the Jordan Plantation, approximately 60 miles south of the modern city of Houston, Texas, archaeologist Kenneth Brown uncovered an assemblage of artifacts apparently used in healing and divination rituals. The Jordan plantation operated as a slave-worked plantation from 1848 until emancipation, and continued with wage laborers, many of whom were former slaves of the plantation, until 1890. Nine cabins were excavated and the materials from several individual cabins revealed evidence of the specialized activities of a carpenter, seamstress, cattle herder (cowboy), and a shaman/healer. The materials from the shaman's cabin consisted of the bases from cast iron kettles, pieces of utilized chalk, fragments of a small scale, bird skulls, an animal's paw, medicine bottles, ocean shells, doll parts, spoons, nails, knives, and chert scrapers. Many of these objects could have functioned in other activities and most likely did at various points in their lives. But when the artifacts are taken together, they suggest some form of ritual use. Support for this thesis comes from abundant ethnographic studies conducted in the Caribbean and parts of Africa that describe the use of wooden or metal trays, white chalk or powder, metal staffs, bird symbolism, and other objects used in healing rituals.

The assemblage of artifacts from the Jordan Plantation presents an excellent example of African Americans using mass-produced and reworked objects for a special African American meaning. Another example of the special use of manufactured objects is the occurrence of colored glass beads, particularly blue beads, that are found on slave sites throughout the south from Virginia to Texas. William Adams, an archaeologist at Oregon State University, recently suggested that blue beads may be related to a widespread belief in the Moslem world, including parts of Africa, that a single blue bead worn or shown on clothing protected the wearer against the Evil Eye. Undoubtedly, other artifacts uncovered from African American sites have been ignored by archaeologists who have been unable to decipher the special function certain objects occupied in African American culture.

ARCHAEOLOGICAL EVIDENCE OF FREE AND FREED AFRICAN AMERICAN COMMUNITIES

Slave sites, the primary focus of African American archaeology, sometimes contain deposits that date after emancipation. Plantation sites containing deposits dating from before and after emancipation often reflect continuity from slave to free labor, as was the case at the Jordan Plantation. However, a wide variety of African American sites have been studied; in fact, archaeological investigations at African American sites have been undertaken in at least 30 states, Canada, and several Caribbean islands. These investigations range from the home sites of well-known, often prominent individuals such as Benjamin Banneker, Frederick Douglass, and W. E. B. DuBois, to entire towns such as Allensworth, California, and Buxton,

Iowa. Archaeologists have also examined African American neighborhoods in several cities and isolated rural settlements. For many of these sites, archaeology is the only source of information that describes the everyday lives of people who once lived at these locations.

Studies of free and freed African American communities have addressed questions similar to those of slave sites: What were the living conditions and basic material culture of these communities? What aspects of the archaeological record related to ethnic behavior and what aspects to economic and social conditions? Unlike the growing evidence at slave sites for ethnic behavior in ceramic production and use, architecture, and ritual objects, archaeological evidence of ethnicity at nonslave sites varies from site to site and is much more subtle. In some cases, for example at Benjamin Banneker's home site, no evidence of Banneker's ethnicity is revealed from the archaeological record. The assemblage from his eighteenth-century farmstead in rural Maryland was found to be identical to those recovered from sites of European American settlers of similar social and economic status living at the same time as Banneker. This degree of assimilation may characterize many other free African Americans living during the time of slavery who owned property and enjoyed a material life beyond bare necessities. However, bound by race, free blacks occupied a tenuous position, where they were at the constant mercy of whites, regardless of their material wealth.

A comparison of poor African Americans and poor European Americans suggests a similar pattern. Archaeology at Millwood, a plantation worked by tenant farmers and wage laborers from 1865 to 1925, revealed that the quality of material life was not based upon ethnicity or race but upon one's position in the plantation hierarchy. Archaeologist Charles Orser identified five classes of occupants living on the plantation (landlord, millwright, tenant, servant, and wage laborer), and observed that blacks and whites of the same class experienced similar material conditions.

Archaeological studies of African American neighborhoods in Alexandria, Virginia, and Washington, D.C. suggest that ethnic behavior is most evident in food preferences. In both studies, the archaeological records of the African Americans were compared with those of European Americans of similar economic status. Although subtle differences were evident in purchased ceramics and other artifacts, the most striking difference was found in foodways (encompassing everything from food procurement and preparation to consumption habits), an aspect of culture that frequently indicates ethnic preferences. The African Americans at both sites consumed much more pork than European Americans and displayed a particular preference for pigs' feet. Floral and faunal analyses indicated that an African American community in Washington also consumed collard greens and opossum.

Archaeology can also be used to examine material conditions associated with special circumstances experienced by African Americans. For example, preliminary work I conducted on sites associated with recently emancipated slaves suggest that former slaves living along the Georgia coast were, in some cases, materially "worse off" in the first years of freedom than they were as slaves. Structural remains from the cabins of freed men and women indicated that the chimney was constructed of reused brick, haphazardly built on a bed of oyster shell. Tools were used until they were completely worn, and occupants of the site subsisted almost entirely upon wild game: turtle, fish, and small mammals. A recent excavation of another refugee camp of former slaves should provide additional information of the immediate material effects of emancipation.

THE DIET AND HEALTH OF SLAVES AND FREE BLACKS

Archaeological studies of nutrition are particularly important to discussions of slave nutrition, a realm of slave life that has been greatly debated by students of slavery. One school of thought suggests that slave diet was nutritious and that caloric intake often exceeded modern recommended levels of chief nutrients. The more accepted view is that slave diet was inadequate, and malnutrition was a frequent problem reflected in high child mortality and in the prevalence of diseases resulting from nutritional deficiencies. The analysis of food remains can contribute to this discussion by documenting the kinds of foods slaves consumed. Studies conducted by zooarchaeologists (archaeologists who analyze food bone) indicate that slaves supplemented their mundane plantation rations of cornmeal and fatback with small mammals they hunted and fish they collected in nets. Several studies of faunal remains collected from sites in the southeastern United States suggest that food-collection activities of slaves accounted for 35 to 40 percent of the meat in the slave diet.

Analyses of human remains provide a wide range of information on nutrition, pathological conditions, and occupational stresses. One of the largest skeletal samples of African Americans was unearthed from an abandoned cemetery of Philadelphia's First African Baptist Church (FABC), which served as a burial ground for free African Americans between 1823 and 1843. More than 140 adult and child skeletons were analyzed and reburied. Analyses revealed that the quality of life and the health status of free black Philadelphians and various slave populations were similar. These conditions were particularly evident in the analysis of dental enamel undertaken by Michael Blakey, a physical anthropologist at Howard University. Blakey introduced a new method that gives a record of fetal and childhood health by measuring defects in the dental enamel of adult skeletons. Results show that their lives were particularly harsh, especially as fetuses (linked to maternal health) and as children. This finding came as a surprise to Blakey who thought that free African American children would have had somewhat better health than did slave children.

Occupational stress in the FABC population was particularly evident among females, many of whom were laundresses. The stress of laundering is evident in their well-developed triceps and pectoral muscles and fingers. One individual displayed evidence of cervical breakdown, perhaps from carrying the laundry as a head load, and of bending stress on lower vertebrae. Tuberculosis, iron deficiency anemia, arthritis, and cholera are among the diseases the cemetery population suffered.

The healing paraphernalia uncovered from the Jordan Plantation in Texas suggest the kinds of folk medicine sought by African Americans, but excavations of slave cabins and plantation infirmaries give indications of the kinds of medications slaveowners administered to the slaves. Excavations of slave cabins along the Georgia coast indicate that slaves regularly consumed patent medicines with high alcoholic content and brewed alcoholic beverages. While some of this consumption was perhaps recreational in nature, the plantation records of a slave site I excavated indicated that patent medicines and homemade rum regularly were dispensed to the slaves as a preventative for rheumatic diseases. Future excavations of plantation infirmaries will possibly turn up medical instruments and other objects used to treat slaves.

From this brief overview of African American archaeology, it should be apparent that this research presents new and provocative information on the lives of African Americans. Critics of historical archaeology often claim that all this information is in the written record; I challenge them to find it.

UPDATE

This research area continues to grow, and is increasingly referred to as either African American archaeology or the Archaeology of the African diaspora in the Americas. In recent years, there have been numerous investigations, new research directions and findings, and several book-length publications.

Perhaps the most significant development is a shift in emphasis from identifying African elements and describing material possessions, food habits, or health status to undertaking more in-depth social analysis. For example, archaeologists are attempting to understand how artifacts shed light on the ways in which African Americans actively resisted aspects of white American culture and structured their own cultural identity. Most of these studies examine acts of slave resistance that had to be concealed for fear of punishment from slaveholders. Cultural anthropologist John Scott refers to hidden or covert acts of resistance as *hidden transcripts*, the responses of subordinates to the power of the dominant.

A recurrent archaeological transcript of slave resistance is suggested in the underground storage pits found within the interior living spaces of many slave quarters. These storage pits were apparently used to store food as well as to conceal valuables, possibly pilfered goods. In several storage pits, farm tools have been recovered that may have been deliberately buried in the pits as a subtle way to slow down work on the plantation. Written sources indicate that slaveholders tried to prevent enslaved people from digging pits by raising dwellings on piers or by backfilling those that came to their attention, but the enslaved continued to dig pits.

Other hidden transcripts of cultural resistance may be revealed from the growing archaeological evidence of African American folk beliefs and practices. A variety of objects, including cowrie shells, beads, ornaments, pierced coins, polished stones, reworked glass, and ceramic objects recovered from numerous sites, have prompted several archaeologists to suggest that these objects reflect conjuring, divining (predicting the future), and healing practices. Despite the eventual adoption of Christianity, enslaved African Americans did maintain some African religious beliefs, but these often were concealed for fear of punishment from slaveholders. The need to conceal these activities may explain why a presumed cache of divining materials recovered from the site of the Carroll House in Annapolis, Maryland, was apparently intentionally hidden. As oral and written sources from former slaves reveal, these practices provided a source of strength and empowerment for many African Americans.

The study of African American resistance is also beginning to include the settlements of maroons—black freedom fighters who successfully escaped enslavement and formed their own autonomous communities. Archaeological studies of maroons have been conducted so far in Brazil, Cuba, the Dominican Republic, Jamaica, and Suriname. Most of these investigations are still in the preliminary stages of locating and identifying these sites, which were almost always in remote areas such as mountainous terrains or dense tropical forests. To be viable, maroon communities had be located in places that were inaccessible to the penetration of militias or patrols who could attack and reenslave them. Archaeological research on maroon communities is expected to provide clues to how maroons overcame these hostile environments and established social, political, and economic systems—remnants of which have survived to the present day.

In addition to the new analytical frameworks and research directions, a debate is currently being waged regarding the social responsibilities of archaeologists engaged in this research to descendant African American communities. Some archaeologists believe African Americans can inform and enrich this research in ways that Euro-American practitioners of archaeology have not; therefore, African American input should be incorporated in every phase of research—from the formulation of research questions to the development of public programs. Other archaeologists believe that African Americans constitute one of many audiences for this research, and that archaeologists should avoid getting entangled in the political agendas of the communities. Further, they feel that only archaeologists can generate questions and interpret findings without bias.

This debate stems from larger issues currently being discussed in many scholarly disciplines concerning who owns the past, or how should people who are the subject of research be represented by those studying them? While the solution to these questions is unclear, more and more archaeologists are beginning to recognize that they cannot continue to ignore the desires and needs of descendant communities. One can only hope that African American archaeology will benefit from this discussion, and that future studies will encourage more African American participation than is the case at present.

FURTHER READING

Agorsah, Kofi E., ed. 1994. *Maroon Heritage: Archaeological, Ethnographic and Historical Perspectives*. University of West Indies Press.

Armstrong, Douglas V. 1990. *The Old Village and the Great House: An Archaeological and Historical Examination of Drax Hall Plantation, St. Ann's Bay, Jamaica*. University of Illinois Press.

Deetz, James. 1993. *Flowerdew Hundred: The Archaeology of a Virginia Plantation, 1619–1864*. University Press of Virginia.

Ferguson, Leland. 1992. *Uncommon Ground: Archaeology and Early African America, 1650–1800.* Smithsonian Institution Press.

Orser, Charles E., ed. 1990. Historical Archaeology on Southern Plantations and Farms. *Historical Archaeology* 24(4).

Singleton, Theresa A. 1995. "The Archaeology of Slavery in North America." *Annual Review of Anthropology* 24:119–40.

Singleton, Theresa A., and Mark D. Bograd. 1995. "The Archaeology of the African Diaspora in the Americas." *Guides to the Archaeological Literature of the Immigrant Experience in America,* no. 2, Society for Historical Archaeology, Tucson, Ariz.

Yentsch, Anne E. 1994. *A Chesapeake Family and Their Slaves: A Study in Historical Archaeology.* Cambridge University Press.

OUR MANY CULTURES

Why Do We Live in Such Diverse Cultures?
How Do Anthropologists Study Other Cultures?
How Have Cultures and Cultural Anthropology
Changed over Time?
How Has Culture Helped Humanity Survive?

19 IDENTITY TRANSFORMATION IN COLONIAL NORTHERN MEXICO

William L. Merrill

Con gran facilidad mudarán a semejanza de los mulatos y mestizos su traje, dejando crecer el cabello, trocando la tilma por un capote; pues con esta transformación se llaman gente de razon, y se eximen de pagar tributo.

—A Jesuit Priest, 1754

n 1754 Spanish officials and Catholic missionaries in the province of Sinaloa, located in northwestern Mexico, debated the wisdom of requiring local Indians to pay tribute to the king of Spain while exempting certain non-Indian settlers from such payments. A Jesuit missionary, whose opinion but not his name is preserved in the historical record, argued against the measure, indicating that the Indians would simply change their identity: "With great ease they will come to resemble mulattos and mestizos in their dress, letting their hair grow and exchanging their capes for cloaks, and with this transformation they call themselves people of reason and are exempted from paying tribute."

HISTORICAL BACKGROUND

During the century following the Spanish conquest of the Aztec capital of Tenochtitlan in 1521, Spanish settlers spread from central Mexico as far north as what is now the southwestern United States. Drawn especially by major strikes of silver and gold in the modern state of Chihuahua, miners were joined by missionaries, ranchers, farmers, and merchants in an effort to establish firm Spanish control over the northern frontier.

At the time of European contact, Chihuahua was populated by a num-

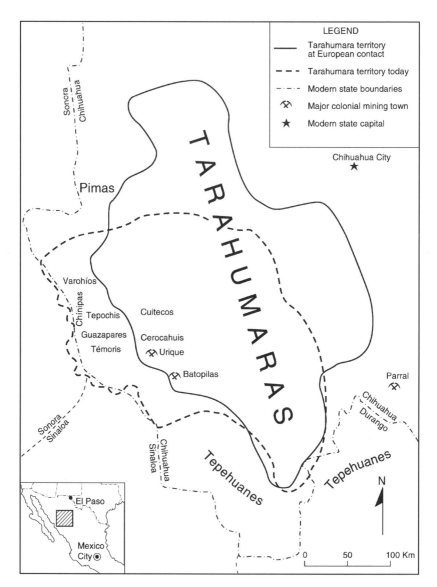

TARAHUMARA TERRITORIES

ber of distinct Indian groups speaking mutually unintelligible languages. Nomadic, hunting-gathering bands lived in eastern and northern Chihuahua, while in central and western Chihuahua sedentary societies supplemented their agriculture with extensive collecting of wild resources. All these societies were egalitarian and locally autonomous. At the time of contact, there were no native conquest states in this region (such as the Aztec and Inca farther south) and, while local groups probably formed alliances during times of conflict, no political organization existed that encompassed more than a few small bands or contiguous rancherías.

Franciscan and Jesuit missionaries first contacted the Indians of Chihuahua in the second half of the sixteenth century, but they did not begin to create a network of permanent missions until the early decades of the seventeenth century. Indian revolts throughout the second half of the seventeenth century disrupted their efforts, but by the early eighteenth century this mission system covered most of central and western Chihuahua. In 1767 King Charles III of Spain expelled the Jesuits from all of his New World empire, and Franciscan missionaries and diocesan priests divided the responsibility for their missions in northern Mexico.

CONCEPT OF IDENTITY

The expansion of the Spanish colonial system and particularly the Catholic mission system in the region brought about important changes in local Indian identity. Identity is one of the few concepts to have made the transition from the social sciences to popular culture with its technical definitions largely intact. Academic and popular views of the concept of identity agree that identity is, in essence, who I think I am and who others think I am, or, on a more sociological level, who we think we are and who others think we are. These views also concur that identity is the product of the interplay between these insider and outsider perspectives, and that it is subject to change as the circumstances change within which an individual or group operates.

Although the concept of identity is relatively uncomplicated—we might even say self-evident—this fact does not diminish its importance as a central feature of human existence. Moreover, although we may have a clear idea of what identity is, we still have much to learn about how identities are created, maintained, and transformed.

Colonial contexts offer an excellent opportunity to examine these processes. The expansion of colonialism usually involves the formation of new kinds of social, economic, and political relations among the members of societies and between societies that have had limited previous contact with one another. In such settings, existing schemes of identity classification must be revised and the significance and implications of these classifications defined. Seldom do the colonized passively accept the classifications that their colonizers intend to impose on them, for important political and economic and psychological interests are at stake. More frequently, identities and the relations of inequality typically assigned to them are openly contested.

Here I explore processes of identity formation, maintenance, and transformation during the colonial and immediate postcolonial periods in the Tarahumara region of central and western Chihuahua. At the time of European contact, the Tarahumara, who today call themselves "Ralámuli," farmed, hunted, and gathered in a territory that covered about 50,000 square kilometers in central and western Chihuahua (see map). During the past 400 years, they have been displaced from much of their original territory and are found today in the foothills, mountains, and canyons of western Chihuahua. They speak a language that is related to the languages spoken by their neighbors in northern Mexico—the Guarijío, Tepehuan, Pima, Yaqui, and Mayo—as well as more distant Indian societies such as the Comanche, Hopi, and Aztec, all of which belong to the Uto-Aztecan language family.

ETHNIC CLASSIFICATIONS

When the Spanish arrived in northern Mexico, they brought with them a scheme of ethnic classification derived ultimately from Iberian and European concepts of ethnicity and modified during the previous century on the basis of their experience in other parts of the New World. The basic distinction in this scheme was that between "Spaniards" and "Indians." The category of "Spaniard," itself a subcategory of "European," was divided into two principal subcategories, the first encompassing Spaniards born in Spain (*peninsulares*) and the second Spaniards born in the New World (*criollos*). The category of "Indians" also was subdivided. Distinct Indian groups were labeled according to tribal identities, which were cross-cut by several general categories. For example, Indians were classified as being "civilized" or "barbaric"—a distinction that reflected the prejudices not only of Europeans but also of central Mexican Indians—depending primarily on the complexity of their societies. Those Indians who converted to Christianity were called "Christians" (*cristianos*), "baptized people" (*bautizados*), or "converts" (*conversos*), and were distinguished from those who did not, who usually were referred to as "gentiles."

Christian Indians were further distinguished according to their inclination to accept the conditions of colonial existence that their colonizers attempted to impose upon them. There were "good Christians," who tended to accept these conditions, and "bad Christians," who did not. Those "bad Christians" who abandoned their mission pueblos and the Spanish economic centers to live in areas beyond Spanish control were in addition characterized as "apostates," "fugitives," or "cimarrones." The term "cimarrones" originally meant "runaways" and is the source of the name "Seminoles," which labeled Indians and African slaves who sought refuge from European colonialism in remote areas of Florida.

Apostate and fugitive Indians often moved into established communities of gentile Indians. In fact, people in Chihuahua today use the terms "gentiles" and "cimarrones" interchangeably to designate the descen-

dants of those Indians who remained outside the colonial system. However, not all gentiles rejected baptism and incorporation into the mission pueblos. Many remained outside the mission system simply because the opportunity to join had not presented itself or because they did not want to abandon their rancherías, which frequently were located long distances from the mission pueblos. As the mission system expanded into their areas, they often accepted baptism. Thus, over the course of the colonial period, the number of Indians identified as "gentiles" tended to decrease and to include primarily those Indians who intentionally rejected an affiliation with the Catholic mission system.

Joining the categories of "Spaniards" and "Indians" in the Spanish ethnic classification was a third division composed of a complicated set of categories that labeled individuals of mixed European, Indian, and African genetic heritage. These categories, theoretically infinite in number, were collapsed under the general term of "castes" (*castas*). The people so classified also were categorized collectively as *gente de razón*, a term that literally means "people of reason" but was originally used to designate non-Spaniards and especially people of mixed genetic heritage who were able to speak the Spanish language. Today non-Indians in Chihuahua sometimes refer to all local non-Indians as *gente de razón* regardless of their genetic heritage. However, colonial documents reveal that many Spaniards carefully distinguished themselves from the ethnically mixed *gente de razón*, whom they tended to consider of inferior status.

The Indians of Chihuahua maintained their own schemes of ethnic classification, but it is impossible to determine with any confidence what these schemes might have been because all of our information is filtered through documents produced by Europeans. From the evidence that is available, it appears that the Indians emphasized language as the principal marker of ethnicity, further distinguishing among speakers of the same language on the basis of locality. There was some blurring of identity along the borders of different language groups, where speakers of distinct languages intermarried, lived in the same or adjacent rancherías, and occasionally shared political leaders. Yet, even in such border areas where bilingualism was the rule, a person's first or preferred language appears to have been the key element in determining his or her ethnic identity.

The Spanish and Indian schemes of ethnic classification probably differed primarily in the degree to which the categories they included were ranked. In the Spanish scheme, Spaniards and other Europeans were located at the top, *castas* in the middle, and Indians at the bottom. In specific areas, however, Indians and in particular "good Christian Indians" were considered by Europeans to be morally if not socially superior to certain people of mixed heritage whose libertine ways were felt to jeopardize the progress of "civilization" on the frontier.

Given the egalitarianism of the Indian societies in northern Mexico, it is unlikely that their schemes of ethnic classification were as hierarchical as that of the Spaniards, although they may have thought of themselves as superior to the Spaniards. Today the Tarahumara Indians classify all non-Indians as "whiskered ones" (*chabochi*) and say that they are the children of the Devil, while considering themselves and all other Indians to be equals and the children of God.

FEWER INDIAN IDENTITIES

One of the most notable features of the history of identity formation in colonial northern Mexico is the decline in the number of distinct Indian groups noted in the documentary record between the seventeenth and eighteenth centuries. In some cases, especially among nomadic Indian societies in eastern Chihuahua, entire groups disappeared because the majority of their members died in epidemics or conflicts with the Spanish, the survivors joining other Indian groups or assimilating into the emerging mestizo population. Epidemics and military conflicts also had an important impact on the more sedentary Indian populations in central and western Chihuahua. In these areas, however, the reduction in the number of distinct Indian identities appears to have been due primarily to the emergence of more inclusive categories of ethnicity and a better understanding of the linguistic and cultural relationships among the Indians on the part of missionaries and colonial officials.

At the time of European contact, the greatest ethnic diversity in the region was reported from the mountains and rugged canyon country of western Chihuahua. The first missionaries to visit and work in this area identified these Indians as comprising a number of distinct "nations" (*naciones*): Chínipas, Varohíos, Guazapares, Témoris, Tepochis, Cuitecos, Cerocahuis, and so on. However, their perspectives on local ethnic diversity was strongly affected by their previous experience in the Sinaloan missions to the south, where the Indians belonged to a number of politically autonomous groups and spoke many distinct languages. When they arrived in western Chihuahua, these missionaries failed to realize that the various politically autonomous groups that they encountered probably were subdivisions of but two ethnic groups: the Varohío (known today as

Guarijío) and the Guazapar, who probably spoke a dialect of Tarahumara rather than a distinct language.

In 1632 the Varohíos and Guazapares expelled the missionaries and other outsiders from their territories. It was not until the late seventeenth century that the Spanish had an opportunity to acquire a more profound understanding of the cultural and linguistic affiliations of these groups. From that point on, the missionaries began using fewer terms to distinguish among the Indians in the region.

It is also likely that the influx of Tarahumaras and Indians from other areas into western Chihuahua resulted in some cultural and linguistic homogenization across the region. Large numbers of Tarahumaras began migrating into this area during the major revolts in the mid and late seventeenth century, and the immigrants probably included both rebels fleeing from the Spanish military and other Tarahumaras who sought to avoid the violence altogether.

Where the number of Tarahumara immigrants was small, they were absorbed by the local communities, eventually substituting local Indian identities for their own. A similar loss of identity may also have occurred where the number of Tarahumara immigrants was more substantial, but the outcome for ethnic identity was not always the same. The large numbers of Tarahumara immigrants who entered the Varohío area of western Chihuahua apparently were assimilated into the Varohío communities: the Varohíos continue to live today as a distinct ethnic group in roughly the same area as they did in the seventeenth century. In contrast, the Tarahumaras who migrated to the neighboring Guazapares region did not lose their identity but instead, by the eighteenth century, the Guazapares became known as Tarahumaras and apparently identified themselves as such.

If comparable numbers of Tarahumaras migrated into the Guazapar and Varohío areas, how can we explain the fact that the Varohíos retained their distinct identity while the Guazapares lost theirs? I believe that the key lies in differences in the degree to which the languages spoken by the Varohíos and Guazapares were similar to the Tarahumara language spoken by immigrants into their communities. Although closely related to Tarahumara, Varohío is nonetheless a distinct language. The Guazapar language, on the other hand, probably was a mutually intelligible variant of Tarahumara. Assuming an identity as "Tarahumaras" thus would have been simpler for the Guazapares than for the Varohíos. Indeed, given the linguistic and cultural similarities between the Guazapares and the Tarahumaras, it is possible that the Guazapares identified themselves as Tarahumaras before the arrival of the Spanish, who might have concluded incorrectly that "Guazapares" labeled a separate ethnic group rather than a subdivision of the Tarahumaras.

In the eighteenth and nineteenth centuries the Spanish expanded the semantic scope of the term "Tarahumara" to label both Tarahumaras and other Indians who closely resembled them. They did this even in the case of Indians who did not identify themselves as Tarahumaras. This reformulation of the category "Tarahumaras" by the Spanish may have paralleled and even contributed to the adoption of the term as a more encompassing ethnic label by the Indians in the region. During the colonial period, Indian groups from widely separated areas came into contact with one another in Spanish mines, haciendas, and other population centers. It is reasonable to assume that this increased interaction, combined with the growing presence of non-Indians with whom to contrast themselves, encouraged the emergence of a sense of common identity among the Indians, an identity that came to be labeled as "Tarahumara."

Today the Tarahumaras consider the term "Tarahumara" to be a Spanish word, and they refer to themselves as "Ralámuli." The term "Ralámuli" has meanings on four increasingly specific levels of significance. At the most general level, it designates "human beings" in contrast to "nonhumans." At the second level, it labels "Indians" in contrast to "non-Indians." At the third level, it refers only to Ralámuli Indians in contrast to the members of other Indian groups. Finally, at the most specific level, it designates Ralámuli men in contrast to Ralámuli women. A recognition of these different senses clearly indicates that the term "Ralámuli," semantically one of the most complex words in the Ralámuli language today, was adjusted, if not created, to accommodate the distinction between Indians and non-Indians that impinged itself upon the Ralámuli and other Indian people in the colonial period.

The word "Ralámuli" first appears in the historical literature in 1826 in a sermon prepared in the Tarahumara language by the Franciscan missionary Miguel Tellechea. Given its late appearance, I am inclined to conclude that the Tarahumaras adopted the term during the course of the colonial period to label the more inclusive ethnic identity that was being forged out of the multiple and often very localized identities of the precontact period. Because the term "Tarahumar" was used by the Spanish from the time of their arrival in Chihuahua, the Tarahumaras later on in the colonial period might have identified it as a Spanish rather than native word, as they do today. If so, they may have rejected it as an inappropriate label with which to distinguish themselves from non-Indians.

THE SPATIALIZATION OF IDENTITY

The Tarahumaras responded to the Spanish colonial system in a variety of ways, ranging from enthusiastic acceptance to near total rejection. Through time these differences in attitude became increasingly associated with communities located in different areas rather than being replicated within each Tarahumara community.

By 1767, when the Jesuits were expelled, the Tarahumaras who rejected most aspects of the Spanish colonial system lived in the remoter reaches of western and southern Tarahumara country, far from major Spanish settlements and economic centers. There they were little affected by labor drafts, Spanish encroachment on their lands, and the programs of directed culture change administered by the Catholic missionaries.

These isolated communities of Tarahumaras contrast with those located in and around the missions and Spanish economic centers of east central Chihuahua and northern Durango. Here the Indians participated extensively in the regional colonial economy and were described by the missionaries and Spanish colonial officials as having accepted much of Spanish colonial society and culture. Between these two groups were the Tarahumaras who lived within the mission system but some distance from major Spanish economic centers. These Indians created a synthetic culture that combined both indigenous and introduced ideas and practices. They also retained their distinct Indian identity, which they modified to reflect their affiliation with the Catholic mission system.

SUMMARY

In this essay, I have discussed three basic processes related to the formation and transformation of Indian identity in colonial northern Mexico. All three processes took place simultaneously and were inextricably linked to more general processes of the colonial endeavor.

The first process involved modifications in the Indian schemes of ethnic classification. Unlike the Spanish, who employed essentially the same scheme in northern Mexico as the one they had developed earlier in central Mexico, the local Indians modified their preexisting schemes rather extensively. They created new terms to label non-Indians, as well as new or modified terms to label the emerging category of "Indian." They also adopted ethnic labels from the Spanish to designate subgroups of Indians who varied from one another in their responses to the colonial system.

The second process was the reduction in the number of terms used to label local groups. In other areas of the New World, the emergence of more inclusive ethnic categories often resulted from the consolidation of remnant groups into new ethnic units. In central and western Chihuahua, in contrast, most Indian groups were sufficiently large to sustain their biological reproduction and avoid reduction to the status of remnant societies, at least until the twentieth century. The Spanish began using fewer terms to label these groups because they gradually came to recognize the cultural and linguistic affinities among them. In northern Mexico, as in other areas of the New World, they sometimes carried this process too far, lumping together Indians who probably were sufficiently different to warrant designation as distinct groups. During the same period, the Indians in the region also apparently began employing broader ethnic labels to designate themselves, in part because the Spanish were using these terms in a more inclusive sense, in part because of the cultural and linguistic homogenization that resulted from population movements, but most importantly because they were forging a sense of common Indian identity to contrast with that of non-Indians.

The third process was the spatialization of identity, in which internal divisions within the more inclusive Indian identities became associated with distinct geographical areas. These divisions were defined in terms of the different stances that different Indian people and groups took with respect to the Spanish colonial and mission enterprise and, on a superficial level at least, the Spanish and Indians agreed on what the distinctions were.

The interplay of both external and internal factors is evident in all three of these interconnected processes. Colonial categories and policies forced people to be "Indians" as well as specific kinds of "Indians," but at the same time they motivated Indian people to create a common identity as "Indians" that at different times and places served as the basis for political solidarity against the Spanish. Yet, while the Spanish presence engendered solidarity at one level, it produced internal divisions and conflicts at another. At no time during the colonial period did all the Tarahumaras unite to support or oppose the Spanish.

The Spanish presence also stimulated the movement of Indians out of their home communities, either to avoid contact with the Spanish or to trade with and work for them. People from many different ethnic groups, often including both Indians and non-Indians, came together in refuge areas, in missions near Spanish settlements, and in Spanish economic centers, where identities were both reinforced and revised. One result was the transformation of large numbers of Indians into mestizos, either because of their assimilation into the emerging mestizo society or because of the creation of offspring of mixed ethnic and genetic heritage through inter-ethnic marriage or sexual relations.

Although less frequent, the transformation of non-Indians into Indians also occurred. Non-Indian criminals and other fugitives from Spanish society sometimes joined communities of fugitive and gentile Indians, many of whom themselves came from distinct Indian societies. The emergence of a common identity within these communities depended upon overcoming the ethnic diversity of their members, a process no doubt facilitated by the physical isolation of the communities and their marginal and often oppositional stance with respect to the Spanish.

Despite the transformations that have taken place in their lives since European contact, many Indian societies in northern Mexico have succeeded in maintaining their distinctive identities. During the past century, several developments in Mexico—including the *indigenista* movement, the organization of Indian communities into collective landholding and economic units called *ejidos,* and changes to the Mexican Constitution, which now acknowledges that Mexico is a multiethnic and multicultural society—have promoted the persistence of separate Indian identities. However, Indian people have never depended on external structures and forces for the maintenance of their identities. Instead they have produced and reproduced their identities as part of their pursuit of the goals and interests that they have defined as fundamental to their survival.

FURTHER READING

Barth, Fredrik, ed. 1969. *Ethnic Groups and Boundaries: The Social Organization of Culture Difference.* Little, Brown.

Cohen, Ronald. 1978. "Ethnicity: Problem and Focus in Anthropology." *Annual Review of Anthropology* 7:379–403.

Eriksen, Thomas H. 1991. "The Cultural Contexts of Ethnic Differences." *Man* 26:127–44.

Merrill, William L. 1988. *Raramuri Souls: Knowledge and Social Process in Northern Mexico.* Smithsonian Institution Press.

Merrill, William L. 1993. "Conversion and Colonialism in Northern Mexico: The Tarahumara Response to the Jesuit Mission Program, 1601–1767." In Robert W. Hefner, ed., *Conversion to Christianity: Historical and Anthropological Perspectives on a Great Transformation,* pp. 129–63. University of California Press.

Spicer, Edward H. 1971. "Persistent Cultural Systems." *Science* 174:795–800.

20 ANDEAN WOMEN

United We Sit

Catherine J. Allen

During my first month of fieldwork in Sonqo, a Quechua-speaking community in the highlands of southern Peru, I found myself extremely irritated by the apparently secondary status of women. They seemed to me like a flock of morose and timid crows—all dressed alike, hanging back at public assemblies, allowing themselves to be greeted and served last, and watching their menfolk eat at fiestas while they themselves went hungry. Frequently I had to choke back an urge to jump up and start lecturing them with evangelical zeal. None of these facts has changed, but my perception of them has. Sonqo's women no longer seem subordinate to their menfolk; indeed, one might argue, also erroneously, that the opposite is true.

TRADITIONAL SEX ROLES

Traditional Andean ideology, which is very strong in rural communities like Sonqo, is based on a principle of dual organization that structures the whole of society and the cosmos. In this dualistic mode of thought, the two parts of any given entity are related in a dialectical fashion, often expressed in the word *tinkuy,* the encounter that creates unity out of opposition. *Tinkuy* refers, for example, to the turbulent convergence of two streams, as well as to ritual battles between the two halves or moieties of a community.

Obviously, this way of thinking affects the way the sexes are conceptualized and how they are expected to behave toward each other. The household, as a functioning production unit, is built around the married couple, called *warmiqhari,* literally "woman-man," the fusion of two different but interdependent kinds of human being, with separate but complementary knowledge, interest and abilities. This relationship is summed up in various ways:

> "Women know how to work with their hands; men know how to work with their feet." So women spin, weave, and cook in or near their homes, while men plough the earth and travel.

> "Women are horizontal, their place is the *pampa,* the flat ground; men are vertical, they perform their activities standing or sitting on seats." So the vertical upright loom with foot pedals is suitable for males, while the horizontal loom is suitable for females. The great extensive earth is female, *Pachamama* or Mother Earth, while the high snow-capped mountains are male, called *Apus* (Lords) or *Taytakuna* (Fathers).

> "Men don't know how to take care of growing things." On the other hand, "Men know how to talk in the Assembly; women don't know how." So women bear and tend children and look after the animals. Men pass through a hierarchy of community offices. At public functions men sit on seats in a line, roughly in order of seniority, while women sit in a crowd on the ground.

The image of Woman evoked by these dichotomies is characterized by immobility. While the men are coming and going, building and talking, and passing vertically through a civil-religious hierarchy of offices, the women are sitting on the ground covered by layers of heavy skirts, their hands busily reaching in all directions. How beautifully this idea is expressed in dancing, as the women bend over their full skirts and twirl around in place, while the men go stamping and leaping around them! It is also well expressed in the different expressions of respect suitable for men and women: a prosperous influential man is called *qhapac,* which can be translated as "noble" or "mighty." The comparable term for women is *wira,* which means "fat" or "substantial."

Although a woman may not have a man's mobility, she is neither inactive nor passive. On the contrary, she has a female way of asserting herself. Women support and anchor the life of the community and household, and it is in this that their power resides.

THE ALL-MALE ASSEMBLY

Turning to the realms of community politics, this sexual ideology would seem to (and in certain respects does) put women at a distinct disadvantage in relation to men. The central governing body of Sonqo is the Assembly, considered the voice of the *Ayllu Runa*, the people of the community. The constitutive units of the Assembly are households, not individuals. Each of Sonqo's 84 households is represented by its senior male member. The women in attendance seldom number more than four or five, consisting of widows and women whose husbands are ill or absent. These women sit in a group apart from the men, sometimes at such a distance that it is difficult to hear the proceedings, much less take part in them.

The president of administration presides over the Assembly, accompanied by a vice president and secretary, and often by the *Alcalde* (mayor) with his staff of office. Often they are "assisted" by a school teacher or government agent. The presiding officers are elected by the Assembly and serve for a term of two years. As the president represents the community to the national government and its agents, his position provides opportunities for self-aggrandizement and exercise of personal power. Sonqueños are keenly aware of this danger and repeatedly emphasized to me that it is the Assembly and not the president or other officers that makes decisions. On one occasion the president was nearly impeached for having accepted a government loan of eucalyptus trees without consulting the Assembly. So the individuals who hold political office are not supposed to wield political power; they simply proclaim and carry out the collective will. The *Alcalde,* in particular, with his staff of office, is a validator and by his presence makes the *Ayllu*'s decisions official.

But what *is* the *Ayllu*? Is it the group of men and few silent women who meet at intervals to argue and vote? Initially this seems to be the case; watching the Assembly gives the impression that decision making is vested in a group of young and middle-aged males, with females and old men excluded from the political process. But this is a mistaken impression, similar to that created by a play, which fixes our attention on the actors on the stage and makes us forget that the observable action is produced

and directed from behind the scenes. In Sonqo, while vigorous men play out the public drama of political life, the women and old men are the invisible production crew. While we focus our attention on the public stage, we miss half the action, and inevitably must fail to understand how community politics function.

Although during my fieldwork I lived in the president's house and attended the Assemblies, I usually had the feeling that the way things were "really" getting done was eluding me. I wondered whether there was a "council of elders," but eventually I realized that no such council exists. Decision making goes on through seemingly casual visiting, as influential men and women (the *quapac* and the *wira*) call on each other in the evening or before breakfast, to chat and chew coca, or as they talk soberly during communal work parties while younger men work noisily at heavy tasks.

In this elusive process of sub rosa decision making, the opinions of the substantial women (*wira warmi*) carry a great deal of weight. In Assemblies, the *Mamakuna* (mothers, mature women) and *Kuraq Taytakuna* (elder fathers) are a significant, albeit invisible, presence. The men in the Assembly do not represent themselves as individuals, but represent their households, including their wives and aged parents, and are accountable to them. This makes the decision-making process difficult to understand for the government agent, school teacher, or anthropologist who watches only the public drama.

THE POWER OF WOMEN

But what about situations in which women have to enter the public arena to achieve a goal that cannot be achieved otherwise? Clearly a woman without a husband for a mouthpiece, or who is seriously at odds with her husband, is at a great disadvantage. The most unpleasant incidents I witnessed in Sonqo were those in which women tried to address the Assembly as individuals, inevitably without success. In one case, a woman who had married into Sonqo but returned to her natal community after her husband's death, showed up in the Assembly to demand her widow's rights of seed potatoes and labor. She was rejected without hesitation, and her gift of *trago* (cane alcohol) was returned unopened by the president.

Having failed to press her case as a single woman in a male forum, the widow changed her tactics. She did have a certain amount of sympathy from other women who had married into Sonqo. At the next communal work party these women appeared among the kinswomen of the hosting officials, bringing food and *chicha* (corn beer) for the laboring menfolk. After the work was finished, the gathering divided into the usual male and female groupings, who sat around chatting and chewing coca. At this point the widow appeared again and was loudly welcomed by the women who sympathized with her. Sonqueños consider it impossibly rude to turn away a guest who has been invited by even one member of a party, so, while most of the men and many of the women were quietly displeased, the widow settled down and was offered coca and *chicha*. After a few minutes she presented the president with two bottles of *trago*. To my surprise, he accepted them and had them served to the gatherings. The husband of another woman, who had also married in, rose to argue the widow's case. Even before he began it was clear that she had already won, and the ensuing debate centered not on whether she would be helped, but on how much she would be helped.

Later I asked the president why he accepted the *trago*, when it committed the *Ayllu* to an unwelcome contract it had previously refused. "The *Mamakuna* accepted her," he answered, "so we had to accept her too."

The widow achieved her goal by confronting the men, not on their own terms, but on a woman's terms. She recruited a collective base of female support at a gathering properly attended by both sexes. This group of women cleverly maneuvered the men into risking a serious breach of etiquette. Finally, they exploited a male representative. This collective female support with a male mouthpiece won the day before a word was spoken.

In another incident a woman proved able to enforce the *Ayllu*'s will when the men were unsuccessful. In 1975 the *Alcalde*-elect announced that he would not accept his office. In spite of his public election and unremitting pressure from his elders and peers, he stubbornly held out into December, only a few weeks before his inauguration. Backed by a group of women, his mother coerced him into serving, exploiting a religious feast day, another occasion on which both men and women gather to eat and drink together. Seated next to a big jar of *chicha*, surrounded by a crowd of women, she began to scream at her son, "What are you? Are you a Quechua person?" continuing with a long stream of condemnations. Although most of the men agreed with her, they begged her to be quiet in a subdued chorus. Eventually she subsided, and the feast continued. The next day the word was out that the *Alcalde*-elect had agreed to accept his office.

To summarize, female power is exerted collectively and consists essentially in the power of veto and commentary. Those who have spent time in Quechua households will find this familiar—recalling how as a man of the house prepares his family offering to *Pachamama* and *Apus,* his wife sits at his side selecting the ingredients and correcting his invocation; how as a man tells traditional stories, his wife coaches him and he accepts her corrections. The political sphere is not essentially different; in Assemblies the *Mamakuna* are not physically at their husbands' sides, but their invisible presence weighs heavily nonetheless. When, in extreme cases, women as a group decide to "go public," they cause a kind of social earthquake—an upheaval of the private substream of public life.

This way of operating does not sit well with a modern professional woman, eager to meet men on her own terms in a public forum. But there is much to be learned from it: that this is not a simple matter of female subordination but something much more subtle and complex; and that the powers as well as the limitations of Sonqo women are inherent in the total sociocultural system, a system whose resilience and strength resides to a great extent in the invisible, elusive—and potentially violent—character of female power.

FURTHER READING

Allen, Catherine J. 1988. *The Hold Life Has: Coca and Cultural Identity in an Andean Community.* Smithsonian Institution Press.

Bastien, Joseph W. 1985. *Mountain of the Condor: Metaphor and Ritual in an Andean Ayllu*. Waveland Press.

Isbell, Bille Jean. 1985 [1978]. *To Defend Ourselves: Ecology and Ritual in an Andean Village*. Waveland Press.

Meyerson, Julia. 1990. *'Tambo: Life in an Andean Village*. University of Texas Press.

Nash, June, and Helen Safa, eds. 1986. *Women and Change in Latin America*. Bergin and Garvey.

Rosaldo, Michelle Z., and Louise Lamphere, eds. 1974. *Woman, Culture and Society*. Stanford University Press.

21 WHOSE PAST IS IT ANYWAY?

Three Interpretations of History

Loretta Fowler

My work with Plains Indians began in Wyoming, where I studied the way of life of the Arapahoes on the Wind River Reservation. I went to Fort Belknap, Montana, because the Gros Ventres there are a related people. In fact the Gros Ventres and the Arapahoes used to be one people. They speak the same language, though different dialects. But when I got to Fort Belknap, I was amazed to find the Gros Ventres so different culturally from the Arapahoes.

Fort Belknap proved to be a very complicated community, with two tribal groups—the Gros Ventres and the Assiniboines—sharing a single reservation. Between these two groups there was a lack of agreement about the meaning of shared cultural symbols and about the interpretation of their common past. In addition, there was a pronounced generation gap between the views of Gros Ventre elders and youths concerning culture and history.

The cultural complexity within a small, "face-to-face" reservation community forced me to ask some very difficult questions. Should I treat this complexity as factionalism, as many anthropologists have done in their work on the Plains? Should I adopt one particular interpretation, such as one age group's views, and ignore the others? Should I concentrate exclusively on the Gros Ventres, even though they literally live side by side, interact intensively, and intermarry with the Assiniboines?

My decision to confront the cultural complexity at Fort Belknap led me to some new ways of doing Plains anthropology. I decided to use a variety of methodologies to understand this contemporary Indian society. The three methodologies I used in examining the relationship between past and present were ethnohistory, cohort analysis, and the analysis of folk history.

ETHNOHISTORY

Ethnohistory is a term used differently by many people. I use it to mean interpreting documents from an anthropological perspective. For example, one aspect of the anthropological approach is to try to see interconnections between different aspects of life: how politics is affected by economics; how artwork is tied to worldview; or how religion is related to economics. For example, in my first Arapahoe study I obtained important information about politics from looking at museum files on art. These documents became, in a sense, my informants, enabling me to learn something about the whole culture from one aspect of it.

For my Gros Ventre work, the first thing I did was study every document written over the past 200 years that I could find about these people. I looked at records of traders in Canada and Montana. I also consulted anthropologists' field notes, including those of Regina Flannery, who did an excellent study on the Gros Ventres in the late 1930s and 1940s. Her unpublished notes were a wonderful source of information about people born in the 1850s. She had recorded their conversations—what they thought of life, of each other, of particular families and events. Several women, for example, had grown up in polygynous households, where they had been one among several wives. They had tanned buffalo robes and forded the Missouri River to trade their robes at Fort Benton and elsewhere.

In doing ethnohistory, you have to play detective. You try to put yourself back in time and figure out where people would have left a trace of what they were doing and then try to find that trace. This ethnohistorical approach taught me a lot about Fort Belknap. For one thing, it demonstrated quite clearly that, contrary to what other writers have reported, there were real continuities in Gros Ventre culture, in what Clifford Geertz has called "ethos," the kinds of motivations and perceptions people have about things, the style they have in coping with life.

ETHNOHISTORY

FOLK HISTORY

COHORT ANALYSIS

ENEMY-FRIEND RELATIONSHIP

One of the continuities was that the Gros Ventres at Fort Belknap, as far back as the late eighteenth century, were very competitive with other Gros Ventres and with other peoples. For example, in the late eighteenth century through the early twentieth century, Gros Ventres had an institution called the enemy-friend relationship. A man would pick another Gros Ventre, and when he went to battle and captured a trophy, perhaps a shield, he would bring it back as a gift to his enemy-friend. The gift meant that the enemy-friend was obligated to do something just as brave and generous in return. Sometimes an enemy-friend would feast widows and orphans and then his enemy-friend would be obligated to do something equally generous. Competition reinforced sharing, establishing a system in which goods, food, and property circulated through the society. In this way people who could not go out and hunt would still eat, and people who could not obtain hides would be able to clothe themselves. Competition for war honors became more intense, escalating intertribal fighting, after the introduction of guns by European traders.

There are recurrent references to the Gros Ventres as the most competitive of the northern Plains people in the accounts of traders in the late eighteenth century and early nineteenth century. Traders noted that the

Gros Ventres always brought in the best-prepared robes, and that they took pride in getting a higher price for their robes than other tribes. The Gros Ventres' emphasis on competitiveness and on the pursuit of public recognition of prominence through generosity (as in large public give-aways of property) is evident. It can still be observed today. By looking at a culture over a long time span, by studying documents as well as living people, I can see continuities that other researchers have missed by look-ing at only one particular era. I can correct other kinds of misinterpreta-tions as well. Gros Ventre cultural identity was not anchored in particular ceremonies or customs. Rather, it hinged on the Gros Ventres' interpre-tations of change. The giveaway held at powwows (intertribal celebra-tions, including dancing)—although a twentieth-century phenomenon—expresses the same value on competitive generosity as the enemy-friend relationship and thus is viewed by the Gros Ventres as "traditional."

COHORT ANALYSIS

The method of cohort analysis comes from the sociologist Karl Mann-heim, who developed this approach to better understand the relationships between generations. Mannheim argued that people who are born within a particular time span often have shared experiences that significantly dis-tinguish them from other cohorts in their society.

The first step is to identify cohorts and to determine what distinguishes them from one another. I found two cohorts at Fort Belknap, one I called the elder cohort, the other the youth cohort. Members of the elder cohort, today ages 56 to 90, were born between 1895 and 1929. They were all children when Gros Ventre ceremonial life was in its heyday. As children or young adults, they were not considered mature enough to hold posi-tions of ritual responsibility, but they attended the ceremonies. They at-tended secular dances in which they saw elderly warriors acting out what they had done in battles.

The elder cohorts' parents encouraged them to speak English, and their schoolteachers threatened with severe punishment those who continued to speak their native language. Although they spoke English in the schools, they spoke Gros Ventre with their grandparents.

Their elders did not encourage them to pursue an interest in native re-ligion. They were told that Gros Ventre religion would not be of use to them in the future. Elders insisted that it was more important for them to learn skills that would enable them to compete successfully with non-

Indians. Gros Ventre adults in the early twentieth century wanted their children, those born between 1895 and 1929, to compete successfully with non-Indians so that they would not be exploited or abused. When elders told one young boy (now 70 years old) that he was not going to be a warrior like his grandfather, but that instead he must get an education to learn to compete successfully with the non-Indian, the boy saw schooling as a kind of warfare. He would not ride into battle against the Piegan or the Sioux, but instead compete against non-Indians. As a child, the elder cohort of today was strongly motivated to go to school, get an education, and find a trade. Nothing was too difficult for the Gros Ventre child who was reared by the old warriors and medicine men.

Members of the youth cohort, today ages 30–55, were born between 1930 and 1955. What sets this group apart is that they were too young to have experienced Gros Ventre ceremonial life in its heyday. They never saw a medicine man cure a patient nor did they attend a religious ritual. They never went to a dance in which warriors acted out their battle exploits. Youths did not speak the Gros Ventre language as children. Many of them had grown up off the reservation with only occasional contact with Fort Belknap.

On the other hand, they were the right age to take full advantage of new opportunities in the late 1960s and 1970s—the affirmative action programs, the educational grants for Vietnam veterans, and self-determination legislation affecting tribal governments. New jobs opened up to them through minority recruitment. And many moved back to the reservation to accept the new jobs. In school they were exposed to a positive view of Indian culture and history through Native American studies programs. The youth cohorts, then, experienced the 1960s and 1970s differently from the elders who could not take advantage of college or job opportunities to the extent that youths did.

THE GENERATION UNIT

In my cohort analysis, I also found Mannheim's concept of a generation unit useful. Within a single cohort or generation, there are people who experience life differently, who make different choices. At Fort Belknap there were two generation units that I called the education clique and the militants. The education clique were people who went to college in Montana. Their concept of Indianness developed or was embellished on Montana campuses, at Missoula, Bozeman, or Billings. Even though as children they had not been involved with Gros Ventre religion, at college many of them had roommates from other tribes where native religion was more important. The college campuses also had Indian clubs that put on powwows to which they invited singers and dancers from other tribes. This was the first ceremonial experience of this kind for many of the Gros Ventres. They became part of a network of powwow people and made contacts throughout Montana. They also got involved in politics by going to the state legislature and persuading the legislators to make college tuition free for Indians on Montana campuses. This group of Gros Ventres became aware of their potential and, with the encouragement of their parents, they set high goals for themselves. They returned to Fort Belknap and set out to achieve greater self-determination for the Indian people and to revive ceremonial life.

The militants were people who developed or embellished their concept of Indianness outside of Montana, where they lived in urban areas. Many of them attended colleges such as the University of Washington in Seattle, the University of California at Los Angeles, and Harvard in Boston. They took jobs in urban poverty programs and became involved in social protest movements that were much more active than those in Montana. Many took part in confrontations such as sit-ins or marches.

POWWOWING

What insights were obtained by comparing interpretations of culture and history in elders and youths? It is clear that the contrasting experiences of these cohorts, and of the education clique and the militants, have shaped the way Fort Belknap culture and society are changing today. We sometimes tend to think that change in Indian communities comes only from ideas and customs introduced by non-Indians. But a great deal of change and the way change is made culturally acceptable comes from the interplay and exchange of different interpretations held by cohorts. To youths, reviving Indian ceremonies such as the powwow is an important goal. Thus they have organized and expanded these dances.

In the powwow sponsored by the education clique, one major theme is hospitality to visiting tribes. Much effort is exerted to raise money for dance contest prizes and to purchase groceries to distribute to visitors. Moreover, the veteran plays a prominent role in the powwow. There are flag-raising ceremonies and special dances done by veterans. But to the militants the U.S. military represents an oppressor, and so they deemphasize flag symbolism or veteran participation in the powwow they sponsor, the Chief Joseph powwow. An aspect of this powwow is the laying of wreaths or other kinds of grave offerings at the site of the Nez Perce's battle with the U.S. military. The battle site is 20 miles west of Fort Belknap. There, Nez Perce people were killed by the army while trying to cross the border into Canada. For the militants, Chief Joseph symbolizes resistance to an unjust U.S. government.

Both elders and youths participate in powwows to varying degrees. But the powwow has come to symbolize different things to elders and youths and to the education clique and the militants. For the education clique, for example, the powwow is a vehicle for expressing Gros Ventre competitive drive. One of their goals is to attract bigger crowds than do powwows on other reservations. Militant youths interpret the powwow as a vehicle for the expression of protest against the U.S. government. These interpretations reflect the youths' contrasting involvements in the Native American pride movements of the 1970s.

FOLK HISTORY

The third method I used was the analysis of the stories that people tell about their past. Gros Ventres and Assiniboines have shared a reservation since 1878, and they have participated in the same events. Their ancestors sat together at the same councils and attended many of the same ceremonies. Although they were participants in the same events, they perceived them very differently. I was interested in looking at folk history as an entry to contemporary symbols and their meanings, not in looking at the stories in terms of whether or not they were accurate or compatible with the documentary record.

Gros Ventre and Assiniboine versions of the history of the U.S. government's relations with the Fort Belknap peoples are quite different. In stories about events from the late nineteenth century to the present, the Gros Ventres portray themselves as fully capable of managing their community by themselves and capable of competing successfully with whites if given a fair chance. Gros Ventres attribute reservation problems to the failure of Assiniboines—Assiniboines are not assertive enough with federal officials. Assiniboines portray themselves as expert in living harmoniously with others. In their stories, reservation problems are attributed to the obstinate nature of Gros Ventres. Folk history serves to orient social action. The contrast in Gros Ventre and Assiniboine interpretations of history works to stimulate flexibility, maneuverability, and creativity. Individuals have a wider range of potential strategies and choices. Variant interpretations encourage intertribal competition, as well. Each tribe presents the other somewhat negatively. The competitive component of symbols of identity fosters a sense of cultural distinctiveness that is important to Indian people today. As one youth told me, "When the new Indian awareness came, it wasn't enough just to realize you were Indian; it was what kind of Indian [that mattered]."

Each of the three ways of interpreting the past contributed to my understanding of Fort Belknap. Ethnohistory made clear that long-term cultural continuities were possible even though the Gros Ventres had to change their way of life to cope with their changing environment. Cohort analysis revealed that age groups differed in their interpretations of their past. Folk history was a good way to learn how images of the past contribute to cultural identity, and how these same images motivate behavior.

By combining the three approaches, I was able to reach an understanding of the dynamics of culture change: how change actually occurs, and how people accept it or initiate it. At Fort Belknap, innovation has come about as generations and tribes, Indians and whites, continually adjust and reformulate their notions of the past and the present in order to cope with the conflicting interpretations of one another. By influencing one another, they influence the way in which their society changes. The anthropologist, by confronting the complexities of culture, can see things about a society that would not be seen by focusing on one group's perspective or on one point in time.

UPDATE

My research on the culture and history of the Gros Ventre people at Fort Belknap Reservation spanned 1979–85 and culminated in the publication of a book in 1987. In the book, I draw some conclusions about why life was changing in a particular direction for the Gros Ventres during 1979–85 and about why the Gros Ventres have been able to maintain a distinct cultural identity despite extensive changes in their circumstances during the past 200 years and despite the fact that intermarriage has taken place between Gros Ventres and other peoples. The conclusions I reached had their basis in the research theory and method described in "Whose Past Is It Anyway?"

The different and conflicting views of elders and youths, Gros Ventres and Assiniboines, led to ritual and political innovations in the 1980s and gave shape to more recent developments. By 1997 the youths of my study had become middle-aged or elderly.

Ritual activity and symbolism at Fort Belknap was changing at a very fast pace when I was there. Gros Ventres were sponsoring ceremonies associated with the late nineteenth and early twentieth centuries, that is, "reviving" traditional rituals. The clash in views between elders and youths led to an emphasis on secular rituals, such as naming ceremonies, memorial rituals, and the "powwow," rather than religious ones. In this way, youths reached an accommodation with the elders, who believed that the youths were not qualified to attempt the religious rituals they had experienced in the early twentieth century. Youths drew on knowledge and recollections of elderly Assiniboines to organize powwows, reinterpreting the meanings of various phases of powwow ritual to fit Gros Ventre perspectives. And gradually they interpreted some of the powwow features as sacred. By the 1990s the youths in my study began to introduce religious ceremonies based on nineteenth-century rituals, this time without opposition, for the elders of the early 1980s were deceased.

The innovations in the 1980s not only were a result of the youths' relations with Gros Ventre elders but also were made possible by the influence that Assiniboine ideas about ritual innovations had on Gros Ventre youths. From the Assiniboine perspective, dreams gave supernatural validation to innovation, and favorable response to the requests of others for help brought a supernatural blessing. Thus Assiniboines, acting on their own interpretation of the history of their relations with the Gros Ventres, helped Gros Ventre youths sponsor powwows and other rituals. The new ritual activity could be viewed as traditionally Gros Ventre in large part because a competitive element had been introduced by the youths; that is, as the Gros Ventres had done for generations, they competed with the Assiniboines and others—in this case, to make the Gros Ventre powwow more elaborate or larger than others. This emphasis on the quest for primacy has been viewed by the Gros Ventres as a "natural" outgrowth of their tenacious nature and an important element of Gros Ventre identity, at least since the early nineteenth century. In the 1980s, competition in the ritual sphere was one means of expressing Gros Ventre identity.

Another arena for innovation at Fort Belknap was tribal government. The War on Poverty programs and the opportunities posed by the Self-Determination Act of 1975 (which allowed tribes to contract for programs previously administered by federal agencies) worked to draw back to Fort Belknap many individuals who had moved to towns and cities in the 1950s to find employment in the aftermath of the collapse of an agricultural economy on Fort Belknap Reservation. Many of the Gros Ventre youths had acquired skills, as well as a commitment to reviving Native American traditions, in universities or urban areas in the 1960s and early 1970s. They began to return to Fort Belknap and assume managerial positions in the new programs or the local federal bureaucracy. At the same time, housing projects and other new services attracted Gros Ventre elders in their retirement years. The youths had political contacts with young people on other reservations whom they had known at universities or people who had been members of national Native American advocacy groups. The reservation government was a joint Gros Ventre–Assiniboine "business committee" in the 1970s. By the mid-1990s, youths had established separate tribal governments. The movement for separation from the Assiniboines also resulted in the creation of new criteria for legal enrollment in the Gros Ventre tribe. To Gros Ventres, these political developments expressed their "traditional" commitment to establishing Gros Ventre primacy at Fort Belknap.

Anthropologists proceed from detailed case studies to comparative studies in order to make broader generalizations about sociocultural change. I was able to compare my earlier study of the Arapahoes with my Gros Ventres research, placing the history of both these peoples in regional context. The Gros Ventres were situated on the Northwestern Plains, where they had an advantageous position in the fur and robe trade. Traders courted individuals and promoted interpersonal rivalry among the Gros Ventres. Also wealthy in horses, because of their easy access to groups that could obtain large numbers of horses from the Southwest, the Gros Ventres used their wealth in horses and trade goods in competitive rituals. Lavish and generous distribution of property bought prestige and leadership positions to individuals and allowed the Gros Ventres leverage against neighboring groups. On the Northwestern Plains, groups were spared the large-scale intrusions of settlers and troops in the 1850s and 1860s. The Gros Ventres never had a hostile encounter with troops and, in fact, were military allies with troops and traders against more hostile peoples, such as the Sioux groups who moved into Montana. After the Gros Ventres moved onto their reservation, settlers began to pressure the federal government to move them. Not viewed as a military threat, the Gros Ventres were thought to be vulnerable to dislocation. In this context, then, the Gros Ventres allied with Catholic missionaries and the powerful Catholic lobby in Washington, D.C. to persuade the government to honor their title to the reservation. In 1896 they could not prevent the cession of a southern portion of their reservation that was rich in mineral resources. This left them unable to develop the reservation economy after the collapse of agriculture in the 1930s and led to the exodus of young people from the reservation in the 1940s and 1950s.

The Arapahoes are a good comparison to the Gros Ventres, for at one time these two peoples were one. They settled in different regions and their histories took different turns. The Arapahoes occupied the Central Plains. There, all the groups had easy access to horses but the volume of trade was less than on the Northwest Plains. Arapahoe ceremonial life did not place as much emphasis on lavish generosity or on competition. When settlers began moving west, they crossed through the best hunting territories of the Central Plains, and they and American troops came into conflict with the native peoples there. The Arapahoes fought the army for several years. Even after the Northern Arapahoes settled on a reservation in 1878, they were regarded as a potential threat to the settlement of the Western United States. They, in turn, were suspicious of officials and missionaries. They gave the appearance of being accommodating, in allowing Catholic missionaries to live on the reservation, but retained their commitment to their own religious rituals. The Northern Arapahoes' reservation in Wyoming had rich oil deposits and was too arid for profitable agriculture. They retained their land base with its mineral resources and, in the 1940s, Arapahoe leaders persuaded Congress to allow them to collect the royalties from the oil production. With a monthly per capita payment from the tribe's oil royalties, Arapahoe young people continued to live on the reservation and elders continued to preside over Arapahoe ritual life, giving direction to the lives of their juniors and schooling young people in ritual leadership during the florescence of Indian identity in the 1970s. By comparing the Gros Ventres with the Northern Arapahoes (and comparing other groups in the various Plains regions), anthropologists can better understand why native peoples' cultures and histories developed in particular ways over time.

FURTHER READING

Flannery, Regina. 1953. *The Gros Ventres of Montana. Part I: Social Life.* Catholic University of America Press.

Fowler, Loretta. 1987. *Shared Symbols, Contested Meanings: Gros Ventre Culture and History, 1778–1984.* Cornell University Press.

Fowler, Loretta. 1994. "The Civilization Strategy: Gros Ventres, Northern and

Southern Arapahos Compared." In Raymond J. DeMallie and Alfonso Ortiz, eds., *North American Indian Anthropology: Essays on Society and Culture,* pp. 220–57. University of Oklahoma Press.

Geertz, Clifford. 1973. *The Interpretation of Cultures: Selected Essays.* Basic Books.

Mannheim, Karl. 1952. "The Problem of Generations." In Paul Kecskemeti, ed., *Essays on the Sociology of Knowledge.* Oxford University Press.

22 DOING ETHNOGRAPHY AT MACALESTER COLLEGE

"From the Inside Out"

Ruth Osterweis Selig

Armed with a tape recorder, anthropologist David McCurdy spent his sabbatical a few years back doing fieldwork—at a local stockbroker's office. Everyday he visited his informant, watching him "picking up his mail," "checking the Journal," "searching for ideas," "posting his books," "massaging clients," and "making cold calls." McCurdy socialized with his informant and his fellow brokers after work, and on their lunch break played racket ball. He attended "dog and pony shows" and went to "due diligence meetings." In this way, by learning a new language "from the inside out," McCurdy began to learn the intimate culture by which brokers conduct their lives.

David McCurdy states the facts simply: "Meeting Jim Spradley changed my life." For several generations of anthropology students, the names Spradley and McCurdy have been inseparable, known as joint authors and as creators of an innovative fieldwork approach to teaching anthropology. Few people, however, know the story behind this remarkable collaboration or that Jim Spradley died in 1982—of leukemia—at the age of 48. Dave has made sure that Spradley's name, contribution, and memory live on.

In 1969 David McCurdy, the only anthropologist at Macalester, hired a second anthropologist to help him develop an anthropology program for undergraduate students. Thirty-three-year-old James Spradley had just completed his ethnographic study of skid row alcoholics living in Seattle, Washington. For that study, Spradley had adapted a new research technique called *ethnographic semantics,* based on a theoretical approach pioneered by Harold C. Conklin, Charles O. Frake, and Ward H. Goodenough. Spradley believed that his methodology, largely dependent on learning the way people categorize, code, define, and describe their experience through language, enabled him to understand and analyze the culture of "tramps." The title of Spradley's highly acclaimed book, *You Owe Yourself a Drunk: An Ethnography of Urban Nomads* (1970), comes from the phrase these men used to describe their feelings after being released from jail. As you learn people's own language, Spradley believed, you learn their culture from their point of view—"from the inside out."

AMERICAN SUBCULTURES

A brilliant and charismatic teacher, James Spradley urged anthropologists to take the ethnographic study of American culture and subcultures seriously. During the 1960s he came to believe that American urban crises demanded that people in our cities be understood from their point of view—not ours. As he explained in his book, "by defining people as bums, Skid Road alcoholics, vagrants, common drunkards, or homeless men, the average citizen or even the professional knows these men only through the values and language of their own culture—through a popular, medical, sociological, or legal framework" (p. 68).

To develop policies and laws that could help these men, one first had to understand who these men really were and why they lived as they did. Spradley believed that anthropology could contribute vital information to public policy and to practical solutions for social problems, if anthropologists could demonstrate their ability to analyze and describe the culture of others "from the inside out." In the anthropological lexicon, this analysis of the "culture-bearer's" world from the inside is called "the emic" view as opposed to the outsiders' view that is called "etic." Anthropologists have long believed that one of their discipline's unique strengths lies in its ability to understand and describe cultures from the emic point of view, and that this view is essential to understanding human cultures worldwide.

ETHNOGRAPHIC SEMANTICS

You Owe Yourself a Drunk is an eloquent, highly detailed ethnographic study of the way tramps organize and identify their life experiences by means of a specialized vocabulary of English, a lexicon that Spradley believed held the key to understanding their culture. Learning this complex language enabled Spradley to identify five major cultural scenes that tramps find themselves in: buckets (jails), farms (treatment centers), jungles (encampments), skids (skid rows), and freights (railroad cars). Within each of these scenes, Spradley identified the various terms that help tramps understand and organize their world: for example, they distinguish 15 kinds of tramps, 100 types of sleeping places ("flops"), and various strategies for survival while "making the bucket" (the cycle of getting arrested, pleading guilty, and doing time in jail).

Ethnographic semantics and related methodologies such as componential analysis were developed in the 1960s to apply explicitly "scientific" analytical frameworks to the analysis of cultural phenomena. These techniques sought to determine the definitive attributes of various local terms and cultural concepts in order to get at culturally important distinctions.

Throughout his book, Spradley used ethnographic semantics, identifying the terms tramps used and organizing these terms into chart form in order to create "hierarchical taxonomies." For example, he charted the terms used by the tramps for the people that tramps interact with "in the bucket" (jail), the inmates, bulls (people with power), and civilians. Inmates, in turn, include drunks, lockups, and kickouts; bulls include matrons, bailiffs, sergeants, court liaison officers, and others; civilians include cooks, doctors, and nurses.

The organization of these terms into chart form transforms a collection of "folk terms" into a "hierarchical taxonomy," with each group of terms categorized within its proper "domain." Hence, people "in the bucket" are divided into three "domains": inmates, bulls, and civilians. On another and even more complex level, Spradley analyzed the various dimensions or "attributes" that explain the differences among domains. In the above example, the distinction among inmates, bulls, and civilians is the relationship each has to the system (inmates are held by the system; bulls run the system; and civilians are employed by the system). Such a "componential analysis" results in the creation of "paradigms," a charting of attributes that show exactly how people divide up the various experiences they have. For Spradley's tramps, for example, whether a man travels, how he travels, what kind of home base he maintains, and what livelihood he utilizes turn out to be the four "attributes" by which these men divide themselves into fifteen types of tramps. The key role of mobility led Spradley to call tramps "urban nomads"—since that term most closely describes the way these men view themselves.

THE SPRADLEY/MCCURDY TEAM

At Macalester College, Spradley and McCurdy became a team, developing a new approach to teaching anthropology to undergraduate students and coauthoring numerous publications based on their understanding of culture and their approach to doing ethnography. Spradley and McCurdy increasingly came to believe that students could best learn anthropological concepts, perspectives, and even theory by doing fieldwork. The anthropologists' challenge was developing a systematic, focused, and rigorous methodology for students to use within a realistic time frame to complete a fieldwork project. Ethnographic semantics applied to the study of microcultures provided this methodology and structure.

Inseparable as friends, colleagues, and daily racquetball partners, Spradley and McCurdy worked together over a period of thirteen years, changing the way anthropology was understood and taught to undergraduates—at least at Macalester. According to former student and anthropologist Marlene Arnold, "We didn't learn theory, we were doing ethnography and discovering theory ourselves. Anthropology students became famous on the Macalester campus because we worked so hard and became so totally involved in the ethnographic studies we were carrying out in the community. Many of the studies by my classmates were published by Spradley and McCurdy in their book, *The Cultural Experience: Ethnography in Complex Societies.*" This volume, first conceived by McCurdy, details the fieldwork approach for students and includes twelve ethnographic reports written by Macalester students. This book is still used in classrooms today.

With standing offers from some of the best universities in the country, Spradley and his family elected to remain at Macalester, where he could work with McCurdy, pioneering their new approach to anthropology and coauthoring several publications, including the widely used *Conformity and Conflict: Readings in Cultural Anthropology,* now in its ninth edition. Tragically, Spradley died in 1982, but the Spradley/McCurdy legacy remains vital even today, through McCurdy's popular courses at Macalester and through their joint publications that McCurdy faithfully rewrites, updates, and reprints. In all the publications, culture is the central focus.

CULTURE AND ETHNOGRAPHY

Culture, as defined by Spradley and McCurdy, is not behavior. Culture is a kind of knowledge, the acquired knowledge that people use to generate behavior and interpret experience. As Spradley and McCurdy explain, as we learn our culture, we acquire a way to interpret our experience. One example they cite, based on McCurdy's field experience in village India, is the comparison of the American and Indian conception of dogs.

> We Americans learn that dogs are like little people in furry suits. Dogs live in our houses, eat our food, share our beds . . . villagers in India, on the other hand, view dogs as pests. . . . Quiet days in Indian villages are often punctuated by the yelp of a dog that has been threatened or actually hurt by its master or by a bystander. Clearly, it is not the dogs that are different in these two societies. Rather, it is the meaning that dogs have for people that varies. And such meaning is cultural; it is learned as part of growing up in each group. (*Conformity and Conflict,* p. 7)

CRITIQUES

As Spradley and McCurdy became better known, anthropologists responded to their work, and to the more general question of whether undergraduates can or should do fieldwork, regardless of what methods they use. Many anthropologists use the field approach to teaching anthropology, particularly in courses on methodology. As Ruth Krulfeld of George Washington University explains:

> In my methods class, I always have my students do a fieldwork project. They don't usually use ethnographic semantics, but they read Spradley and McCurdy, and they develop a focus and methodology best suited to the project they choose. They can't do the sort of in-depth, sophisticated study a graduate student can do, or an anthropologist who does a two year field study, but, nevertheless, they learn a great deal about culture and about anthropology from their participant-observation study. Through their own projects, many students become so excited about what they are learning that they decide to pursue graduate work in the field.

Anthropologist and the former dean of Beloit College, Lawrence Breitborde, explains the appeal of the Spradley/ McCurdy approach:

By utilizing a highly structured and precise methodology, Dave McCurdy is able to give his students, even first year college students, a practical and systematic way to get into the field, and to understand culture from the insider's point of view. I admire the precision and the structure, and it's been an influential force in teaching anthropology, spreading to a number of departments across the country. (Breitborde, personal communication)

In the 1970s the early promise of ethnoscience—to provide a scientific basis for ethnography—was never fully realized. Anthropologists could see that language was only one important "window" to another culture, and that ethnographic understanding required several methodologies. Defining groups within the urban underclass as separate cultures or microcultures also was criticized for suggesting that the behavior of these individuals was due to cultural transmission of different values rather than to common reactions to similar pressures of the larger society. (e.g., Liebow, 1967:208–31) In the 1980s, ethnography itself, and in particular the writing of ethnography, came under serious attack, as revisionists (postmodernists) asserted that an anthropologist's understanding of another culture is so filtered through his or her perceptions, language, and culture, that any description of another culture is suspect.

Not surprisingly, Spradley and McCurdy's approach to teaching ethnography has generated some controversy. Some anthropologists assert that unsophisticated undergraduates cannot do ethnography because they know so little anthropology, and, in particular, know so little theory; that practical considerations rule out the approach for most departments and most professors; and that student ethnographers will, in fact, make mistakes and run the risk of engaging in unethical behavior, such as not protecting informants, or trying to study illegal activities, such as groups involved with drugs or alcohol.

McCURDY RESPONDS

At the 1990 meetings of the American Anthropological Association, McCurdy described his approach to student ethnography and answered these criticisms. To those anthropologists who assert that undergraduates are not trained to do fieldwork and need to learn theory first, McCurdy pointed out that although an overall grasp of theory can, in fact, be important to providing structure, definition, and focus to field research, there are other ways for students to focus their research. By beginning to collect and analyze data using one highly structured technique, the student can come to understand the theoretical basis of that technique and its limitations, and can also develop hypotheses and interpretations based on the analysis.

McCurdy gave several examples to support his assertion that students can arrive at theoretical hypotheses through their own research. One student, for example, studied paramedics working on ambulance teams. The student discovered that these paramedics used three separate languages to convey the same information, depending on who received the message: a radio language, a technical-medical language, and a slang language. The student hypothesized that slang (for example, *crispy critter* denoting a badly burned patient) developed for functional purposes, easing the terrible emotional stress paramedics endured while caring for seriously injured and often mutilated human beings.

McCurdy offered several suggestions to ease the practical problems of teaching field research to students, although admitting that this is a problem with large classes of undergraduates. He suggested assigning limited problems for students to research in short papers (for example, ask students to report on the ways people celebrate birthdays); lecturing on field methods and using hand-outs; having graduate students or section leaders handle student discussion of their projects as they develop; or running a seminar in interviewing and field research or a summer field school.

Regarding ethical problems, McCurdy was emphatic. Students must learn from the beginning that informants need to be protected. Student researchers must explain to their informants and anyone they come into contact with who they are and what they are doing. No student can study any illegal activity. All students must read the AAA Code of Ethics and informants' privacy must always be the paramount consideration. Ethical risks exist, McCurdy stated, but they exist for all ethnographers, no matter how well trained or sensitive they are. McCurdy summed up his response:

> I have argued that ethnographic research is a central and unique property of cultural anthropology. Ethnography can be undertaken by undergraduate students without theoretical training; it may actually be a useful way to bring students to theory. Although teaching ethnography may place a strain on faculty time, adaptive measures make it practical even for fairly large classes. Similarly, ethnography always entails ethical risk, but such risk may be reduced by openly facing ethical consequences.

Recently, McCurdy was asked to comment on his career at Macalester:

When I take stock of Macalester's anthropology program these days, I can't help but be pleased by its progress. The faculty has doubled in the last 20 years; it attracts a larger number of undergraduate majors than at many large universities. It has ranked first in the number of students per faculty member for five of the last twenty years, and it has never ranked lower than fifth. A significant number of our students go on to graduate school, and scores of them claim the value of anthropology in their lives. Although one can never be sure, I like to think that ethnography, and the approach that Jim Spradley and I developed together, had something to do with it.

FURTHER READING

American Anthropological Association. 1997. *AAA Code of Ethics.* Arlington, Va.

Liebow, Elliot. 1967. *Tally's Corner: A Study of Negro Street Corner Men.* Little, Brown.

Spradley, James P. 1979. *The Ethnographic Interview.* Holt, Rinehart and Winston.

Spradley, James P. 1980. *Participant Observation.* Holt, Rinehart, and Winston.

Spradley, James P. 1988. *You Owe Yourself a Drunk: An Ethnography of Urban Nomads.* University Press of America.

Spradley, James P., and David W. McCurdy. 1980. *Anthropology: The Cultural Perspective.* 2d ed. Wiley.

Spradley, James P., and David W. McCurdy. 1988. *The Cultural Experience: Ethnography in Complex Society*. Waveland Press.

Spradley, James P., and David W. McCurdy. 1990. *Instructor's Manual: Conformity and Conflict: Readings in Cultural Anthropology*. 9th ed. Scott Foresman/Little Brown.

Spradley, James P., and David W. McCurdy. 1997. *Conformity and Conflict: Readings in Cultural Anthropology*. 9th ed. Scott Foresman/Little Brown.

23 ANOTHER MAASAI STORY

Naomi Kipury

was born and raised in a village known as Ilbisil (Anglicized as Bissel), located in Kajiado district in Kenya, one of the country's two Maasai districts. Ilbisil was and still is such a small place that everyone knows everyone else and social relations are very personal. Because of this, I grew up not always quite knowing who was and who was not a relative. Although Ilbisil is the meeting place of two major Maasai groups called *iloshon* (sections), Ilmatapato and Ilpurko, the separation was not always clear. My inability to identify my relatives was made even more difficult by the fact that my parents belong to these separate *iloshon,* in effect making everyone a relative to some degree.

As I grew older and learned to distinguish the various kinship categories, the many "relations" began to fall into place. In our little town, other social relationships also included Ethiopian, Somali, and Asian families who had been trading in the area for many years and who seemed to be part of the community. Cultural heterogeneity was an integral part of my experience growing up.

Editors' note: Naomi Kipury is a Maasai woman. The unique perspective of anthropology is a holistic and cross-cultural view, and a central "rite-of-passage" for anthropology students is immersion in another culture through fieldwork. This experience gives a more detached perspective on one's own and other cultures. How is this experience defined for the anthropologist of non-Western origin? Has such a person already gained a perspective on cultural differences through exposure to non-Western and Western cultures? Why is it important to encourage students of different backgrounds to enter this discipline?

Although Ilbisil is a small village, it is not isolated from national and international affairs. Tanzania's border lies only 30 miles away, and the highway connecting the capital cities of Kenya and Tanzania runs between our home and the school, which was opened in 1951 by the colonial governor. Less than 20 miles away sits the police headquarters and the government administration and less than 200 yards from our home stands the village church, with its strong stone walls, symbolizing the religious persuasion into which the Maasai were inducted. The church was allegedly built single-handedly by an Anglican priest who was determined, like others before him, to wipe out "paganism" among the Maasai. But judging from records of church attendance and villagers' comments, the physical strength and architectural tastes of the priest/builder more impressed our people than the spiritual message he tried to convey.

EARLY EDUCATION

When I was about six, I attended Ilbisil primary school, the only school in the area. The idea of going to school was extremely exciting to me, mainly because my elder sister was already attending, as were other "big" girls, but also because it was an adventure, something out of the ordinary. In those days (the late 1950s), the colonial government forced children to attend school through the establishment of a quota system. Each district and location supplied a given number of children to the newly constructed government school. It was the responsibility of the newly appointed chiefs and headmen to locate prospective students to fill the quotas. Teachers were equally difficult to induct into this new educational process. Only a very good excuse would relieve them of this wage employment. As can be expected, there was always a severe shortage of teachers.

In filling the student quota, chiefs and headmen ensured that their own children and those of their friends and clansmen were not selected. This gave special relevance to clans, subclans, and any other indigenous social divisions as people attempted to evade the new system. Animosity suddenly shrouded our own little community following the establishment of the schoolhouse. My story was different, however. Since my father already had been coerced into attending school, he was determined to send his children as well. Thus, unlike our friends, who were able to stay away from school, we could never dream of doing so. Actually, I was absolutely elated at the opportunity to attend school and could not understand why my grandmother cried and why the majority in my community considered school such a dreaded place. I was yet to be inducted into the horrors of the school experience.

At the age of about seven, I traveled by car to the first all-girl's school in the district at Kajiado, the administrative headquarters. The headmistress was a dedicated and talented South African missionary who spoke our language so well that she even composed songs in Maa. She was affectionately nicknamed "mother of girls." Despite what seemed like fine living conditions, boarding school was a miserable experience for most of us and entirely different from anything we were accustomed to.

The food, for instance, consisting of vegetables, maize, beans, and ugali (made from maize meal), was strange to most of us. Only two or three of us had ever tasted any vegetables. Cabbage and carrots, overboiled in the typically English style, were quite unpalatable. As essentially cattle pastoralists, the Maasai subsist primarily on milk and occasionally on meat. We are popularly known to exist on blood; however, consumption of it occurs only during very hard times or during convalescence. Since we all were from a pastoral community, where milk was our only food, lack of it was interpreted by us and by our folk as either starvation or malnutrition, and, at times, as both. Once during a drought, boiled maize was our only sustenance, and since most of us did not eat it, we often went hungry.

School was further made difficult by rules we thought unnecessarily strict. For instance, two girls were not allowed to sleep in the same bed. Yet for most of us, sleeping in one's own bed was a new experience. We found sleeping alone cold and scary, and so most of us often broke the rules to sleep with friends. Picking berries near the school during the weekends was also not allowed. For these reasons, and because we were homesick, we had crying sessions every evening during the first weeks of school. Cultural differences made home more interesting than school; consequently, many girls ran away with hopes they would not be recaptured, as often happened.

ON BECOMING AN ANTHROPOLOGIST

I was one of 4 of the original 80 girls at the school who went on to high school in Kajiado, and, later, to the University of Nairobi. I survived the dropout rate because I felt I was too far entrenched to quit, so I continued. I am certainly glad to be literate, unlike my mother who never got the chance. Not all that we learned in school, however, was relevant to my education, just as not all that our community had to offer was irrelevant.

After years in the "culture" of boarding school, away from my family and community, I felt somewhat alienated from my own culture and sure that I had missed out on a great deal of valuable knowledge. Perhaps my decision to become an anthropologist was partly influenced by my desire to investigate my own society. I found I had a particular interest in social change, the transformations that have been taking place at different levels of society, and how people have reacted to them. These became the focus of my interests in graduate school. In particular, I am examining the complexities of class and gender during the transition from precolonial times to the present.

CULTURE CHANGE AMONG THE MAASAI

A discussion of change among the Maasai might sound like a contradiction in terms, since we are often perceived as conservative and impervious to change. In earlier anthropological literature we would have epitomized the concept of the "noble savage." However, the Maasai, like everyone else, have experienced an incredible amount of change that has affected every aspect of their lives. Change as we know it is part and parcel of human survival.

The most pronounced changes to have taken place over the past twenty years are economic, political, and social. The early encounters with colonialism led to expropriation of land through treaties similar to those signed with the American Indians. In subsequent years, commercialization of land and livestock led to further economic constraints.

Politically, the Maasai, like other small Third World societies, have been incorporated into modern states and the world system, whose ideology is radically different from their own. How do we gauge the effect of these transformations within the family level? Although all of these processes have been deeply felt by all levels of society and by all categories of people, the manner in which women have been affected has not been adequately covered in the anthropological literature, partly because of the androcentric biases of earlier studies. I hope my study and those of others, who are now addressing this issue, will bridge that gap by focusing on women within the total system in which they operate both historically and culturally.

As members of a pastoral society, women "traditionally" had significant control over the herds and the household economy. While men may have controlled the exchange of livestock mainly for the elaboration of affinal and other ties, women controlled the products of the stock and were primarily responsible for feeding the household. At marriage a woman received a certain portion of the household herd, which remained under her jurisdiction throughout the marriage. A portion of this stock she allotted for her son's inheritance. As managers of the production and distribution of the milk and staple products, women played an important role in ensuring the productivity of the herds for sustenance and for future redistribution. Only through negotiation could any livestock under their jurisdiction be disposed of, loaned out, or sold.

Since colonialism, our pastoral economy, and consumption primarily of dairy products, and hence women's economic role within the household and community, have been undermined by changes that have significantly affected relations between people and among people, their land, and their animals. The commercialization of agriculture, for instance, has led to environmental overuse from the reduction and degradation of our rangelands, necessitating the herding of stock to more widely dispersed areas in search of water and grass. While the mobility of herders has increased, the mobility of women with children attending primary day school has been restricted, so that they are often separated both from the men and from the herds that usually provide their sustenance.

The commercialization of livestock has led to a shift in the focus of pastoral production, from milk to meat products. Since meat production requires the calves to be kept with the mother for a longer period, the availability of milk for family consumption or exchange is reduced. This, in turn, has reduced women's economic importance, as have the more recent development policies that have created a new role for the male "head-of-household" as property-owner and taxpayer. This new system does not accommodate the shared "ownership" of livestock within the household or the differential control of livestock products. The denial of women's traditional residual rights in the cattle of marriage-exchange and sons' inheritance has reduced their productive role still further and has fostered economic dependence. Increasingly, women are finding it difficult to feed their households, and, men, often separated from wives and children, are similarly unable to devote adequate means to household sustenance, partly because of economic constraints, but also because they lack the cultural training as providers of daily food.

I do not believe that my society is unique, nor are the changes that Maasai women are experiencing. Therefore I hope that my study will contribute to scientific discourse and to the manner in which peoples like my own are adapting to economic, political, and social changes. Anthropology is sometimes considered a Western system of thought that grew out of imperialism, but I do not believe that it should be condemned to stay so. If anything, the discipline should be able to provide tools with which to conceptualize cultural change in transitional societies. To be able to do this, and for the sake of its own survival, the discipline has had to adapt. The contribution of Third World students could certainly enrich the discipline even further.

FURTHER READING

Arhem, Kaj. 1985. *Pastoral Man in the Garden of Eden: The Maasai of the Ngoro Ngoro Conservation Area, Tanzania.* Reports in Cultural Anthropology. University of Uppsala, Department of Cultural Anthropology.

Jacobs, Alan. 1965. "African Pastoralists: Some General Remarks." *Anthropological Quarterly* 38:144–54.

Kipury, Naomi. 1988. "Change and Gender in Pastoral Ideology: East African Pastoralists in Perspective." Paper presented at the African Studies Association Meeting, October 28–31.

Kipury, Naomi 1988. "Focusing on the Feeders: Women in Pastoral Development." Paper presented to the Office of Research and Evaluation, African Development Foundation, September.

Rigby, Peter. 1985. *Persistent Pastoralists: Nomadic Societies in Transition.* Zed Books.

24 MAYAN INDIANS AND THE PASSAMAQUODDY OF MAINE

Anthropological Linguists Aid in Cultural Survival

Robert M. Laughlin and Kathleen J. Bragdon

ME AND SNA JTZ'IBAJOM (THE HOUSE OF THE WRITER)

Robert M. Laughlin

My work with the Mayan Indians of Chiapas in southern Mexico began in 1959. I was a member of the Harvard Chiapas Project, the goal of which was to document culture change in a Mayan community. There I met Romin Teratol, a Tzotzil Mayan Indian who was employed as a puppeteer at the National Indian Institute (INI). My wife and I moved briefly into his mother's second house and began learning his language. My predecessor in the project, Lore Colby, had typed up a provisional dictionary, but it was just a start. Soon I was collecting folk tales and thereby adding vocabulary to the dictionary. Then I collected dreams. When I suggested the possibility of publishing those dreams, however, I was advised that I should be able to analyze them according to Freud, Jung, and who knows who else. So I decided it would be easier to compile a thorough dictionary. This process took the next 14

Editors' note: This chapter consists of two separate pieces written by anthropological linguists who have gone beyond the traditional work of accumulating vocabularies and grammars to bring their linguistic expertise back to the Native American speakers whose languages they have studied. Robert Laughlin and Kathleen Bragdon describe, respectively, their work with a Mayan community in Chiapas, Mexico, and the Passamaquoddy of Maine.

years, and in 1975 *The Great Tzotzil Dictionary of San Lorenzo Zinacantán* was published. In 1980 I published *Of Shoes and Ships and Sealing Wax: Sundries from Zinacantán,* based on the journals of Romin and his neighbor, Antzelmo Peres, who had become my collaborators. They had twice traveled to the States to finish our opus and offer a description of life in another world.

Eventually the collections of folk tales and dreams were published in Tzotzil and English: *Of Cabbages and Kings: Tales from Zinacantán* (1977) and *Of Wonders Wild and New: Dreams from Zinacantán* (1976). Selections from these were published in *The People of the Bat: Mayan Tales and Dreams from Zinacantán* (1988; 1996 [paperback edition]). My publication *The Great Tzotzil Dictionary of Santo Domingo Zinacantán* (1988) is a translation and reordering of a sixteenth-century Spanish-Tzotzil dictionary that I found in my home town of Princeton in 1974.

In 1982, aided by the Mayan poet Jaime Sabines, brother to the governor of Chiapas, Mexico, a group of Tzotzil Mayan Indians who had worked with me or with anthropology colleagues over many years secured funding for a writers' cooperative and published two bilingual booklets. However, the governor's term was ending and, lacking further support, this line was permanently cut. I was then approached by the late Romin's son, Xun, by Antzelmo Peres, and by Maryan Lopis Mentes of neighboring Chamula, whom I had known for many years. I had hoped, during the years of my anthropological and linguistic research, that somehow my work might return to Zinacantán. I saw this as an opportunity—an opportunity to help bring Mayan literacy to Chiapas.

By chance, a conference that same year celebrating "40 Years of Anthropological Research in Chiapas" was scheduled to begin. I urged my Mayan friends to address the many assembled anthropologists and linguists. This they did, explaining, "You have awakened our interest in our own culture, you have published many studies, but always in other countries where we never see the results. Our young people are now literate in Spanish and think they are very smart, but they don't know a quarter of what their fathers know. We would like, at least, to put on paper our customs for the sake of our children and grandchildren."

The next few years, aided by Cultural Survival, a human rights nonprofit organization, we founded Sna Jtz'ibajom, a Tzotzil-Tzeltal writers' cooperative. Currently the cooperative publishes bilingual booklets in two Mayan languages; these booklets cover history, oral history, and customs. The cooperative has also established a puppet theater, a live theater, and a weekly Tzotzil-Tzeltal radio program. The puppet theater draws on folk tales but also presents didactic skits on alcoholism, medicine, and bilingual education. The live theater has dramatized a folk tale and created a family-planning play.

The cooperative also has started a Tzotzil literacy project. Initially I contacted two religious scribes and a secretary of the school committee of Zinacantán to teach. Currently the teachers give two-hour classes in Tzotzil twice a week in their own homes to 10 to 12 of their neighbors. The interest in the project was so great that one teacher requested to teach overtime.

Those eligible to participate in the literacy program must already be minimally literate in Spanish. Initially there was some discussion as to whether women should be allowed to take classes. The idea of women and men spending time together in the evening at first made many feel uncomfortable. One prospective student thought that learning Tzotzil would enable him and his girlfriend to write secret messages to each other since his

father only knew Spanish. In two years, the project has awarded 500 diplomas to men, women, and children in two communities. At present we have 2 directors, 14 teachers, and 144 students enrolled each semester. Although Tzotzil is not the government or official language, that has not discouraged the Mayans' enrollment in the evening language classes. Students are encouraged to record personal and family histories as well as to produce creative writing. Stories are reviewed and edited by Sna Jtz'ibajom. The federal publisher has agreed to print 3,000 copies of each work submitted by the cooperative. Students give the following reasons for learning Tzotzil: to improve their Spanish by working with translations, to learn, to become smarter, and to appreciate their own tradition. Besides the personal enrichment the students receive from learning to read and write their native language, the Mayan society also benefits through the national and international recognition the cooperative is receiving. The cooperative's success has been due in part to the talent of its members as writers, actors, artists, and teachers, and also to the great pride that the people have in their culture and their new desire to be literate in their mother tongue, to "become smart."

We have already come a long way since our beginning eight years ago. We next would like to see the establishment of culture centers in each community, linked to a Mayan Academy of Letters based in San Cristóbal, where teachers could be trained to spread our activities throughout the Mayan areas of the state.

My first responsibility to the cooperative as an anthropological linguist has been to train its members to write their language correctly. While spelling is quickly learned, the decision as to where words begin and end is a problem even for linguists. For example, should the particles *to* (indicating an incomplete or future action) and *ox* (a completed or future action), when they occur together to mean "used to—," be kept separate or merged?

Second, the economic crisis in Mexico, severely restricting government funding, combined with the lack of a tradition of charitable giving in Mexico, forces the cooperative to look outside for support. Very few foundations grant internationally, and of those a very small number support cultural projects. Even then, support is limited to two to three years, so it is difficult to plan for the future. I have been able thus far to steer the cooperative to appropriate foundations. For a weaving cooperative, self-sufficiency may be possible, but for writers?

As a member of Sna Jtz'ibajom, I see the significance of the project as strengthening the Mayan culture for the Mayans themselves and offering an alternative to the non-Mayan media barrage. Just as important, the cooperative is awakening an interest among non-Indian Mexicans in their Indian heritage and informing the outside world that Mayan culture is alive and flourishing.

UPDATE

In the past five years The House of the Writer has achieved international renown. The Spanish versions of two of its folk tales have been published by the Mexican Department of Education in two editions totaling 71,500 copies. The first three volumes of *Colección de Letras Mayas Contemporáneas, Chiapas,* edited by Carlos Montemayor, are dedicated to six of our plays in Spanish and Tzotzil. Recently acquired computer equipment gives us a desktop publishing capability.

The theater has given over 380 performances in Chiapas. This theater gave rise to Mexico's first two Indian women playwrights, who have won several state and national prizes and participated in women playwrights' conferences in Canada and Australia. They separated from our cooperative to create La Fomma, an association dedicated to the Indian women and children now living in the city, providing them with a day care center and training in native literacy and theater. One of its founders, Petrona de la Cruz Cruz, has just been made the first Indian member of the state's human rights commission. The president of Sna, Diego Méndez Guzmán, has taken an active role in the dialogue between the Mexican government and the Zapatista rebels, demanding that Indian culture be given new respect and support in his country. Under our guidance, Casas de Cultura have been established in many of the Indian towns.

As the members have gained confidence and a new awareness of social forces, the subject of our plays has evolved from the dramatization of traditional folk tales to the discovery of ancient Mayan history and an exploration of current social problems. The performance of a play in Immokalee, Florida, inspired the audience of Guatemalan and Mexican field hands to create a workers' cooperative that held its first strike and that is about to found its own theater.

Our literacy project now teaches Tzeltal as well as Tzotzil. It is in such demand among the Tzeltal people that teachers are accepting students who are totally illiterate and who, nevertheless, are able to complete their training. Nearly 2,000 men, women, and children have received diplomas.

The Chiapas Photography Project, directed by Carlota Duarte, has provided our members with darkroom experience, leading to the production of photo comic books and exhibits in Mexico City and the United States. The photographs of Maruch Sántiz Gómez, Mexico's first recognized Indian woman photographer, have also been on exhibit in Johannesburg, South Africa. Sna has contributed actors and film to the production of video documentaries by Mexican and foreign studios.

AN ANTHROPOLOGICAL LINGUIST
LOOKS AT PASSAMAQUODDY

Kathleen J. Bragdon

The mist was rising off the inlet, the tall spiky outlines of the weirs just visible through the haze, as I drove for the first time into the small Passamaquoddy Indian reservation at Pleasant Point, near Perry, Maine. The reservation is spread out in a sinuous pattern, running along the shore of the inlet and ending short of a narrow isthmus that bears the road running toward Eastport, a fishing/resort community on the coast. The conspicuous landmarks of the community include the Wabanaki Mall, where signs for the restaurant, auto repair shop (now closed), and grocery store are in Passamaquoddy and English, the native-run supermarket, and the Passamaquoddy Museum, home of the Passamaquoddy Bilingual-Bicultural Program.

I have come to begin a study of the Passamaquoddy-Maliseet language. Passamaquoddy is a language of the eastern subgroup of the Algonquian language family. I am already familiar with a related language, Massachusett, which I have studied with Ives Goddard, with whom I co-authored *Native Writings in Massachusett*. Massachusett, however, is an extinct language, and what is known about it comes from writings left by native speakers who became literate in their native language in the seventeenth and eighteenth centuries. My plan is to study Passamaquoddy and thereby to familiarize myself with a living Algonquian language, for the comparisons it will make possible with Massachusett and for the insights it will give me into language use. For instance, do people within the community use Passamaquoddy in formal as well as informal situations, and does speech differ among different age groups?

At the Wabanaki Mall, shoppers and employees speak softly in Passamaquoddy. I catch perhaps one word in five. Fortunately for me, all speak English as well. I purchase a basket and ask about the maker, a woman still living at Pleasant Point and well known for her skill. I am then directed to the Passamaquoddy Museum to meet Joseph Nicolas and David Francis, two Passamaquoddy men who have been most influential in sustaining the Bilingual-Bicultural Program at Pleasant Point.

Both men are articulate about the needs of their community and their concern for the preservation of the Passamaquoddy language. Both spend much of their time creating and editing materials for school use, taping stories, and working on translations. The museum, the center of the Title-Four funded educational program, consists of two rooms filled with displays of baskets and other objects, as well as murals and life-size models dressed in traditional clothing.

As a newcomer to Pleasant Point, I am more a receiver of knowledge than a giver. Both here and at Peter Dana Point, where Wayne Newell oversees the vigorous sister program, materials traditionally supplied by the linguist, such as dictionaries, grammars, and translations, have been begun or completed by community members, with the occasional assistance of other linguists and educators such as Phillip LeSourd, Robert Leavitt, and Carl Teeter. Here, as elsewhere in native communities across the United States and Canada, the people are beginning to take a more active role in generating information, and in making important decisions for the future, about their language and culture.

As an outside observer, it is this native involvement that I can perhaps describe and analyze whereas a community member could not. In pursuit of such understanding, I have begun to interview various community members about their use of and feelings about their native language. These interviews, in combination with well-established ethnographic techniques of field observation, allow me, even as a novice in the language, some insight into the way Passamaquoddy is being used, by whom, and for what reasons.

Fortunately, I encounter little resistance and hostility. The people of Pleasant Point and Peter Dana Point are proud of their language, proud of the fluency of their leaders and elders, and proud to discuss and describe their language to an outsider. As a beginner, I am dependent on them for information, which they generously supply. Their attitude greatly encourages my study and creates enjoyable working conditions.

As the work of a number of modern sociolinguists has shown us, language preservation is not simply a question of recording texts, or creating grammars and dictionaries, but of working to create and foster natural (as opposed to formal teaching) situations in which the native language can be used (for example, teaching basket making or revitalizing fishing and hunting skills). In other words, language preservation can encourage social contexts in which the native language has a legitimate and valued place. Here, comparative information, derived from studies like mine of languages that did not survive, is important, as is the information from other successful language preservation programs in other contemporary native communities.

Yet all of this is in vain if the people of the community cannot or do not wish to make the enormous commitment that is required to sustain preservation. Among the biggest problems facing the Passamaquoddy and others like them today is the conflict between their increasingly strong desire to preserve their language and culture and their need to provide relevant education, job training, and an acceptable standard of living for community members, especially the young. In Pleasant Point today, the percentage of people under 30 who are fluent speakers of the language is declining, and young parents are not using the language with their children. Although native language classes are held in the elementary schools, these classes are seen by the children as having little relevance to their daily lives. There is relatively little published material in Passamaquoddy, and all technical and advanced educational literature is in English. Studies elsewhere have shown that only when native students are "immersed" in the language, and only where all official agencies provide truly bilingual services will the language have any hope of survival.

Leaders of the Bilingual-Bicultural Program at Pleasant Point and Peter Dana Point are aware of this and are actively searching for new ways to involve the community in the language preservation effort. Some options to provide natural contexts for native language use include native language newspapers, closed-circuit native language television shows, and the encouragement of traditional subsistence and manufacturing skills. The use of Passamaquoddy in newly composed songs, poetry, and literature offers another intriguing avenue of potential involvement.

As an anthropological linguist, I have found the efforts of the Passamaquoddy communities fascinating and informative. I now have a deeper understanding of the relationship between anthropology and education and of what makes a successful bilingual cultural program, information I am sharing with colleagues.

In an era when native people are becoming increasingly active in disseminating information about their own languages and cultures, the work of anthropologists and linguists takes on a different kind of significance. Scholars are now being called on to witness a revitalization of native awareness of their languages, and in many cases to assist native-run programs of language preservation. It is a great privilege to be allowed to observe and to assist in such efforts.

UPDATE

Since I first wrote about my fieldwork with Passamaquoddy in *Anthro-Notes*, I have visited the two reservations at Peter Dana Point and Pleasant Point three times, staying approximately three to four weeks each time. I have worked with nearly a dozen native consultants, ranging in age from 21 to 94, and have collected close to 100 hours of tape-recorded texts and conversations. I have also taken many photographs and shot several videotapes, and I have administered 75 questionnaires on native language use in both communities.

Although my knowledge of Passamaquoddy itself is progressing more slowly than I would like, my familiarity with the communities where it is spoken has greatly increased, and I now have insight into issues of language use and preservation that I did not envision when I first began my study. In particular, I have been interested in the changing direction of local programs of language preservation, away from text-based, classroom-oriented memorization and instruction, toward an increased emphasis on "natural" language learning, through conversation and description in the context of "real" work (see chapter 25).

The complexities of this shift in orientation are numerous. Much more is demanded of community elders and fluent speakers than in the previous program, in which a specially trained teacher conducted instruction in more standard classroom settings. Teacher pay is not high, and many fluent speakers cannot afford to devote their full time to language instruction of any kind, nor can all fluent speakers meet the requirements for state and local teaching certification.

Efforts to involve adults in language learning have also increased, since it has become clear that children are most likely to learn (or to be enthusiastic about learning) their native language if adults whom they admire make use of it also. The problems connected with adult education are predictable: most adults are busy with jobs and family and cannot devote significant time to language study. Many also feel uncomfortable with classroom instruction and are ambivalent about having to admit that they need such instruction.

At the same time, many more young people are expressing an interest in native language and culture and are acutely aware of the risks of losing their connections to their cultural heritage. A significant number of people in their 20s are using or learning to use the language and teaching it to their children as well. They see my efforts as parallel to theirs, with a similar goal of entering into, and celebrating the richness of, Passamaquoddy culture and history through language.

FURTHER READING

Bragdon, Kathleen J. 1996. *Native People of Southern New England, 1500—1650*. University of Oklahoma Press.

Breedlove, Dennis E., and Robert M. Laughlin. 1993. *The Flowering of Man: A Tzotzil Botany of Zinacantán*. Smithsonian Institution Press.

Frischmann, Donald H. 1994. "New Mayan Theatre in Chiapas: Anthropology, Literacy and Social Drama." In Diana Taylor and Juan Villegas, eds., *Negotiating Performance: Gender, Sexuality and Theatricality in Latin/o America*. Duke University Press.

Goddard, Ives, and Kathleen J. Bragdon. 1988. *Native Writings in Massachusett*. American Philosophical Society.

Laughlin, Robert M. 1975. *The Great Tzotzil Dictionary of San Lorenzo Zinacantán*. Smithsonian Institution Press.

Laughlin, Robert M. 1976. *Of Wonders Wild and New: Dreams from Zinacantán*. Smithsonian Institution Press.

Laughlin, Robert M. 1977. *Of Cabbages and Kings: Tales from Zinacantán*. Smithsonian Institution Press.

Laughlin, Robert M. 1980. *Of Shoes and Ships and Sealing Wax: Sundries from Zinacantán*. Smithsonian Institution Press.

Laughlin, Robert M. 1995. "From All for All: A Tzotzil-Tzeltal Tragicomedy." *American Anthropologist* 97(3):528–42.

Laughlin, Robert M., coll. and trans., and Carol Karasik, ed. 1988. *The People of the Bat: Mayan Tales and Dreams from Zinacantán*. Smithsonian Institution Press. (Paperback edition, 1996. *Mayan Tales from Zinacantán: Dreams and Stories from the People of the Bat*.)

Laughlin, Robert M., with John B. Haviland. 1988. *The Great Tzotzil Dictionary of Santo Domingo Zinacantán*. Smithsonian Institution Press.

Leavitt, Robert M., and David A. Francis, eds. 1986. *Kolusuwakonol: Phillip S. LeSourd's English and Passamaquoddy-Maliseet Dictionary*. Passamaquoddy-Maliseet Bilingual Program, Pleasant Point, Perry, Maine.

Montemayor, Carlos, ed. 1994. *Colección de Letras Mayas Contemporáneas, Chiapas*. Vols. 1–3. Instituto Nacional Indigenista.

25 MEDICINE, LAW, AND EDUCATION

A Journey into Applied Linguistics

P. Ann Kaupp

W hat do medicine, law, and education have in common? Each involves specialized communication between a practitioner and members of the general public, within a distinct social context. Each is, further, the subject of a new area of study: applied linguistic analysis.

In recent years the role of linguistics in anthropology has focused increasingly on the study of communication behavior and its relationship to the culture as a whole. This approach can be used not only to further the research interests of anthropologists but also to address and possibly resolve common everyday problems in communication linguistics. New subfields in linguistic behavior have arisen, such as *sociolinguistics,* the study of the structure and use of language as it relates to its social setting; and *psycholinguistics,* the study of the structure and use of language behavior, how it is learned, produced, and understood. The application of studies of linguistics to real life problems is the concern of *applied linguistics.* Traditionally, applied linguistics has dealt almost exclusively with language learning and teaching. Recently, however, its focus has been expanded to other issues such as those described here, reflected in publications by Georgetown University linguistics professor Roger Shuy. Some of the latest applied psycho- and sociolinguistic communication research is taking place in the fields of medicine, law, and education.

LANGUAGE AND MEDICINE

Shuy points out that recent linguistic work on medical communication assumes that talk between patients and doctors has "deep clinical significance" (Shuy, 1984:422). This research involves the analysis of "the speech event itself rather than the physician's interpretation of the patient's responses" (Shuy, 1984:422–23).

The medical profession claims that 95 percent of treatment success depends on the physician's ability to elicit accurate information from the medical interview. Physicians' use of tenses, hedges, euphemisms, ambiguous adjectives, intensifiers, tag questions (questions that almost invariably influence the respondent to agree with the speaker's proposition, whether or not one wants to agree), and question-answering avoidance techniques influence patient behavior and can lead to misunderstandings between the doctor and patient that grow out of "differences in experience, needs, goals, and world knowledge" (Shuy, 1984:424).

Shuy and his colleagues conducted research on cross-cultural communication problems of black, inner-city patients and their physicians, analyzing their attitudes toward medical delivery service and the communication breakdowns that occurred in the tape-recorded interviews. They discovered that patients speaking vernacular English "worked very hard at learning the vocabulary, question response routines, and perspectives of their physicians during the interview, but that there was little, if any, reciprocal learning attempted or evidenced by their physicians" (Shuy, 1984:423). In addition, the doctors' categories of questions "severely limited the patients' opportunities for providing adequate and even accurate information" (Shuy, 1987:423). From more than 100 taped interviews, they concluded that the tremendous asymmetry in such communication almost assured misunderstanding and miscommunication.

According to Shuy, the impact of this recent linguistic research on medical communication has been meager. One reason may be that the field of medicine has not felt a particularly strong need for it (1984).

LANGUAGE AND THE LAW

One area of linguistic study focuses on written and spoken language in the courtroom.

Language in the Courtroom

The study of courtroom language ranges from the perceptions and evaluations of jurors to the actual language used by witnesses, judges, attorney, and defendants, to the language of question asking, jury instructions, defendant's constitutional rights, and interpreter competence. One example of jurors' perceptions in the courtroom setting is an experiment carried out by a Duke University research team.

When a witness was permitted to respond at length with considerable

WITNESS RESPONDING AT LENGTH WITH "NARRATIVE TESTIMONY"

freedom, that testimony (called "narrative testimony") elicited more favorable responses from jurors than did the more common courtroom style of highly controlled, brief answer testimony (called "fragmented testimony"). Interestingly, male responders believed that the attorneys who interrupted and talked over the witnesses the most were the most skillful and competent, while the female subjects disagreed, ranking such attorneys as less competent and less likeable (Shuy, 1986:429).

One group of researchers studying witnesses' responses to the wording of an attorney's courtroom question found that answers to the question, "About how fast were the cars going when they smashed into each other?" more consistently mentioned higher speeds than answers to the question, "About how fast were the cars going when they hit each other?" A week later, the subjects were asked whether they had seen any broken glass in the filmed accident stimulus used in the experiment. Those who had been asked the question with "smashed" in it responded "yes" twice as often as those who had been asked the question with "hit" in it, even though the film showed no broken glass at all. This kind of research on the psychology of eye-witness testimony and memory is of great significance to both linguists and legal practice. It demonstrates, for one thing, that language form and content affect mental processes such as situation and memory of important details, and it strongly suggests that attorneys need to take into account lexicon, syntax, semantics, pragmatics, and social context in their litigation efforts (Shuy, 1984:427).

Language as Evidence

Another area of linguistic study concerns the use of language as evidence. Secondary evidence from witnesses becomes less useful when jurors are able to hear tape-recorded, or primary, evidence, which is thought to speak for itself. The applied linguist, however, knows that a tape-recorded event is not the real event. Audiotape tells a great deal, but it tells little about how far away from each other the speakers were or, in fact, who was actually talking with whom. Although videotapes may give better evidence of speakers and distances, they may also provide misleading appearances (Shuy, 1984:431).

For example, the many Abscam conversations videotaped in the rooms of the Marriott Hotel in Arlington, Virginia, were in black and white, which made the expensive rooms look "grimy, run-down, and dark" and thus gave support to the appearance of sleaziness that the FBI hoped to demonstrate.

Linguists assist attorneys in preparing their cases for trial, and, in some cases, appear as expert witnesses in criminal and civil court cases. In one instance, a man accused of making a bomb-threat during a telephone call to an international airline was acquitted when a linguist compared the speech on the tape-recorded call with that of the defendant and showed it to be a quite different dialect.

Indeed, when tape-recorded evidence is available, linguists play an important role in helping the jury understand the case. Linguists can help the jury determine who said what to whom, discern speakers' intentions from available clues in the tapes, and identify the conversational strategies of the speakers (Shuy, 1984:432).

LANGUAGE AND EDUCATION

As a composition teacher for nine years at both the secondary and college levels, Roger Shuy realized that it was easier to edit student papers with such remarks as "monot." or "awk." than to explain why the papers read that way. Our educational preoccupation is with language forms (phonology, morphology, vocabulary, syntax) rather than with language functions (using language effectively in life functions such as requesting, denying, asserting). How people use language to get things done turns out to be a higher-order skill or competence than the simple mastery of grammatical forms.

As Shuy explains, our tradition of teaching reading, writing, and foreign languages has developed not holistically (taking into account both linguistic environment and social context) but in the opposite direction, from surface to deep, from form to function, from part to whole. We teach language, then expect people to use it. Recent studies on teaching English as a second language to adult foreign students demonstrates that learning improves when form follows function, when language is taught within the context of its practical use. The experiment consisted of a control class using traditional form-oriented teaching and an experimental class using the functional approach, in which students were involved in typical life situations. At the end of the year, the latter group was considerably ahead of the control group "not only on how to use the language to get things done (such as to complain, to request, to deny, to clarify), but also in sheer fluency and, most surprisingly of all, on skill in English forms (past tense, etc.) even though such forms were not directly instructed" (Shuy, 1981: 19–20).

Holistic language training also considers social contexts. For instance, the British Council's English for Special Purposes teaches adults in a work context. "Turkish mechanics are taught English through a curriculum which has as its content the topic of mechanics. Such an approach contextualizes the learning into the learner's world and frame of reference" (Shuy, 1981:18).

Dialogue Journals

Large classes and the traditional emphasis on paying quiet attention and on taking turns can thwart the improvement of oral language ability. Classroom talk usually consists of question-answer sequences. Dialogue, on the other hand, is a natural learning device for language acquisition, which begins with the dialogue between parents and child. Efforts are being made to bring dialogue back into the classroom by way of dialogue journals between teacher and student. Dialogue journals are conversational in style and allow the teacher and student to discuss important topics. Unlike the classroom setting, dialogue journals enable the student to generate the topics for discussion.

Oral language research has shown that teachers in elementary classrooms talk about 95 percent of the time; this talk is divided about equally between asking questions, giving directions, and evaluating. In dialogue journal writing, however, Shuy found that these forms of teacher communication were cut almost in half. "The big difference, though, was in the type of questions asked. In the classroom, teachers ask test-type questions—ones that the teacher already knows the answer to. In their journals, teachers' questions were new, information-type questions, genuine requests for knowledge of something that only the students had" (Shuy, 1987:894).

The following is an example from the dialogue journal of a second-grader having difficulty learning to read and to write in the classroom but eager to write to her teacher and to receive her responses:

> *Kelly:* I have problems some times well I have this problim it is I am not very god on my writeing.
>
> *Teacher:* I think you *are* a good writer. Keep on trying your best. I like the Little Red Hen, too, Kelly. Keep on writing!
>
> *Kelly:* Oh kay. Do you have a problem. if you do I will help you and what are going to be for Halloween.
>
> *Teacher:* I am going to be a farmer. . . . Everybody has problems, Kelly. Some problems are big and some are small. One of my small problems is I can't stop eating chocolate when I see it!

Language functions of predicting, evaluating, and complaining, which take more thinking and reasoning skills, increased from 3 percent in classroom talk to 23 percent in journal writing. In journal writing, students also increased by 50 percent the number of information questions they asked of the teacher (Shuy, 1987:895).

Effective Complaints

Another important aspect of dialogue journal writing is that it provides the student an opportunity to complain which is an important language function (Shuy, 1988:143). Student complaining can be instructive for the teacher, providing important information about how students perceive what is going on, which in turn enables the teacher to determine what to reinforce, repeat, stop, supplement, or avoid. More important, says Shuy, complaining is a thinking process. Complaints can be true or false. But to be felicitous (or effective), they must be uttered sincerely, or rather the speaker must *believe* that the complaint is true.

In examining six sixth-grade student journals consisting of student-teacher exchanges for one school year, Shuy tallied 365 student complaints in three basic areas: academic concerns (134), student and teacher relationships (198), and personal matters (33) (Shuy, 1988:149). Of the 365 complaints given, 167 were structurally felicitous ("with stated conflict, an account given and new information provided" [Shuy, 1988:153]) and were convincing. The most felicitous complaints were those relating to student-teacher relations and personal matters. Although the students were at different stages of developing communicative competence in complaining, over the year they all found that their ability to produce a felicitous complaint had improved, and most even reduced the number of complaints (Shuy, 1988:156).

Willy is an example of an effective complainer, one who mitigates his directness with positive evaluation. He has learned how to use the social skills of language effectively, with the aid of the following strategies: direct discontent, mitigation, indirect discontent, and positive evaluation. An excerpt from his journal reveals some of these characteristics.

> Feb. 29: I hope we don't keep studying about India to the end of the semester because truthfully I'm getting tired of studying about India every morning. I like studying about it and all but I think we are spending too much time on India and its getting kind of boring although I like making maps. (Shuy, 1988:145)

Other Studies

Sex differences in classroom response are just beginning to attract the attention of researchers. As part of a linguistic study of a high school class, led by Secretary of Education William Bennett, Shuy looked at male-female responses. He found male students responded more frequently than female students to the teacher's (Bennett's) questions and that males answering the teacher's questions were interrupted less (19 percent) by the teacher than were the females (27 percent) (Shuy, 1986b:319).

Also noted were Bennett's responses to the student's answers. He gave four types of evaluative responses to their answers: negative, challenge, neutral, and positive. Of particular interest were his neutral and challenge evaluations:

> Neutral evaluations neither praised nor condemned. They usually took the form of "Okay" or "Alright," spoken with flat intonation. Bennett's challenges usually repeated the words of the student in a question intonation . . . indicating that part of the answer was right but not all of it, or he asked the student to say the answer in another way. (Shuy, 1986b:322)

In fact, Bennett offered challenges only to male students and neutral evaluations only to females. Although aware that this is a limited study, Shuy asks if teachers do tend to challenge males more than females and if male teachers challenge males, while female teachers challenge females. These are questions that teachers as well as linguists ought to consider.

CONCLUSION

As Shuy (1984:439) states: "What is glaringly omitted in all three professions [medicine, law, and education] is the use of functional, interactive, self-generated language performance data as the major source of diagnosis and evaluation for medical service, legal evidence, and learning/teaching." As is clear from Shuy's update, however, some progress fortunately has occurred in more recent years.

The fact that there are common research methods that cut across as well as emerge from these linguistic studies may have encouraged a more widespread use of linguistic approaches in other professions, such as law, medicine, and teaching. These similar methods include: (1) a reliance on *direct observation* of the communicative event, (2) analysis of the *interactions* themselves, (3) discovery of the *structure* of the communicative events to obtain a holistic, contextualized perspective, (4) inclusion of the *perspective* of the patient, defendant, plaintiff, and learner as well, (5) use of *technology* (audio- and videotaping, for example) to capture and freeze event, and (6) *construction* of meaning, referential and inferential, by the interaction of conversing participants (Shuy, 1984:440). Shuy's research strongly suggests that if lawyers, doctors, and teachers would use linguistic studies more widely, they would better serve not only their professions but also their own clients.

UPDATE

Roger W. Shuy

The journey of linguists into related fields such as medicine, law, and education continues to be healthy some eight years after the preceding essay appeared. New linguistic subfields have emerged, such as discourse analysis and pragmatics, aiding the quest considerably. If anything can characterize the state of contemporary linguistics, it seems to be the split between the study of forms, universals, and the mind versus the study of language in context, variation, conveyed meaning, and discourse. Fortunately, there is room (and need) for both kinds of linguistic analysis, and both feed the type of applications discussed here.

In 1988 the impact of linguistic knowledge on medical communication seemed meager. Today, however, scholars who have endured the unenthusiastic responses of the field of medicine are beginning to see hopeful gains. Some medical training programs, such as the Rochester University Medical School, now train future physicians in effective communicative strategies. Likewise, a growing interest in the elderly has spawned research in more effective communication across age groups, including the more specialized focus on Alzheimer's patients.

The relationship between language and law has also grown considerably. We now see books with titles such as *The Language of Judges, Forensic Phonetics, Language and the Law, Language Crimes, Trial Language, Language in the Judicial Process,* and *The Acoustics of Crime.* There is even a new association called the International Association of Forensic Linguistics, with its own journal, *Forensic Linguistics.* Attorneys for both the defense and the prosecution are regularly calling on linguists to assist them, either as case consultants or expert witnesses. It appears that this area of applied linguistics is maturing nicely.

Language impact in the field of education has taken a somewhat different turn. In the 1960s and 1970s linguists were called on regularly for guidance in the field of general literacy education. This has died down considerably, perhaps because so few linguists expressed interest in problems of reading and writing but, I believe, also partly because the American Association of Applied Linguistics (AAAL) separated itself from mainline linguistics as represented by the Linguistic Society of America. AAAL now meets and publishes separately and has tended to focus primarily on first- and second-language learning and teaching. The good news is that the type of applied linguistics described here is beginning at last to make some inroads in AAAL.

The area of applied sociolinguistics that seems to attract the most attention today, however, is gender-related studies, thanks mostly to the pioneering and effectively communicated contributions of scholars such as Deborah Tannen and Robin Lakoff. This field transcends the more particularized areas of medical communication, law, and education and has created renewed interest in issues such as language in the workplace, therapy, gender relationships, and the socialization of both men and women.

Other areas of applied sociolinguistics have also emerged in recent years. Geis has produced one useful book on the language of advertising and another on the language of politics. These areas appear to be emerging as important thrusts of the work of linguists and bear watching in the near future.

It has been said that there are two types of scholars: those who work on minute, theoretical issues and those who expose their work, like missionaries, to allied fields. In my opinion, it is unfortunate that the label "applied linguistics" has been limited only to first- and second-language learning and teaching. Although this is an important focus, there is far, far more territory to cover.

FURTHER READING

Baldwin, John, and Peter French. 1990. *Forensic Phonetics*. Pinter Press.

Berk-Seligson, Susan. 1990. *The Bilingual Courtroom: Court Interpreters in the Judicial Process*. University of Chicago Press.

Cushing, Steven. 1994. *Fatal Words: Communication Clashes and Aircraft Crashes*. University of Chicago Press.

Geis, Michael L. 1987. *The Language of Politics*. Springer-Verlag.

Geis, Michael L. 1995. *Speech Acts and Conversational Interaction*. Cambridge University Press.

Gibbons, John, ed. 1994. *Language and the Law*. Longman.

Hollien, Harry. 1990. *The Acoustics of Crime: The New Science of Forensic Phonetics*. Plenum Press.

Levi, Judith N., and Anne Graffam Walker, eds. 1990. *Language in the Judicial Process*. Plenum Press.

McMenamin, Gerald R. 1993. *Forensic Stylistics*. Elsevier.

Shuy, Roger W. 1981. "A Holistic View of Language Training." *Research in the Teaching of English* 15(2):101–11.

Shuy, Roger W. 1984. "Linguistics in Other Professions." *Annual Review of Anthropology* 13:419–45.

Shuy, Roger W. 1986a. "Language and the Law." *Annual Review of Applied Linguistics* 7:50–63.

Shuy, Roger W. 1986b. "Secretary Bennett's Teaching: An Argument for Responsive Teaching." *Teaching and Teacher Education* 4:315–23.

Shuy, Roger W. 1987. "Dialogue as the Heart of Learning." *Language Arts* 64(8).

Shuy, Roger W. 1988. "Discourse Level Language Functions: Complaining." In Jana Staton, Roger W. Shuy, Joy Kreeft-Peyton, and Leslee Reed, eds., *Dialogue Journal Communication: Classroom, Linguistic, Social, and Cognitive Views*, pp. 143–61. Ablex.

Shuy, Roger W. 1993. *Language Crimes: The Use and Abuse of Language Evidence in the Courtroom*. Blackwell.

Solan, Lawrence M. 1993. *The Language of Judges*. University of Chicago Press.

Stygall, Gail. 1994. *Trial Language: Differential Discourse Processing and Discursive Formation*. John Benjamins.

26 ANTHROPOLOGICAL PERSPECTIVES ON AGING

Alison S. Brooks and Patricia Draper

Patricia Draper, anthropologist: What is one of the good things about being an old person?

!Kung informant, western Botswana: There is nothing good about being old. An old person can just sit and think about death. If you have a child who takes care of you and feeds you, you have a life.

Old age is often considered to be a unique biological characteristic of modern humans. Physical anthropologists tell us that, like most other mammals, our distant ancestors rarely if ever lived beyond their reproductive years. One evolutionary explanation for old age holds that females who lived longer but whose fertility was curtailed in later adult life were more successful at rearing their last-born children and may have contributed to the reproductive success of their earlier children.

Today, however, many of us live in societies that are grappling with the "problems" of the elderly, and in which the elderly seem increasingly divorced from the productivity and success of everyday life. How similar or different are the lives of elders in modern, complex society as opposed to the lives of elders in more traditional, simple societies? Are there more elderly in our society than in others? Are the elderly in other societies happier or better cared for than in America? How old is "old?" What defines an old person? A "middle-aged" person? Is old age a "good" time of life? Are elders respected or given special status? Why or why not? What kinds of circumstances make for a happy old age or an unhappy one? These and other questions have given rise to a cross-cultural study of aging in seven locations.

THE CROSS-CULTURAL STUDY

Central to anthropology is a cross-cultural perspective that asks the question, "How does the human experience differ from one society or cultural tradition to another?" As many times as this comparative question has been asked, researchers have had to grapple with the problem of which aspects of experience to compare across societies. In the United States, for example, older people value independence. They and their younger kin go to great lengths to arrange for the financial and residential independence of older people from younger kin. In many traditional societies, however, independence of the generations is neither valued nor a practical goal. Therefore, a cross-cultural study of how elders achieve independence in old age would be ill advised. Project A.G.E. (age, generation, and experience), described more fully below, attempted to avoid such pitfalls by investigating the meanings attached to old age by members of several selected communities.

Project A.G.E. is a long-term, cross-cultural study of aging funded by the National Institutes of Health, through the National Institute on Aging, and directed by Christine Fry (Loyola University, Chicago) and Jennie Keith (Swarthmore College). This research project was designed to minimize the opportunity for Western or American assumptions about successful aging to be imposed on respondents in other culturally distinct communities. The study involves seven anthropologists and locations in five cultures: !Kung villages of Northwestern Botswana (Patricia Draper); Herero agropastoralist villages of Botswana (Henry Harpending); four neighborhoods in Hong Kong (Charlotte Ikels); Blessington, Ireland, a suburb of Dublin (Jeanette Dickerson-Putman); Clifden, Ireland, an isolated seaside town in County Galway, Ireland (Anthony Glascock); Swarthmore, Pennsylvania, a suburb of Philadelphia (Jennie Keith); and Momence, Illinois, a small rural community a two-hour drive from Chicago (Christine Fry).

The seven communities were deliberately chosen to maximize diversity in the sociocultural variables: size, social complexity, economy, mobility, scale, and technology, all thought to influence both the sense of well-being of the elderly and their participation in society.

The focus of the project is not simply to study "aging" but to understand how culture shapes the structuring of social roles across the life span. All researchers but one had previously carried out fieldwork as participant observers in the culture under study. Each researcher spent at least

one year at the research site. Before any formal interviewing was done for Project A.G.E., each researcher spent several weeks in the community eliciting information about the vocabulary and semantics of age terminology, so that the basic interview questions could be framed in terms comprehensible to the respondents. The plan called for 200 interviews at each location; 150 subjects evenly divided by sex and (adult) age category, and an additional 50 from the two oldest age groups. Questions about aging were phrased in such a way that differences in people's attitudes about aging (both within and between cultures) could emerge. Questions fell into five categories:

1. Terminology and differentiation: What do you call people of different ages, and how are they different? What are the best and worst aspects of each? What age group are you in?
2. Transitions between age groups: What happened to you to change you from your former age group to your present one? How will you know when you have moved into the next age group?
3. Feelings about age transitions: Do you like your present age? How do you feel about entering the next age group?
4. Evaluative questions about the age groups: In what age groups do you know the most or least people? What age group are you most comfortable with? What are the best and worst ages to be?
5. Past and future questions: Are you better off now than you were 10 years ago? What do you imagine about your life 5 years from now?

PROBLEMS OF RESEARCH AMONG THE !KUNG

These and related questions were readily answered and yielded abundant interesting data in two American sites, in Hong Kong, in the urbanized Irish community (Blessington), and among the Herero. In contrast, the more rural Irish (Clifden) and the !Kung were alternately puzzled, irritated, and amused by the age questions. Many grew visibly anxious at not being able to provide answers. Since both the Irish and the !Kung are famous (at least in anthropological circles) for their talkativeness, this result in two independent communities was puzzling. The informants knew the researchers well and appeared comfortable with them, and great care had been taken to phrase the questions in the local idiom. Moreover, aging and senescence were familiar to every informant. What, then, accounts for the relative failure of this approach in these two sites?

What informants in these two communities share is a low "salience" of aging categories. That is, although age terminology may exist, people do not categorize or identify particular people by their age, nor do they readily generalize on the basis of age. For example, a !Kung informant was asked, "What do you call people of different ages?"

> *Respondent:* Oh, they have all kinds of names. There's John, Sue, Jane, George. . . .
>
> *Pat Draper:* No, I mean, when people have different ages, how do you distinguish among them?
>
> *Respondent:* Well, that's easy. Come on over here and I'll point them out to you. See, there's Jane and Sue is over there. John isn't here now but George. . . .

In this society, personality, residence, sex, and health are more important than age in distinguishing individuals. From start to finish, interviews with the !Kung were like pulling teeth.

> *Pat Draper:* So, you say that for women you would use four age terms . . . young, . . . middle-aged, . . . elder . . . , and aged. . . . For example, let's start with the young women. What is it about the young women that makes them alike? What do they have in common?
>
> *Respondent:* What do you mean alike? They're nothing alike! I've already told you that. Some of them are hard workers, others are lazy; some of them have children, others have no children. What makes you think they are alike? They are all different.

Throughout the study, informants failed to identify age as the key part of the questions.

> *Pat Draper:* If you were at your village one day, and there wasn't anyone to talk to, and you were sort of lonely, wishing for conversation, what age person would you most like/not like to have visit you?
>
> *Respondent 1:* Why would I be alone at the village? If I were alone, I wouldn't want anyone to visit me.
>
> *Respondent 2:* Well, I would prefer that someone I knew would visit me.
>
> *Respondent 3:* I don't like to be visited by a Herero.
>
> *Respondent 4:* Anyone who visits me is welcome. I don't refuse anyone! Children, old people, young adults, they are all welcome. If I have tobacco we will sit together and smoke and talk.

Questions about how many acquaintances an informant had in each age group were unanswerable by !Kung informants who had no indigenous system of counting above three and rarely use "foreign" number systems except for counting cows. The questions about past and future were defeated by the strong theme of empiricism and practicality in the !Kung worldview.

> *Pat Draper*: If you could be any age you wanted to be, what age would you be?
>
> *Respondent*: It is not possible to change your age. How would that happen?

Questions designed to elicit cultural norms or individual feelings about moving from one age to another were also unsuccessful.

> *Pat Draper*: What happens, for example, in a woman's life to move her along?
>
> *Respondent*: Age, just age.
>
> *Pat Draper*: Is there nothing else you can tell me about what happens that makes the difference between, say, a middle-aged woman and an elder woman?
>
> *Respondent*: Well, you see, it is the seasons. First it is winter and dry, then the rains come and then that season is past and then the winter comes along again. That is how it happens that you get older. Now do you understand?

In addition to these problems, the short question-and-answer format of individual interviews violated the normal rules of discourse among the !Kung. In their conversational style several people participate in turn, each speaking for several minutes. Nevertheless, a small number of informants (far below the 200 target sample) did become interested in the issues and provided interesting and informative data on this topic (see below).

PROBLEMS OF RESEARCH IN RURAL IRELAND

Like many communities in rural Ireland, the population of Clifden has been dramatically affected by emigration. If children are excluded, more than 25 percent of the population is over 65, in contrast to 19.1 percent of the adult population of Swarthmore, another study site. In addition to questions of the type posed to the !Kung, residents of Clifden were asked to sort a series of cards on which were written a brief description: for example, "a widow who lives in a nursing home, with married children and grandchildren." Age was not mentioned on the cards, and respondents were asked to sort the cards into age categories and were asked questions about their categories. Over half of the respondents could not complete this task, since, as in the !Kung example, people rarely think of one another in age categories, and generalization based on age has a low "salience." One Irish woman began to ask questions about a card that described a hypothetical person as "a married woman, daughter takes care of her and her husband, has great-grandchildren."

> *Respondent*: Ah, about what age was she when she married? If she married quite young, she wouldn't be that old.
>
> *A. Glascock*: I can't say; you have to use what is on the card.
>
> *Respondent*: Well then, was her first child a daughter?
>
> *A. Glascock*: I don't know, she is not a real person.
>
> *Respondent*: How old was her daughter when she married?
>
> *A. Glascock*: I can't say, all I know about her is what is on the card.
>
> *Respondent*: Ah now, it wouldn't be possible for me to say who this person is without knowing something about her.

Respondents had little trouble naming "women living on Bridge Street," but experienced considerable difficulty in naming "older women living in Clifden." Questions such as "How does your health compare to other people of your age" were answered in many cases by responses such as "I couldn't say, really. Everyone's different and there's no way to say just one thing." In addition, as among the !Kung, the standard questionnaire format violated the normal rules of discourse, which among the rural Irish is indirect and allusive. For example, the local people communicated in various behavioral ways the irritation they felt with the probing nature of the card sort: they moved away from the table, looked away, crossed their arms, changed the tone of their voice. All these behaviors disappeared when the card sort and the interview were finished.

Despite methodological problems, such as the evident absence of a universal age category of "old" and the difficulty people in many societies experience in being asked to categorize people into age classes, the study has yielded interesting results.

AMERICA'S ELDERLY ARE NOT UNIQUE

In the United States, society's treatment of the elderly and the problems of elder care are prominent issues for politicians, community organizers, public health workers, authors and television producers, religious leaders, and even the courts. We often imagine that the problems of our society are unique, that we have more elders than ever before, that they are lonelier, more childless, more single and therefore more dependent on strangers than in other societies. The study suggests, however, that the proportion of individuals over 60 (19 percent in Swarthmore, 30 percent in Momence) in the American study sites is not greater than in some of the other sites. In Clifden, Ireland, for example, more than a quarter of the adult population is over 65, and the proportion of elderly among !Kung and Herero adults is slightly larger than in Swarthmore.

Nor are Americans less likely to have children. In America we often hear that declining birth rates coupled with greater longevity have produced increasing numbers of old people with only one or no surviving child to provide care in their parents' old age. Yet, here as well, Americans are not extreme. About 90 percent of the elderly men in the Swarthmore study and 82 percent of the elderly women had at least one child, in sharp contrast to the !Kung, among whom about 30 percent of the elderly were childless, although in the latter case, a number of parents had outlived their children—only 12–13 percent had never had a child. A similar pattern was observed among the Herero: 25 percent of elderly women were childless, but about half of these women had borne children who later died. In rural Ireland, more children survive but fewer adults have children. While only about 12 percent of elderly women were childless, fully 63 percent of elderly men had no offspring.

Americans also tend to think that the feminization of old age and the tendency for older women, in particular, to be unmarried or widowed is an artifact of demography and is universal. The A.G.E. study suggests that customs and values surrounding marriage have a greater effect than demography on the household composition of the elderly. Elderly people of both sexes in Swarthmore were as likely to be married as were the !Kung. For example, about one-quarter of the women and a smaller percentage of the men in each group were widowed. The !Kung value companionship in marriage and will remarry after the death of a spouse. Among the Herero, on the other hand, while three-quarters of the elderly *men* are married, three-quarters of the elderly *women* are single, widowed, or separated. In this society, marriage sanctified by the exchange of cattle is generally contracted between young girls and older men, who have the most cattle. Only 6 percent of the women never married, but widows do not remarry, and, in any case, do not look to their husbands for care or companionship. In Clifden, Ireland, in contrast, only about a quarter of elderly men *and* women are married. While over half of the elderly women are widowed, almost half of the elderly men (44 percent) in this community have *never* married. This phenomenon has been variously attributed to emigration and the absence of economic opportunity in a culture where men are expected to support wives and children. Unemployment among men is currently 35 percent and about three out of every five adults have lived overseas for at least one year.

It has been argued that the United States is such a mobile society that even if older people do have children, they rarely live close enough to be helpful. Among the !Kung, the Herero, and in Clifden, a large proportion (77 to 85 percent) of the elderly who had children had at least one living nearby. This proportion was somewhat smaller in Swarthmore, but of the Swarthmore elderly with children, about 60 percent had at least one child living in Swarthmore or within one hour's travel time. While child mobility is greater in the American sample than among the !Kung or Herero, it is even greater in the Irish sample. Many of the children of Clifden residents have emigrated and live abroad. The study found that 90 percent of the older people with children had at least one child overseas.

WHO CARES FOR THE ELDERLY?

In all the study sites, families, loosely defined, provide the majority of elder care, whether this is limited to economic assistance (provisioning) or extends to help with daily tasks. Yet both the definition of responsibility for elder care and the type of care expected differ markedly from site to site. In the United States, elders expect to be financially independent, even when they need help with daily tasks. In rural Ireland, where so many of the elderly, particularly men, are unmarried or childless or whose children live far away, and where economic assistance is provided by the state, daily or occasional help with living tasks is often provided by collateral relatives such as siblings, nieces, and nephews, or simply by close neighbors. About one-quarter of the Clifden elderly have no close relatives at all in Clifden, and about a third of older men have only one close relative in the community, usually an older sibling. A third of the elderly in this community live alone. Among the !Kung, who have no government help or stored capital, food and other economic assistance, as well as help with daily tasks, are expected from adult children but may also be provided by other close relatives living together in a small village. The presence of two or more adult children was correlated with an increase in the life expectancy of elderly mothers, but not of elderly fathers. Young children are not expected to care for the elderly on a regular basis. Because of remarriage, spouses are more available for care among the !Kung than among the Herero or Irish.

If demography accounts for all the differences in elder care, why are the elderly Herero, with their high rate of childlessness and large number of old unmarried women, not in trouble? Instead, the proportion of elderly Herero in the adult population, in general, and among women, in particular, is slightly higher than among the !Kung. Each Herero belongs to a cattle-holding lineage group, whose members are responsible for the economic well-being of its members. In addition, much as Americans and other societies derive great self-esteem from the care given to their children, a Herero draws more of his or her self-esteem from the care given to parents and older relatives. Since many elders are childless or have children away at school, young children are loaned or even fostered out to elders for the express purpose of providing care. Approximately 40 percent of all Herero children are reared by foster parents.

What happens when an elderly individual becomes frail and unable to care for himself or herself? In rural Ireland, behaviors that would signal an end of independent living in America—leaving the stove on, forgetting to turn on the heat, inability to drive, falling down the stairs, not recognizing friends and family—do not endanger the person or others to the same extent as in America. Houses do not have second stories, most older people do not drive in any case, and shopping can be done on foot. Neighbors and the community's visiting nurses make sure that the chimney has smoke coming out of it on a cold day. An old man who does not really recognize his surroundings might be escorted to and from the pub, where he will spend the day in a warm corner. Inappropriate behavior is explained as "He's a bit mental, you know."

ARE THE ELDERLY HAPPY?

One of the striking contrasts is the degree to which elderly Americans described themselves as happy, whereas the younger members of the American population were more negative in their self-evaluations. Americans place great emphasis on economic independence, and the elderly have this to a greater extent than the young and middle-aged. The elderly Irish of Clifden were also very happy with their lives, in part because they have a degree of economic security in the government dole, in part because they have access to good, almost free, low-tech health care. Two doctors and several visiting nurses make sure that every sick or frail individual is seen on a daily basis if necessary. The Clifden elderly also remember that life was much harder in this community 40 to 60 years ago, when they were young. The !Kung elderly, in contrast, rated their quality of life low, but only slightly less than the self-ratings of the middle-aged. Old Herero were at the opposite end of the scale in describing their age in the most pessimistic terms of any age group, despite what an outsider might see as a very high level of social support. In a somewhat rosy view of an imagined past in which old age was happily spent in the bosom of one's family, we tend to forget that modern society has mitigated many of the real discomforts of the elderly. The good to excellent level of social support routinely available in the two African sites cannot begin to compensate for the absence of furniture, mattresses, running water, central heat, antibiotics, eyeglasses, Tylenol, and false teeth.

A source of unhappiness in the American communities, but less so in Ireland or among the Herero or !Kung, was the degree to which American elderhood is marked by abrupt transitions, such as retirement or change of residence in order to be in a more manageable house or nearer to a child. Elders in the other societies more often continued their adult patterns of work, residence, and social interaction into elderhood. The abrupt transitions that mark elderhood in America, and which are less pronounced in a rural community such as Momence, are in part a corollary of the economic independence and wealth of elders. If private housing were uncommon and economic interdependence the norm, elders would find it easier to get help without compromising their cultural values.

THE A.G.E. PROJECT

The comparison of aging in seven locations has demonstrated that the living conditions, concerns, and even the definition of the elderly are strongly conditioned by cultural values and societal variables. Very different networks have been developed for caregiving in each society. The relatively high status of elderhood in some societies (e.g., in China, or among the Herero, where the elders nominally control the ownership and disposition of lineage cattle) does not appear to be correlated with happiness among the elderly. Though elders in more traditional societies are more likely to remain situated in supportive families and familiar communities, they feel keenly the physical losses of aging under circumstances in which there are few cushions or prostheses to ease their discomforts. Indeed there is a fine irony in the finding that traditional and modern societies satisfy different and mutually exclusive goals of the elderly: social connectedness in traditional societies and freedom from physical discomfort in more modern societies.

FURTHER READING

Draper, Patricia, and Anne Buchanan. 1992. "If You Have a Child You Have a Life: Demographic and Cultural Perspectives on Fathering in Old Age in !Kung Society." In Barry S. Hewlett, ed., *Father-Child Relations: Cultural and Biosocial Contexts,* pp. 131–52. Aldine de Gruyter.

Draper, Patricia, and Anthony P. Glascock. n.d. "Can You Ask It? Getting Answers to Questions about Age in Different Cultures." Unpublished manuscript.

Draper, Patricia, and Henry C. Harpending. 1994. "Work and Aging in Two African Societies: !Kung and Herero." In B. R. Bonder, ed., *Occupational Performance in the Elderly,* pp. 15–27. F. A. Davis.

Draper, Patricia, and Jennie Keith. 1992. "Cultural Context of Care: Family Caregiving for Elderly in America and Africa." *Journal of Aging Studies* 6(2): 113–33.

Fry, Christine L., and Jennie Keith, eds. 1986. *New Methods for Old Age Research: Strategies for Studying Diversity.* Bergin and Garvey.

Sokolovsky, Jay, ed. 1990. *The Cultural Context of Aging: Worldwide Perspectives.* Bergin and Garvey.

27 ETHNOGRAPHIC FILM

Then and Now

John P. Homiak

T
ime was when ethnographic films were rather straightforward visual documents that depicted ceremonies, socialization patterns,
or phases in the subsistence cycles of small-scale traditional societies. Films such as *Trance and Dance in Bali* or *Bathing Babies in Three
Cultures* by Margaret Mead immediately come to mind. Such films served
as visual illustrations of the concepts or cultural categories about which
anthropologists most frequently wrote (e.g., ritual, myth, socialization, or
identity).

The authority of these films rested, by and large, not in their images,
but in the commentary spoken over the image track. For good reason: the
images of ethnographic film typically confront us with cultural differ-

Editors' note: In recent years, anthropology, like other disciplines, has undergone a radical transformation in the wake of new intellectual currents. As anthropologist John Homiak explains in his discussion
of recent trends in ethnographic film, "There has been a shift from objectivity and 'facts' to subjectivity
and 'points of view.'" Anthropologists, in addition, have had to come to terms with the legacy of their
discipline's colonial roots, as the world's indigenous peoples increasingly engage in their own self-study
and representation. In writing ethnographies and in making ethnographic film, most anthropologists today would subscribe to the belief that understanding another culture can at best be only partial and always filtered through the lens of one's own limiting cultural perspectives. In addition, all films reflect the
filmmaker's gender, race, experience, and degree of familiarity with the culture. In analyzing recent ethnographic films, Homiak focuses on two major perspectives—the "indigenous perspective" and the
"global perspective"—that help explain challenges to and changes in ethnographic filmmaking and cultural representation.

ences—with scenes of people in faraway places engaged in seemingly exotic behaviors. The sound track carries the burden of meaning by explaining to viewers the significance of such unfamiliar behaviors and events.

Before the subtitling of native speech in the early 1970s, it was usually a "voice-of-god" narration that provided this translation in definitive and unequivocal terms. At times, the narration even took on an omniscient quality, as in the case of *The Hunters* (John Marshall, 1957) or *Dead Birds* (Robert Gardner, 1963). The narrators of these films liberally attribute thoughts to the subjects and seemingly know their every feeling, thought, and desire. Until recently (the past 15 years), this was not a problem for anthropologists because, like the general public, we accepted the conventions of cinematic realism by which these films were constructed. Never mind that the giraffe hunt in *The Hunters* was constructed from footage shot of various hunts; or that the tribal battle in *Dead Birds* was similarly constructed. As long as it was seen to serve the end of ethnographic "truth," such continuity editing was not seen as particularly problematic.

This, of course, has made "authenticity" a somewhat more complex issue in ethnographic film, but we generally assume that unrehearsed "naturally occurring" events are being recorded. All of this is supported by the unobtrusive camera associated with the documentary mode, the so-called fly-on-the-wall perspective that remained dominant from Robert Flaherty's *Nanook of the North* (1922) until at least the early 1970s. This style of shooting makes an implicit claim to observational neutrality as seen, for example, in such made-for-television films as *National Geographic Specials,* Granada Television's *Disappearing Worlds,* and the BBC's *Under the Sun* series. One of the primary reasons why these visual texts continue to be popular among general audiences is that they appear transparent and objective.

ETHNOGRAPHIC FILM TODAY

> CUT! CUT! I want camera one to come in tight on the Shaman's face. . . .
> Let me see the anthropologist actually talking to him. . . . The subject has
> to speak. . . . All right, Take Two. . . .

Today, the encounter between ethnographic filmmakers and what we fashionably call "the Other" has dramatically shifted. Filming as if the camera were not there has given way to a more frank admission of the fact

that ethnographic films entail an encounter between the members of two cultures. In this regard, many films are now reflexive, incorporating strategies of presentation so that the terms, and even meanings, of an encounter between filmmaker and "Other" are foregrounded as part of the context of the film itself. Now we not only see the Other but we also see the filmmaker showing us the Other. In theory, this serves to destroy any illusion that film is or can be an unambiguous representation of "reality" by giving viewers access to the intersubjective basis on which ethnographic knowledge and understanding is constructed. This helps viewers remain aware of the fact that films, like written texts, adopt particular perspectives and reflect points of view—rather than express some transparent representation of "the truth." Many filmmakers now go out of their way to make clear that anthropologists traditionally engaged not in silent observation but in speaking and interacting with their subjects. The filmmaker/anthropologist is part of the plot. Being open about this dialogical process and about the intentions of filmmakers and subjects alike is also seen as a way to humanize anthropological subjects rather than treating them as examples of abstract or formal principles. This is part of a "postmodern" turn that, to a considerable degree, has served to collapse the separation between a traditional "them" and a modern "us."

In visual ethnography—as in its written counterpart—there has been a shift from objectivity and "facts" to subjectivity and "points of view." Following upon the impacts of interpretive, Marxist, and feminist theory in anthropology, we recognize that even the cultures of small-scale societies that were previously the stock-in-trade of the discipline can no longer be presented as unified and homogeneous realities. We understand that meanings are contested and negotiated in these (as in our own) societies—reflecting factors of age, gender, class, status, and power. In recognition of this complexity of society, films more often feature multiple voices and contested versions of reality. "Closed" didactic readings of societies by the anthropologist and filmmaker have yielded to "open" expressive readings that reflect more direct access to the "lived experiences" of subjects.

This latter effort to resituate the individual as the primary focus of ethnographic filmmaking grades over into postmodern concerns with voice and authority. The omniscient voice-of-God noted above is now déclassé and politically under attack. Filmmakers increasingly listen for indigenous voices "speaking with" or alongside their subjects with the intent of allowing subjects to voice their own concerns. Some advocate a kind of "participatory cinema" initiated by the most prolific of French ethnographic filmmakers, Jean Rouch. In this approach, filmmaker and subjects seek to work out an authentic collaboration that provides the latter a greater role in constructing their own images or that results in films that take us where their subjects want to go.

Around the globe, however, many of the traditional subjects of the filmmaker's gaze argue that anthropologists and other professionals should have no authority at all to represent them. Indigenous groups feel that the only way their stories can truthfully be told is if the means of production

are wholly in native control. It is in this climate that native filmmakers have emerged as "professional Others" who seek to "speak back" to the dominant culture in their own terms.

THE MARGARET MEAD FILM FESTIVAL

The annual Margaret Mead Film and Video Festival, held at New York City's American Museum of Natural History, typically covers all the kinds of documentary genres discussed above and also showcases new and innovative works by independent, ethnographic, and indigenous filmmakers. The Seventeenth Festival, held in October 1993, included a special focus on indigenous media, featuring several native filmmakers—from Papua New Guinea, Native American and Canadian Inuit communities, Japan, and Ghana.

In what follows I review one film that illustrates reflexive and participatory approaches, then turn to others that demonstrate the diversity of approaches within the indigenous perspective. Two final films reflect the growing concern with global and transnational outlooks.

The Earth Is Our Mother

This 1992 film depicts the encounter between Danish documentary filmmaker Peter Elsass and a community of Archuaco Indians in Colombia.

Inhabitants of a coca-growing region contested by the Colombian state, drug lords, and guerrilla forces, the Archuaco find their way of life and their communities caught in the struggle between these warring elements. The Archuaco and their elders were the subject of Elsass's first film, *The Earth Is Our Mother,* which shows the role played by Archuaco elders in passing on and preserving the traditional culture of their people.

Elsass returns six years later to document the Archuaco response to the first film and to follow up on the impact that this film has had upon the community. *The Journey Back* insightfully and sometimes humorously explores the politics that emerge from this type of collaboration.

The filmmaker chose to advocate the cultural autonomy of his subjects and builds this into the film at various turns. At one point, the Archuaco confront Colombian soldiers who occupy their most sacred ritual site. At another point, they accompany an elder to Bogota, the capital, to protest the murder of three Archuaco leaders believed slain by government security forces. The film thus provides a firsthand look at the conflicts of race and culture in Colombia and the ways in which an indigenous people strive to perpetuate their way of life.

Elsass's two "participatory" films bring the inaccessible and distant— so typically a fixture of ethnographic film—close to our own political homefront. The film underscores the toll that the international drug trade takes on both the producers and consumers. In the global village, the little-known tribulations of the Archuaco are paradoxically juxtaposed with the unrest and violence of our own inner cities.

Inuit-Produced Videos

A series of videos from the festival's indigenous media category are worthy of note. These are three Inuit-produced videotapes on Inuit culture directed and produced by Zacharias Kunuk, an Inuit filmmaker from Igloolik, Northwest Territories, Canada: *Qaggig* (Gathering Place, 1989), *Nunaqpa* (Going Inland, 1991), and *Saputi* (The Fish Trap, 1992). These videos have as their primary audience Inuit peoples themselves. All were made under the direction of Inuit elders and involve the "reconstruction" and representation of various traditional Inuit practices. In contrast to the external contextualizing commentary of the anthropologist, we have only the subtitled dialogue of the Inuit. Re-creating the recent past that exists only in memory, Kunuk seeks to keep alive a sense of identity grounded in a traditional way of life.

Those who have seen films from the Netsilik Eskimo Series will find interesting parallels in Kunuk's videos—but in this case with a different sense of pacing and perspective in imaging the land, and in personal touches that give a sense of psychological realism and intimacy to the social interactions among the Inuit.

Imagining Indians

By far the most notable film in the festival's indigenous category was Victor Masayesva's *Imagining Indians* (1992). This Hopi filmmaker presents a native perspective on the misrepresentation of Native Americans through feature films. Masayesva breaks with strict documentary conventions and feels free to use a combination of scripted scenes, documentary and feature archival footage, and interviews. Weaving a complex narrative, he plumbs the ways in which Native Americans react to, attempt to work with, or overtly resist their representation by the dominant white culture. We get an eye-opening native look at recent popular films by Kevin Costner and Robert Redford. Intercut through all this is a subtheme suggesting that a romanticized "noble savage" view of American Indians has gone hand-in-hand with the commodification (commercialism) and appropriation of their arts and material culture.

Employing a keen sense of irony, Masayesva opens the film with a scene in a dentist's office, the walls of which are covered with broadsides for Hollywood films featuring Indians. The patient, a Native American woman, is seen seated in the dentist chair, her mouth plugged ("silenced") with cotton tubes. The ensuing inability of the dentist to communicate with his patient stands as a metaphor for the misunderstandings explored by the filmmaker—just as the visit to the dentist (read: "white man's medicine") constitutes a metaphor, which speaks on various levels both to whites and Native Americans. Virtually any viewer will associate the dentist's office with anxiety and discomfort, a sentiment that Masayesva plays out filmically as he registers the sentiments that Native Americans express at being variously patronized and controlled by the dominant white culture. Throughout the film the dentist office scene reappears periodically to frame newly introduced subthemes.

What is most refreshing about *Imagining Indians,* however, is not simply its "indigenous" perspective, but the fact that Masayesva (unlike some other native filmmakers and some anthropologists), recognizes the existence of diversity and even ambiguity within this perspective. There is no single voice that "speaks back" to the dominant white culture—but many competing voices with individual points of view. At one point the filmmaker explores native protest to a recent production by Robert Redford that casts a non-Indian in the starring role as a Native American. The inserts of two Native American "talking heads" appear on the screen, each simultaneously articulating a different viewpoint on the matter.

THE LOCAL IN THE GLOBAL

Culture within the global ethnospace presents another theme that has emerged in ethnographic filmmaking over the past few years. Cultures are becoming progressively "deterritorialized" as native peoples migrate to the colonial motherlands, as traditional art is commodified and produced for consumption within a world system, and as people find different ways of creating ethnicity in different sites of their respective diasporas. We can no longer maintain the fiction of presenting "the local" without reference to the global.

In the 1960s anthropologists began to handle these new realities through network analysis, in the 1970s through recourse to the concept of "world system," and in the 1980s by reference to transnationalism. All along, however, most ethnographic filmmakers remained content to make films in rustic peasant villages or distant islands or other remote "traditional" sites. The formula, in fact, remains popular for the types of made-for-television documentaries noted above. No doubt it produces the familiar feel for the exotic that audiences have come to appreciate in films dubbed "ethnographic."

But the world is now much more complex. Even television—with its current penchant for using images of the Other in advertising—tells us as much. Today Aboriginal Australians control their own broadcasting network and display their art in the fashionable galleries of New York; Buddhist temples exist in the heartland of America; a fair majority of Maori in New Zealand have embraced the creed of Rastafari, a religion and culture "invented" in the African Diaspora; and Songhay and other West African traders ply an international trade on the streets of Harlem. Culture, the so-called object of anthropological study, stubbornly refuses to stay in its place and be properly analyzed regardless of how much we anthropologists long for the simplicity of our pastoral field sites.

While many popular documentaries continue to uphold the fiction of a radical separation between a modern "us" and a traditional "them," the postmodern turn in filmmaking continues to dissolve this fiction. Films such as *Cannibal Tours* (1987), *In and Out of Africa* (1990), *Black Harvest* (1992), and *Valencia Diary* (1992) all show the complex ways in which the local and the global domains intersect and are implicated in one another.

CONCLUSION

Over the past two decades, ethnographic film has undergone a series of transformations, from films that are didactic and ones in which individuals appear as cultural "types" rather than full-bodied individuals, to ones that are reflexive and that incorporate narrative strategies of presentation, providing access to indigenous voices and concerns. Many of these changes in visual ethnography took place before the more talked about postmodern turn in the writing of ethnographic texts. The concern with "dispersed authority"—producing texts that present more provisional readings of cultural phenomena in which the burden of representation is somehow "shared" between ethnographer and subjects—was recognized as an issue in ethnographic filmmaking over a decade before it became a concern in "writing culture." Perhaps one of the reasons for this is that film images are specific and cannot in themselves generalize from the immediacy of the occurrences they record. Film presents behavior and events "fully-formed" and cannot as easily overlook the specific individuals they present to our gaze.

Concerns over voice and authority have led to a repositioning of the subject across broad swaths of ethnographic film. Films are more open to native voices and concerns. In addition, more films seek to produce representations commensurate with the lived experience of the specific and named individuals that they depict. This tradition, of course, has a long history dating to Robert Flaherty's *Nanook of the North*. Now, however, in addition to Nanook, we are more likely to recognize other "stars" of ethnographic cinema—Damoré Zika, !Nai, Onka, Jero Tapakan, and others. Largely because of these developments, more anthropologists now consider ethnographic film to be an alternative means of representation with its own strengths and weaknesses, rather than merely an adjunct to the ethnographic text.

In acknowledging that film is a form of communication (as argued for decades by scholars such as Sol Worth and Jay Ruby), there is an accompanying expectation that more critical skills for "reading" film need to be brought to bear by those who use them. This is especially true given the challenge of "indigenous perspectives" and indigenously produced media. Ethnographic films are not merely depictions of "the real"; they articulate points of view and incorporate ideologies of their own. I concur with the assessment recently put forward by Jay Ruby that "the move to give greater voice and authority to the subject [in film] has now reached a logical but extreme point" (Ruby, 1991:54). What indigenous voices say about themselves and their situation is as much data to be interpreted as it is an insight into the world of the Other.

FURTHER READING

Crawford, Peter Ian, and David Turton, eds. 1992. *Film as Ethnography*. Manchester University Press.

Heider, Karl G. 1995. *Films for Anthropological Teaching*. 8th ed. American Anthropological Association.

Heider, Karl G. 1997. *Seeing Anthropology: Cultural Anthropology through Film*. Allyn and Bacon.

McDougall, David. 1975. "Beyond Observational Cinema." In Paul Hockings, ed. 1975. *Principles of Visual Anthropology*. 2d edition. Mouton de Gruyter.

Rollwagen, Jack R., ed. 1988. *Anthropological Filmmaking*. Harwood Academic.

Rollwagen, Jack R., ed. 1993. *Anthropological Film and Video in the 1990s*. Dual Printing.

Ruby, Jay. 1980. "Exposing Yourself: Reflexivity, Anthropology, and Film." *Semiotica* 30:153–79.

Ruby, Jay. 1991. "Speaking For, Speaking About, Speaking With, or Speaking Alongside: An Anthropological and Documentary Dilemma." *Visual Anthropology Review* 7:50–67.

28 150 YEARS OF NATIVE AMERICAN RESEARCH AT THE SMITHSONIAN

JoAllyn Archambault and William C. Sturtevant

P reserving the past for the future has always been an important mission of the Smithsonian Institution. From the beginning, Native Americans have held a special place in this endeavor, as contributors and users of knowledge. The Smithsonian, a great repository of cultural, social, and biological information, has often assisted tribal groups in preserving, strengthening, and renewing knowledge of their own culture and history. In turn, native people have been actively involved in major contributions to the research goals of the Institution. In honor of the Smithsonian's 150th anniversary celebration, we present here a short overview of the Department of Anthropology's ethnological and archaeological research on the peoples and cultures of the Americas and native participation in this work.

BACKGROUND

The Smithsonian Institution was founded by legislation signed August 10, 1846. Almost immediately it became the leading supporter of anthropological research in America. The first secretary, Joseph Henry, instituted a series of publications called *Smithsonian Contributions to Knowledge* to record "new discoveries in science." Among the earliest volumes was a report on Indian mounds in the eastern United States, which demonstrated that they had been built by prehistoric Indian societies, not by some unknown non-Indian civilization as many scholars thought. Other reports based on investigations of prehistoric and living Indian societies soon followed. Along with the published reports, the Institution began to acquire a vast collection of manuscript descriptions and recordings of Indian cultures and languages. The U.S. National Museum served as the repository for contemporary and archaeological Native American collections and works of art. Many of these collections were gathered by Smithsonian staff members and other people, including Native Americans, and are preserved for exhibition and especially for study to benefit all peoples.

Native American research at the Smithsonian grew rapidly, especially after the founding in 1879 of the Smithsonian's Bureau of American Ethnology (BAE), a research unit independent of the U.S. National Museum that specialized in Native American studies, particularly in ethnology and linguistics. The research of the BAE was preserved and disseminated in several ways. The BAE itself archived the manuscript and photographic results of research. The objects collected by the BAE as documents of both living and prehistoric Indian cultures were preserved by the museum. The BAE published more than 250 volumes describing Native American cultures, languages, prehistory, and history. Much of the information recorded in these volumes and a great deal of the data preserved in manuscripts and photographs archived by the BAE are documented nowhere else. Without active collecting, much of this material would have been lost forever as Indian cultures, societies, and languages underwent rapid changes.

In 1965 the staff and archives of the BAE were merged with the museum's Department of Anthropology, whose primary emphasis was then on archaeology and physical anthropology. Today, the department continues to focus on Native American studies alongside interests in the peoples and cultures of Asia, Africa, Oceania, and South America and involves all subdisciplines of anthropology (ethnology, linguistics, archaeology, physical anthropology and applied).

INDIAN PARTICIPATION

Research and publication on American Indian languages, literatures, history, and social relations depend on contributions by the people who are the bearers of the cultures. To record, analyze, and describe a language, a literature, a traditional history, a religion, or a system of social relations requires the cooperation and the active assistance of those who speak the language and possess the knowledge and beliefs that are recorded. In some cases, Native Americans write the information and organize it for publication. In other cases, they explain to others who serve as recorders and analysts. Archaeology and physical anthropology are less dependent on the active participation of Native Americans although their insight has proven beneficial. The Smithsonian anthropological staff, from its early days, has included distinguished Indian scholars, such as Francis La-Flesche (Omaha) and J. N. B. Hewitt (Tuscarora). Many other Indians were important correspondents and contributors, although not staff members. Among these were Andrew John (Seneca), Phoebe Maddux (Karok), James Murie (Pawnee), Whewa (Zuni), George Bushotter (Sioux), George Washington Grayson (Creek), George Hunt (Tlingit-Kwakiutl), John Squint Eyes (Cheyenne), George Sword (Lakota), Alfred Kiyana (Mesquakie), Henry Tate (Tsimshian), William Jones (Fox), Isabel Meadows (Costanoan), and Seth Newhouse (Mohawk). Scores of individual members of tribes in all parts of North America have contributed knowledge and information that was recorded by Smithsonian staff members and other contributors to the Smithsonian archives and publications. The Department of Anthropology's staff currently includes two archaeologists of Indian ancestry, and the ethnologist director of its American Indian Program is an enrolled member of the Standing Rock Sioux tribe.

One current project of the department is the 20-volume *Handbook of North American Indians,* an encyclopedia summarizing knowledge of the cultures, history, and human biology of all the tribes of the continent. Indians have been active in planning this reference work and in writing many chapters; three of the volumes have Indian editors. Since 1978, 10 volumes have been published, and the rest are in active preparation.

PAST AND PRESENT RESEARCH

Smithsonian anthropologists were prominent pioneers advocating Indian rights and respect for Indian cultures and languages and have remained so. "Anthropologists were among the few who felt that Indian cultures had any value in the late 19th century" says JoAllyn Archambault (Standing Rock Sioux), who directs the American Indian Program of the Department of Anthropology. "They felt that Indian lives and culture had meaning. That is why they wanted to document and save the information and images of our people. And they saved them for future generations of every race."

Anthropologists learned from Indian people and tried, quite successfully, to pass on to others what they learned about the richness and variety of Indian cultures, the complexity and sophistication of Indian thought and belief, the great antiquity of Indian settlement of the Americas, and the thousands of years of inventions and adjustments to the environment. They have continually reminded those who came later how much is owed to their Indian predecessors, and how much was unjustly taken from them.

One of the first Smithsonian anthropologists was Frank Hamilton Cushing, who lived at Zuni Pueblo in New Mexico for four years in the early 1880s. Learning the language, he was adopted by Palowahtiwa, the Zuni governor, and given a ritual position in the Pueblo. Cushing pioneered the anthropological method of participant observation that was reinvented elsewhere in the present century. After he had compiled a valuable record of Zuni culture, he was recalled to Washington because he had defended the Pueblo against the illegal taking of its lands by a politically well-connected outsider.

About the same time another Smithsonian anthropologist, James Mooney, began long-term study of the Eastern Cherokee, recording their historical struggle to remain in their homeland. He collected native curing formulas written in Sequoyah's syllabary and studied ball games and other features of Cherokee culture. In the 1890s he conducted a firsthand study of the new Ghost Dance in the West, interviewing Wovoka, the founding prophet. Mooney demonstrated the religious nature of the movement in an attempt to convince the U.S. government that it posed no military threat. He then began an extensive study of Kiowa heraldry (manifested in designs on shields and tipis) in Indian Territory, which he soon was forced to give up as a result of his activities defending participants in the Native American Church.

Working in Washington, D.C., in the latter half of the nineteenth century, C. C. Royce compiled a detailed study of Indian lands lost throughout the country. The maps he prepared, published by the Smithsonian, served some 50 years later as the fundamental evidence by which Indian tribes were recompensed via hearings held by the Indian Claims Commission.

The first scientifically based and accepted classification of the historical relationships of North American native languages was published in 1891

312 Our Many Cultures

under the direction of John Wesley Powell, the founder and first chief of the Bureau of American Ethnology. Much of the evidence for that classification is preserved in the department's archives; some of it is irreplaceable data on languages that have ceased to be spoken.

In the mid-twentieth century, Smithsonian ethnologist John C. Ewers wrote the standard text used in Blackfeet Indian schools to teach Blackfeet history. Ewers attributed the success of his research to the Blackfeet elders, born in the middle of the last century, who passed on their knowledge to him.

Today, many Tzotzil Indians in Chiapas, Mexico, are producing a literature in their own language, thanks to the literacy program of the Chiapas Writers' Cooperative encouraged and assisted by Smithsonian anthropologist Robert M. Laughlin. Laughlin has devoted 30 years to research in Chiapas, publishing two massive dictionaries of the Tzotzil language. These provide important evidence used in the decipherment of ancient Maya inscriptions that is revealing the history of this Native American civilization. He has also published several volumes of native literature in Tzotzil as well as in English translation.

Ives Goddard, linguist at the Smithsonian, recently published, with Kathleen Bragdon, *Native Writings in Massachusett,* two large volumes that contain all known writings in the Massachusett language by its speakers, together with new translations into English and annotations on the grammar and vocabulary. This language, extinct since about 1826, was spoken by the ancestors of the present-day Wampanoag Indians of Mashpee and Gay Head, Massachusetts (see chapter 24).

William C. Sturtevant, general editor of the *Handbook of North American Indians,* researched the cultures and history of the Florida Seminoles and New York Senecas and over the years has provided expert testimony in defense of Indian land rights and in support of federal recognition of Indian tribes. The testimony of Smithsonian anthropologists, behind the scenes and in formal hearings before the courts and congressional committees, often has proven helpful to Indian communities. Smithsonian anthropologists, known as objective, knowledgeable authorities on Indian history and Indian cultures, have frequently been called on.

The Arctic Studies Center, established in the department in 1988 by William Fitzhugh, is an extension of research begun in the 1860s in Alaska and the western part of Arctic and Subarctic Canada. Other early Smithsonian research, both ethnological and archaeological, was carried out among Indians and Inuit in the eastern Arctic. The new center is involved in research, education, and training of native peoples and the coordination of activities with other government agencies. Fellowships and internships in Arctic and Subarctic studies are available to native individuals. Before and after the establishment of the center, Fitzhugh organized major exhibitions of Arctic native cultures at the Smithsonian, which then traveled to other locations, including cities in Alaska. Special versions were sent to rural locations in Alaska and Siberia making available to native peoples aspects of their own history. Assistance to native museums is a continuing interest of the Arctic Studies Center.

The Archives Program administers both the National Anthropological Archives (NAA) and the Human Studies Film Archives (HSFA). The NAA is the repository for manuscript records on Native American and other cultures and languages, for many thousands of historical photographs of American Indian subjects, and for the papers of Indian and anthropological organizations. The papers of the National Congress of American Indians, the National Tribal Chairmen's Association, Beatrice Medicine, and Helen Peterson are deposited in the NAA. The core of the NAA are the records and photographs collected by the former Bureau of American Ethnology and the museum department since its beginnings. The HSFA collects and documents ethnographic film and video records. It also serves as a clearinghouse for Native American films and videos produced by other organizations and makes films and videos available to Indian communities.

THE AMERICAN INDIAN PROGRAM

The American Indian Program of the Department of Anthropology was founded in 1986 to coordinate and increase Native American involvement with the department. The program provides outreach to Indian communities and individuals, making the department more accessible to native people. It encourages research, collection of contemporary Indian objects, exhibitions, and public programming by and about native people. It has initiated numerous programs with reservation-based community colleges, tribal museums, tribal education departments, and elder groups. Fellows in the American Indian Program are diverse in age, experience, background, and interest. Their projects have been equally diverse, ranging from film research to object collection research by artists to inform their art making. The results of their projects are now used in various community activities in urban and reservation areas. Most recently a group from the Coquille reservation in Oregon found thousands of pages of relevant materials in Washington, had them copied, and has deposited the copies in a local archives where they can be used by tribal members for their own personal research. Several tribes have obtained language materials from the National Anthropological Archives for use in their language programs. Others have used historical photographs to enhance exhibits created for their tribal museums. The program provides technical assistance to tribal museums and cultural programs upon request.

In July 1997 the Department of Anthropology celebrated its 100th anniversary, looking back with pride on its many contributions. At the same time, it is embracing the future, as the field of anthropology continues to change and the department forges new relationships with native peoples.

FURTHER READING

Hinsley, Curtis M. 1994. *The Smithsonian and the American Indian: Making a Moral Anthropology in Victorian America.* Smithsonian Institution Press.

29 RACE AND ETHNICITY IN AMERICA

Alison S. Brooks, Fatimah L. C. Jackson,
and R. Richard Grinker

Varieties of (*Homo sapiens*): "*Africanus negreus (black), Americanus rubescens (red), Asiaticus fuscus (tawny), and Europeus albescens (white).*"

—Linnaeus, 1758

In my opinion, to dismember mankind into races . . . requires such a dis-
tortion of the facts that any usefulness disappears.

—Hiernaux, 1964:43

Race and subrace do represent a truth about the natural world, which cannot be adequately described without consideration of them.

—Baker, 1974:4

Race is a term originally applied to populations who shared close common
ancestry and certain unique traits, but it has been so overworked and its
applications so broad and general that race is nearly useless and is often
replaced by *ethnic group*.

—Molnar, 1992:36

It is important . . . to have a clear . . . understanding of the difference between race and racism, on the one hand, and ethnicity and ethnocentrism
on the other.

—Smedley, 1993:29

Shortly after birth, each American baby is placed in a box—not a
physical box, just a box on a piece of paper. This process, which
counts the child as belonging to one and only one "race" or "ethnic
group," will be repeated over and over throughout an individual's lifetime.

315

Current American "boxes" include: (1) White, (2) Black, (3) Hispanic, (4) American Indian, (5) Eskimo or Aleut, (6) Asian or Pacific Islander. Anthropology departments sometimes receive desperate calls from parents: "I am from Pakistan, should I check 'white' or 'Asian'?" "My wife and I belong to different groups, how do we classify our baby?"

As a child grows, the "box" often will be designated by others, without the person's knowledge or input, as though a simple set of rules could generate a "correct" classification. But is there such a set of rules? Such classification implies that pure races and cultures existed with little intermixture in the recent past. But did such a time ever exist? Before air travel? Before Columbus? Before Marco Polo?

As the initial quotations suggest, anthropologists disagree about the subject of race and ethnicity, and opinions have radically changed over time. Far from reflecting biological and cultural "reality," race and ethnicity are terms increasingly seen as arbitrary constructs fulfilling a social need, with content and limits negotiated among members of each society. How else can we explain why university affirmative action offices in the United States group people from the Indian subcontinent with "whites," whereas, until recently in South Africa, they were officially "Asians." Japanese visitors to South Africa, however, were classified as "whites." In the 1990 U.S. census, every non-Native American who is *not* of Asian descent must be either "black" or "white," while 3,500,000 non-Asian South Africans were classified as "coloured," neither "black" nor "white."

For over 100 years, "science"—particularly its biological and anthropological branches—has been asked three questions: Do races exist? If so, why? What is the most accurate racial classification, whether absolute or relative to geography and history? The larger question, most recently addressed by the scientists themselves, is: Why do we care? Why is the race issue important to scholars, and, even more so, to American society at large?

EARLY CLASSIFICATIONS: EIGHTEENTH CENTURY

Anthropology is the field of knowledge most closely connected to the study of human differences, although attempts to recognize and describe such differences are more ancient than the formal study of anthropology. The French naturalist Georges Buffon, writing in the mid-eighteenth century, may have been the first scholar to use the word "race" to describe the varieties within a single species, whether humans or dogs, and to attribute these differences to local alterations of a single ancestral group. Like more modern biologists, he saw these physical differences as responses to different climates, diets, and even patterns of behavior or cultural practices. We now know that agriculture, for example, resulted in decreasing tooth size in modern humans.

In the eighteenth century, following Linnaeus's classification of the varieties of *Homo,* the German scholar and physician Johann Friedrich Blumenbach developed the concept of human races. He drew up lists of physical and behavioral differences among five major "races": Caucasian (Linnaeus's white or *Europaeus albescens*), Mongolian (*Asiaticus fuscus* L.), Ethiopian (*Africanus negreus*), American (*Americanus rubescens* L.), and Malay, the latter not distinguished in Linnaeus's classification, but added in later editions of Blumenbach's work to encompass the peoples of Southeast Asia and the Pacific. Like Buffon, Blumenbach argued for a single origin of humankind, but thought that some races had "degenerated" from their original state.

RACE AND RACISM: NINETEENTH CENTURY

From Blumenbach on, physicians dominated the study of human physical differences, emphasizing human anatomy rather than a broad natural history viewpoint. Early-nineteenth-century scholars, like the American physician Samuel Morton, used flawed statistics to show that Caucasians had the largest brains, "Negroes" the smallest (Gould, 1981). Morton attributed these differences to separate creation (polygenism), rather than to adaptation or degeneration, and saw them as immutable. Gould, Smedley (1993), and others have argued that this shift reflects the emergence of a worldview in which physical differences or "race" dominated all other kinds of differences such as class or nationality, and were used to justify the oppression of Africans in particular by peoples of European descent.

Smedley's chapter, "Growth of the English Ideology of Race in America," argues that the English, isolated from the more cosmopolitan Mediterranean world, were particularly unprepared to assimilate people with cultural and physical differences. The English colonized Ireland and America at the same time and grouped both Irish and American natives as "heathen," "idolatrous," "wild," and "savage," characteristics used to justify the appropriation of native lands by the more "civilized" English, and the removal or enslavement of the natives themselves.

Anthropologists, though clearly enmeshed in a racist and ethnocentric European and American culture of nineteenth-century scholarship, saw themselves as countering the prevailing theories of the day by asserting human unity. In 1871, Edward B. Tylor, an Englishman and founder of anthropology, defined the discipline as the study of "man and the races of man." Although Tylor was careful to separate race and culture, physical anthropologists, many of whom continued to support polygenism, tended to confuse race and culture as well as to regard psychological traits and cognitive abilities as inborn, as are skin color and hair form.

BIOLOGY AND CULTURE: SEPARATE BUT CONFUSED

The confusion of biology and culture continued into the functionalist era of the 1920s and 1930s, with the application of organic models and adaptationist explanations to social phenomena. For example, it was asserted that just as dark skin evolved to protect humans from excessive ultraviolet radiation, so "joking relationships" with the mother's brother evolved to balance a strict avoidance relationship with the father and his relatives. Many so-called functional explanations of biological traits, in particular, were based on untested assumptions. Black boxes are perfect radiators of heat, so it was assumed that dark bodies would perform better in hot weather. In a series of tests conducted by the French army in North Africa, however, performance differences between whites and blacks under extreme heat conditions failed to materialize. The confusion of biological

and cultural or ethnic differences, together with an extreme view of racial and ethnic separation, derived from the polygenists, was incorporated into Nazi ideas of racial hierarchy and purity.

HOW MANY RACES?

With more than 200 years of scholarship on the topic of human variation, do we know how many races or how many ethnic groups there are? Biologists define races as populations of a species that differ genetically from one another. The emphasis on genetic differences is important, since two unrelated populations that inhabit the same area can come to resemble one another physically as both respond to the same selective forces. Since gene pools change over time in response to natural selection, mutation, random events, and migration or hybridization, biological races are also limited in time. Can the human species be divided into populations that differ genetically from one another?

Many anthropologists today would argue that such a division is impossible, due to extensive migration and hybridization among human groups throughout human history. In a reaction to the discredited studies of the early twentieth century, many anthropologists have pointed to the continuous or "clinal" nature of human variation, arguing that biological "races," in fact, do not exist. There is no line across the middle of the Sahara, or the Mediterranean, that divides people into "white" and "black," nor is there a north-south line in Eurasia dividing "whites" from

"Mongoloids" or "Asians." Even the New World remained in genetic contact with the Old through the intermingling of seafaring peoples from both sides of the Bering Sea, as well as of Inuit and Norse in Greenland. Nor is there a set of criteria that will reliably differentiate members of these large racial groups. The use of skin color will group Africans with native peoples of Australia and south Indians, while the use of hair form and hair color will group the latter two with Europeans.

What about genetics? Should not a comparison of the genetics of different populations allow us to define differences and reconstruct historical relationships? Yes, argues L. L. Cavalli-Sforza of Stanford University, who has used genetic traits determined from blood samples to construct trees of relatedness for large numbers of human groups worldwide. Genetic traits unrelated to surface differences were once considered to reflect a deeper genetic relationship between peoples, unaffected by natural selection. We now know, however, that even such supposedly "neutral" features as your blood group (A, B, AB, or O) are often subject to natural selection in a way that creates similarities in groups that are otherwise unrelated. For example, both the Irish and the Blackfoot Indians have similar frequencies of A blood; this is more likely to reflect a common disease history than any migration event of the past. People with type A blood appear to have been more susceptible to smallpox, while people with O blood were more frequently felled by bubonic plague.

Rebecca Cann, of the University of Hawaii, has constructed trees based on the overall similarity of the mitochondrial DNA genomes in *individuals* of different populations. These trees often cluster individuals from different populations together, particularly in very diverse regions such as Africa. But Jonathan Marks of Yale University, among others, cautions against the too rapid acceptance of population relationships based on DNA similarities. The degree of similarity between two strands of DNA is a subjective judgment, particularly if the strands are of different lengths, due to deletions or repetitions in one, relative to the other. Furthermore, as long as we do not understand the relationship between particular DNA sequences and particular traits, we do not know what we are looking at.

Can we even define a local population of humans for the purpose of sampling it and comparing it to others? On a local level, geographers have demonstrated the existence of breeding populations in humans, reflected in the statistical tendency to select one's mate from within a certain radius. Even in industrialized societies of the twentieth century, this radius may be surprisingly small: a mile or two in mid-twentieth-century England (Molnar, 1992:195).

In each situation, however, the breeding population of "suitable" or even "actual" mates is always culturally circumscribed or expanded in ways that defy geographical proximity. Immigrants may be required to take a mate from their home population or encouraged to marry into the new one. Cultural rules may prescribe marriage to a cousin (Bedouin), or to the most geographically distant person available (*ju/wasi*).

Mates taken from outside the geographer's radius may bring changes to the genetic frequencies of the local population or even create new populations. African American populations exhibit different genetic frequencies from those of their presumed parent populations in West and Central Africa, owing to the American pattern of exogamy (mating outside one's group) *among* once separate African ethnic groups, as well as gene flow with non-African populations in the Americas (primarily western Europeans and eastern Native Americans). In addition, African Americans were exposed to a different set of natural selection factors in America — climatic, nutritional, and disease differences. For example, the Duffy blood group gene Fy^- protects against a particularly deadly form of malaria called vivax malaria. Virtually 100 percent of contemporary West and Central Africans carry the Fy^- gene and are protected against vivax malaria. European, Asian, and Native American populations, on the other hand, maintain low frequencies of the Fy⁻ gene and are susceptible to this infectious disease. Approximately 89–93 percent of African Americans carry the Fy⁻ gene, reflecting the results of the reduced natural selection pressure of vivax malaria in America as well as genetic change in non-African groups. Similarly, the gene frequencies of individuals classed as "white" in America frequently reflect substantial percentages of genes that are more common in "non-whites." This pattern strongly suggests that in the American environment, the flow of genes between formerly geographically distinct peoples has been multidirectional, influencing the subsequent composition of each group.

Restrictions on interbreeding *within* the geographer's average radius, due to caste or religious differences, for example, may *create* genetically differentiated groups that occupy the same local area. This has been the case in Ireland, where Catholics and Protestants rarely intermarry. As a result, differences within populations are often as great as differences between populations, making it almost impossible to assign *individuals* to particular groups, based on physical traits alone. Even in a case where some anthropologists argue for major "racial" differences, for example, Khoisan versus "Negroid," in actuality it is impossible to assign every individual to one or the other of these groups on physical grounds alone, just as it is impossible to assign individuals in America to the categories of the census on physical grounds alone. Within the African continent, for example, there is more physical, physiological, and genetic diversity, than *between* Africans and any other group, or between Europeans and East Asians. At no time in the past did totally "pure" or "isolated" races exist.

A glance at most introductory texts of physical anthropology, however, shows that efforts to list a few major geographical subdivisions are still current, although always qualified by noting that not all individuals or populations can be put into the categories. Most of these lists closely approximate the original five races of Blumenbach, although some also elevate the Khoisan-speaking peoples of southern Africa to that level of distinctiveness, for example, *Homo sapiens hottentotus,* also called Sanids (Baker, 1974:303–24, 624) or Capoids. Interestingly, the greatest variation in these lists is in the treatment of what the U.S. Census calls "Asian and Pacific Islanders." Where Blumenbach recognized only Mongolians and Malays, others, using 1950s studies by Stanley Garn, may divide the latter into Australians, Melanesians, Micronesians, and Polynesians. In addition, some taxonomies separate peoples of the Indian subcontinent as a separate race. Groups that are assumed to lie outside these large categories, or geographical races, from African Americans to the Ainu of Japan, are either subsumed, ignored, or treated as curiosities, isolates, or "hybrids."

ETHNICITY INSTEAD OF RACE

As noted by Molnar, the term "race" is increasingly replaced in public documents and folk taxonomies by the term "ethnic group" or "ethnicity." Ethnicity is a more recent concept in anthropology than "race," although the underlying concept of "ethnos" or "ethnology," denoting a people distinguished by cultural traits is older, dating back to at least the mid–nineteenth century. According to the *Oxford English Dictionary,* the term "ethnicity" was first used in 1953 by the sociologist David Reisman to explain how individuals and groups in multicultural settings shape their identities and their political and economic goals in terms of their interactions with one another.

How do groups (or the scholars who study them) construct or define the boundaries of an ethnic group? As in the case of race, two contrasting views of ethnicity exist. The "primordialists" hold that ethnicity arises from similarities between individuals of the group in physical features and language. These features have the power to impart a sense of group and individual identity, of belonging to the community. Ethnicity in this view is "natural," and is based on biological (skin color, body shape) or linguistic affinities that are distinct from and prior to particular social or historic conditions. In contrast, "instrumentalist" models hold that groups create ethnicity for political and economic interests. In this view, "ethnicity" is rationally oriented toward the fulfillment of specific goals like access to economic power, nationalism, or freedom from colonial rule.

Most scholars today reject these simplistic alternatives and hold the position that neither is sufficient to explain ethnic group structure and sentiment. Primordialism overlooks the fact that ethnic identity is not a natural feeling that simply emerges mysteriously in all human communities, but a complex and dynamic set of symbolic meanings patterned in history. Instrumentalists are so concerned with political and economic *motivations* that they sometimes ignore the question of how the particular elements or symbols of an ethnic identity are chosen. Ethnic consciousness may depend on perceived biological similarities, on a common language or linguistic structure, or on numerous cultural factors and learned behaviors ranging from religion to "styles" of speech and interaction.

Some ethnicities have been determined in large part by recent historical events such as colonization, nationalism, or urbanism. In Ethiopia, the "Falasha" Jews were named by Amharic leaders (Falasha means "exile" in Amharic), while in Europe, the Bosnian Muslims identified themselves as Muslims both as a way to further their political power in previous Islamic states, and, more recently, as a form of resistance to Yugoslavian nationalism.

Other ethnicities have long histories. In Africa, the Hutu and Tutsi of Rwanda, and the Tswana and Sarwa of Botswana predate the onslaught of European colonialism. Nor can the ethnic composition of nations in Europe, (Basques, Flemish), or northern Africa be explained as a correlate of modernity. This is not to imply that ethnic sentiments are "traditional" and unchanging, only that what people believe about their past has a direct relationship to what they are doing in the present. People may *believe* their ethnic ties are ancient, but the meaning and definition of these changes over time and differs according to historical circumstance. Ethnicity among Hutu and Tutsi, for example, while embedded in a long precolonial history, underwent drastic changes in just two years, 1959–61, when the states of Rwanda, Burundi, and Zaire were created. The Muslims of Bosnia, mobilized by ancestry and modern nationalism, do not fit neatly into either the primordialist or instrumentalist conceptions.

ETHNICITY AND STEREOTYPES

Like racial categories, ethnic categories have a static quality that can perpetuate stereotypes of cultural homogeneity and mask within-group variation. Categories such as "European Americans," "African Americans," "Hispanic Americans," and "Asian Americans" comprise many smaller culturally diverse groups. When we fail to recognize this internal variation, we perpetuate stereotypes that often do great disservice and assume that all members of each category are alike.

One benefit of an ethnic focus in anthropology is that it requires us to search for ways in which people, not nature, create their identities. Unfortunately, this emphasis has yet to broaden into public usage.

In the U.S. census of 1970 and 1980, the clearest example of a "race" with little or no biological component was the category "Hispanic." This grouping originally was designed to encompass Spanish-speaking migrants from Latin America, who were also categorized as "brown" owing to various admixtures of Africans, native South Americans, and peoples from Spain, Portugal, and other European (and Asian) countries. But, if the purpose was to define a biological entity, why should Europeans recently arrived from Spain, or non-Latin individuals who have acquired a Spanish surname through marriage, be included? Why should Spanish-speaking immigrants from Latin America with German surnames be excluded? How should Latin Americans of primarily African descent be categorized? In the 1990 census, the category "Hispanic" was redefined as an ethnic group, so that an individual can also classify him or herself by "race" as a "white," a "black," or an "Indian" (American). But what ethnic group combines Portuguese from Brazil and Argentineans of Welsh or Syrian descent, except with reference to the "Anglo" culture of the United States?

In the United States, on the other hand, African Americans or blacks and European Americans or whites remain overemphasized. This practice leads to increasing polarization between these groups, and creates false notions of biological and cultural homogeneity within them. Such practices, rooted in the political, economic, and historical circumstances of this nation, continue to obscure the very real commonalities shared by members of the same sex, class, community, or job category, as well as the common values and beliefs of a uniquely American culture that the two groups have jointly created.

If identities, whether racial or ethnic, are indeed cultural and historical constructs, then they are also changeable. At a time when ethnicity is so often associated with violent conflict throughout the world, a conception of identity as mutable and contingent on circumstance may offer some optimism for the future.

FURTHER READING

Baker, J. R. 1974. *Race.* Oxford University Press.
Crews, D. E., and J. R. Bindon. 1991. "Ethnicity as a Taxonomic Tool in Biomedical and Biosocial Research." *Ethnicity and Disease* 1:42–49.
Gould, Stephen J. 1981. *The Mismeasure of Man.* W. W. Norton.
Hiernaux, Jean. 1964. "The Concept of Race and the Taxonomy of Mankind." In Ashley Montagu, ed., *The Concept of Race.* Free Press of Glencoe.
Jackson, F. L. C. 1992. "Race and Ethnicity as Biological Constructs." *Ethnicity and Disease* 2:120–25.

Marks, Jonathan M. 1995. *Human Biodiversity: Genes, Race, and History.* Aldine de Gruyter.

Molnar, Stephen. 1992. *Human Variation: Races, Types and Ethnic Groups.* 3d ed. Prentice-Hall.

Smedley, Audrey. 1993. *Race in North America: Origin and Evolution of a Worldview.* Westview.

Tylor, Edward B. 1871. *Primitive Culture.* J. Murray.

Wolf, Eric R. 1982. *Europe and the People without History.* University of California Press.

CONTRIBUTORS

Catherine J. Allen is professor of anthropology at the George Washington University, Washington, D.C. She received her Ph.D. at the University of Illinois-Urbana in 1978. For more than a decade, she has been experimenting with the use of theater and actor-training techniques in the teaching of anthropology.

JoAllyn Archambault (Standing Rock Sioux) is the director of the American Indian Program in the Department of Anthropology at the Smithsonian Institution. She received her Ph.D. from the University of California-Berkeley in 1984. She has conducted research on American Indian art, Indian women, the Plains sundance, and Indian-white relations.

George J. Armelagos is professor of Anthropology at Emory University, Atlanta, Georgia. He received his Ph.D. from the University of Colorado in 1968, and his research has focused on diet and disease in human adaptation. He is former president of the American Association of Physical Anthropologists.

Kathleen C. Barnes is an assistant professor of medicine at the Johns Hopkins Asthma and Allergy Center in Baltimore, Maryland. She received her Ph.D. in anthropology from the University of Florida (Gainesville) in 1992, following a career as a registered nurse. Her interests include the genetics and epidemiology of allergic disease in the United States and the Caribbean.

Kathleen J. Bragdon is associate professor in the Department of Anthropology, College of William and Mary. She received her Ph.D. in anthropology from Brown University in 1981 and currently works with native people of New England in the areas of language education and museum exhibit scripts.

Alison S. Brooks is professor of anthropology at the George Washington University, a research associate at the Smithsonian Institution, and visiting scientist at the Carnegie Institution of Washington. She received her B.A., M.A., and Ph.D. in anthropology from Harvard University. She has published on topics in palaeoanthropology as well as the ethnoarchaeology of Botswana's San people. She has done field research in the Middle East, Scandinavia, France, Botswana, and most recently in Ethiopia, Zaire, and China. She was the principal investigator of the George Washington University/Smithsonian Institution Anthropology for Teachers Program funded by the National Science Foundation from 1978–83 and is an *AnthroNotes* editor. She has taught undergraduate and graduate students for more than 25 years and served her university as department chair from 1992 to 1995.

Mark N. Cohen is a Distinguished Teaching Professor in the Department of Anthropology at the State University of New York-Plattsburgh. He received his Ph.D. in Anthropology from Columbia University in 1971. He has conducted field research in South America, Central America, Europe, and North America, and has written articles and books on human populations and ecology.

Tom D. Dillehay is professor of anthropology and chair of his department at the University of Kentucky, Lexington. He received his Ph.D. at the University of Texas-Austin in 1976. He has taught at several universities in Europe, the United States, and South America; his current research interests include complex societies and prehistoric urbanization.

Patricia Draper is professor of anthropology and human development at the Pennsylvania State University. She received her Ph.D. from Harvard University in 1972. Her research interests include biocultural bases of sex roles, cultural ecology, and adult development and aging.

John W. Fisher Jr. is associate professor of anthropology in the Department of Sociology at Montana State University (MSU) in Bozeman. He received his doctoral degree in Anthropology from the University of California at Berkeley in 1987. In addition to teaching at MSU, he gives lectures on archaeology and prehistory to schools in the Bozeman area and to the general public throughout Montana.

William W. Fitzhugh is curator of Arctic archaeology in the Department of Anthropology and director of the Arctic Studies Center at the Smithsonian's National Museum of Natural History. He received his Ph.D. from Harvard in 1970. A specialist in circumpolar anthropology and archaeology, he has spent more than 30 years conducting fieldwork and organizing large exhibitions focused on Arctic peoples and cultures in Canada, Alaska, and Siberia.

Loretta Fowler is professor of anthropology at the University of Oklahoma. She received her Ph.D. from the University of Illinois in 1970. Her research interests include sociocultural anthropology, historical anthropology, politics, and aging, as well as Plains Indian history and culture change.

Diane Gifford-Gonzalez is professor of anthropology at the University of California-Santa Cruz. She received her Ph.D. in anthropology in 1977 from the University of California, Berkeley. For more than two decades, she has worked in Kenya and Tanzania, investigating the early African pastoralists.

Kathleen D. Gordon is a physical anthropologist employed by the Smithsonian Institution's National Museum of Natural History as an exhibit developer. She received her Ph.D. from Yale in 1980. Her research interests and publications focus on paleoanthropology, primate and early hominid feeding behavior, and prehistoric human subsistence and nutrition.

R. Richard Grinker is associate professor of anthropology and international affairs at the George Washington University. He received his Ph.D. from Harvard in 1989 and has been teaching and researching cultural history in the Democratic Republic of the Congo and Korea.

John P. Homiak is the director of the Human Studies Film Archives and the National Anthropological Archives at the Smithsonian's National Museum of Natural History. He received his Ph.D. in Anthropology from Brandeis University in 1985. He has done research in the English-speaking Caribbean since the early 1980s and is currently working on an ethnographic video about traditional forms of Rastafari ritual and worship.

Robert L. Humphrey provides all cartoon illustrations for *AnthroNotes*. He received his B.A. in art history from American University, Washington, D.C., and his Ph.D. in anthropology from the University of New Mexico. During the past 30 years, he has done archaeological research in North Alaska, the American Southwest, Mexico and Central America, and the Potomac Valley. Since 1967 he has been a professor of anthropology at the George Washington University (GW), and has directed the University Summer Field Programs in Mesoamerican Archaeology, Ecology, and History. He founded the Museum Studies Program at GW and was its first director as well as chair of the Anthropology Department for 12 years. He has cartooned since the 1950s, and his cartoons have appeared in *Zoogoer, Faces, Politics,* and *AnthroNotes*. In 1990 he published a book of cartoons, *The Last Elephant,* with the Smithsonian's National Zoological Park. As an artist, he has had several one-person shows, most recently at GW's Colonnade Gallery in 1996.

Fatimah L. C. Jackson is professor of anthropology and Distinguished Scholar Teacher at the University of Maryland. She received her Ph.D. in Biological Anthropology from Cornell University in 1981. Her areas of research include metabolic and genomic effects of exposure to plant phyto-chemicals, biological diversity in contemporary and ancient African peoples, and bioanthropological perspectives on human disease.

P. Ann Kaupp is head of the Smithsonian Institution's Anthropology Outreach Office and managing editor of *AnthroNotes*. She received her B.A. in anthropology from the George Washington University, where she also did graduate work in anthropology. She has worked in the Smithsonian's Department of Anthropology since 1978 and served as administrator of the George Washington University/Smithsonian Institution Anthropology for Teachers Program. She has organized teacher workshops on American Indians, bringing in Native American educators as workshop leaders. She serves on the advisory board for the *Cobblestone* magazines for young readers.

Naomi Kipury served as a fellow in the Department of Anthropology at the Smithsonian's National Museum of Natural History while completing her Ph.D. in anthropology at Temple University. She is currently a lecturer in the Department of African Studies at the University of Nairobi, Kenya.

JoAnne Lanouette is chair of the English Department at the Sidwell Friends School, Washington, D.C., where she has taught since 1984. She received her B.S. in English and Education from the University of Minnesota and an M.A. in anthropology from the George Washington University. JoAnne was the principal faculty member of the George Washington University/Smithsonian Institution Anthropology for Teachers Program from 1978–83. She was a founding editor of *AnthroNotes* and continues to edit all articles for the publication.

Robert M. Laughlin is curator of Mesoamerican and Caribbean ethnology in the Department of Anthropology at the Smithsonian's National Museum of Natural History. He received his Ph.D. from Harvard in 1963. His research focuses on the ethnology, history, and linguistics of the Tzeltal and Tzotzil of Chiapas, Mexico.

James Lin is an anthropology and human biology major at Emory University who is interested in health policy research. He plans to enter an MD-MPH program after spending a research year at Johns Hopkins School of Hygiene and Public Health.

Marilyn R. London is a physical anthropologist trained at the George Washington University (B.A. in anthropology) and the University of New Mexico (M.A. in biological anthropology). Marilyn is the forensic anthropology consultant for the state of Rhode Island's Office of Medical Examiners. She previously worked as a physical anthropology contractor with the Smithsonian's Office of Repatriation. During 1994–95, with Ann Kaupp on leave, Marilyn ran the Department of Anthropology's Outreach Office and served as managing editor for *AnthroNotes*; currently she is a research collaborator in physical anthropology in the Department of Anthropology.

David W. McCurdy is a professor of anthropology at Macalester College in St. Paul, Minnesota, where he served as chair of his department for more than a decade. He received his Ph.D. from Cornell University in 1964. He is the coeditor of the widely used *Conformity and Conflict: Readings in Cultural Anthropology* and served as treasurer and president of the General Anthropology Division within the American Anthropological Association.

William L. Merrill is curator of North American ethnology in the Department of Anthropology at the Smithsonian Institution. He received his Ph.D. in Anthropology in 1981 from the University of Michigan. He has done research among the Rarámuri Indians of Chihuahua, Mexico, as reported in his book, *Raramuri Souls: Knowledge and Social Process in Northern Mexico*. Dr. Merrill's principal interests are religion, historical anthropology, ideology, social organization, and material culture of Native American societies, particularly in the southwestern United States and northern Mexico.

Ruth Osterweis Selig is executive officer for programs in the Smithsonian's Office of the Provost and editor of *AnthroNotes* in the Department of Anthropology. She received a B.A. from Wellesley (history), M.A.T. from Harvard (social sciences), and M.A. from George Washington (anthropology). She acted as codirector (with Alison S. Brooks, principal investigator) of the George Washington University/Smithsonian Institution NSF-funded Anthropology for Teachers Program (1978–83), and director/principal investigator of the Smithsonian Institution/University of Wyoming Anthropology for Teachers Program (1984–85), funded by the Wyoming Council for the Humanities/National Endowment for the Humanities. After ten years of teaching anthropology to high school, undergraduate, and adult students, she established the Smithsonian's first Anthropology Outreach Office, and with JoAnne Lanouette founded *AnthroNotes*.

Roger W. Shuy is Distinguished Research Professor Emeritus in the Linguistics Department at Georgetown University, Washington, D.C., where he taught since 1968. He received his Ph.D. from the Case Western Reserve University in 1962. In 1970 he created the Sociolinguistics Program within his department at Georgetown. His most recent book, *Language Crimes* (1993), describes his linguistic analyses in various criminal trials in which tape-recorded conversations were used as evidence. He is currently writing a book on confession, interrogation, and deceptive language.

Theresa A. Singleton is curator of historical archaeology in the Department of Anthropology at the Smithsonian's National Museum of Natural History, and associate professor of anthropology at Syracuse University. She received her Ph.D. in anthropology from the University of Florida (Gainesville) in 1980. Her research focuses on historical archaeology, with an emphasis on the archaeology of the African diaspora.

Bruce D. Smith is the director of the Archaeobiology Program in the Department of Anthropology at the Smithsonian's National Museum of Natural History. He received his Ph.D. from the University of Michigan in

1973. Dr. Smith is currently doing research on the origins of agriculture in Mexico.

Catherine Cockshutt Smith holds an M.A. degree from George Washington University in anthropology and is currently writing her doctoral dissertation on biological anthropology and archaeology at Harvard University. Her research into past dietary adaptations and the modeling of prehistoric subsistence transitions has taken her from the protohistoric American Southwest to the Plio-Pleistocene African savanna.

J. N. Leith Smith holds an M.A. degree in anthropology from the University of South Carolina and is completing his Ph.D. research in West African archaeology at Syracuse University. He is conducting archaeological investigations in Ghana, West Africa, where he is examining the influence and effects of colonialism and trade on the West African frontier.

Dennis J. Stanford is chair of the Smithsonian's Department of Anthropology at the National Museum of Natural History, and head of its Paleo-Indian Project. He received his Ph.D. from the University of New Mexico in 1972. He has done extensive field research in Colorado, Wyoming, and Alaska.

William C. Sturtevant is curator of North American ethnology in the Department of Anthropology at the Smithsonian Institution. He is also the general editor for the Handbook of North American Indians, published by the Smithsonian Institution. He received his Ph.D. from Yale in 1955.

John W. Verano is assistant professor in the Department of Anthropology at Tulane University. He received his Ph.D. in anthropology from the University of California, Los Angeles, in 1987. He has taught anthropology courses at several universities in the United States and in Peru as Fulbright lecturer at the Universidad Católica in Lima in 1989 and the Universidad Nacional de Trujillo in 1996.

Stephen Williams is Peabody Professor of American Archaeology Emeritus in the Department of Anthropology at Harvard University, and honorary curator of North American archaeology and ethnology at Harvard's Peabody Museum. He received his Ph.D. in anthropology at Yale in 1954 and taught for 36 years at Harvard University. His archaeological research has focused on the southeastern United States, and he is currently researching and writing on the history of the Mississippi Delta and on the history of North American archaeology.

Melinda A. Zeder is associate curator of Old World archaeology and zooarchaeology and serves as a member of the Department of Anthropology's Archaeobiology Program, Smithsonian Institution. She received her Ph.D. from the University of Michigan in 1985. Her research interests include the domestication of animals and the social and environmental implications of early agriculture in the ancient Near East.

INDEX

Page numbers in italics refer to illustrations. Page numbers in bold refer to an entire chapter.